Pregnancy
Birth

Live laugh love!

ALSO AVAILABLE FROM BLOOMSBURY

*The Future Is Feminine: Capitalism and the
Masculine Disorder*, Ciara Cremin
Anarchafeminism, Chiara Bottici
Enduring Time, Lisa Baraitser

Pregnancy Without Birth

A Feminist Philosophy of Miscarriage

Victoria Browne

BLOOMSBURY ACADEMIC
LONDON • NEW YORK • OXFORD • NEW DELHI • SYDNEY

BLOOMSBURY ACADEMIC
Bloomsbury Publishing Plc
50 Bedford Square, London, WC1B 3DP, UK
1385 Broadway, New York, NY 10018, USA
29 Earlsfort Terrace, Dublin 2, Ireland

BLOOMSBURY, BLOOMSBURY ACADEMIC and the Diana logo
are trademarks of Bloomsbury Publishing Plc

First published in Great Britain 2023

Cover design by Ben Anslow
Cover image by Lucy O'Donnell, titled *Sitting with Uncertainty*.
Four drawings in this series, each made from 297 individual works,
measuring 105 × 74mm. Graphite and charcoal on paper, 2019.

A catalogue record for this book is available from the British Library.

A catalog record for this book is available from the Library of Congress.

ISBN: HB: 978-1-3502-7968-1
         PB: 978-1-3502-7969-8
         ePDF: 978-1-3502-7970-4
         eBook: 978-1-3502-7971-1

Typeset by Integra Software Services Pvt. Ltd.
Printed and bound in Great Britain

To find out more about our authors and books visit www.bloomsbury.com
and sign up for our newsletters.

For my sister, Kath

Contents

Acknowledgements

The writing – and not-writing – of this book has taken place through pregnancy, parenting and a pandemic, and there are so many people to thank for their support. Huge thanks must go firstly to Jen Scuro: for such a warm welcome in New York, for reading the first draft of the book so carefully and for your wonderful work and example as a feminist philosopher, artist and educator. I am also extremely thankful for the friendship and dialogue with my colleagues at Oxford Brookes, especially Doerthe Rosenow, Tina Managhan, Maia Pal, Jason Danely, Beverly Clack, Tina Miller and Abbey Halcli, and my co-editors at *Radical Philosophy,* especially Rahul Rao and Hannah Proctor; and for all the support from Stella Sandford and Lisa Baraitser over the past decade. Many thanks to Liza Thompson, Lucy Russell, Dharanivel Baskar and everyone at Bloomsbury whose hard work got this book into print; to the Leverhulme Trust for the Research Fellowship which enabled a year working exclusively on the book; and to the Institute for Research on Women, Gender and Sexualities at Columbia University in New York for hosting me with a Visiting Scholarship during this time. At Columbia, particular thanks to Yasmine Ergas and Nick Bartlett; at Stony Brook, to Victoria Hesford and Lisa Diedrich; and at large, to my brilliant friends, especially Eva Crasnow, Elise McCave, Sally Ferguson, Susanna Hislop, Cat Lynch, Mackenzie Chung Fegan, Chloe Campbell and Helen Rand, for keeping me sane, sustained and amused, and for all the years of talk about gender, politics, pregnancy, miscarriage and mothering. I am so grateful for the love and support of my family, who have had so much faith in me, and looked after me and my children so well when I've needed to write, or needed a break. Particular thanks must go to my mum, Margaret, for her amazing generosity, love and pride in us all; and to Kath and Jamie for sharing so much with us, and for being such an inspiration in how to live with loss. Deepest love and thanks to Theo and Nina, for all the joy and hilarity, and as always to Sam, for the endless patience, insight and care. *You can read me anything.*

Thanks must go, finally, to *Hypatia*, for permission to reprint my article 'A Pregnant Pause: Pregnancy, Miscarriage and Suspended Time', which appears in this book in a slightly amended version as Chapter 4; to *Radical Philosophy*, for permission to reprint amended material from my article 'The Politics of Miscarriage' in Chapter 5; and also to Routledge, for permission to include in Chapter 2 some of the ideas I first explored in my chapter 'The Temporalities of Pregnancy: On Contingency, Loss and Waiting' in the edited volume *Motherhood in Literature and Culture: Interdisciplinary Perspectives from Europe*. And many thanks to Lucy O'Donnell for permission to use her stunning artwork from 'Sitting with Uncertainty' for the cover.

I also want to acknowledge some of the organizations that have informed and inspired this book: National Advocates for Pregnant Women, for their support of pregnant people targeted for state control and criminal punishment in the US (https://www.nationaladvocatesforpregnantwomen.org); The Doula Project in New York, for their full-spectrum pregnancy care and activism (https://www.doulaproject.net); and Maternity Action in the UK, for their campaigning against the charging of pregnant migrants for NHS maternity care, introduced as part of the government's 'hostile environment' policy (https://maternityaction.org.uk/campaigns/nhscharging/).

Preface

I first started to think philosophically about pregnancy when my sister experienced a stillbirth at seven months pregnant.[1] At the time I was working my way through the canon of existential philosophers such as Martin Heidegger and Jean-Paul Sartre, and the way they take birth for granted, as simply an existential precondition, appeared to me as breath-taking arrogance.[2] Feminist philosophy has provided a strong corrective to the traditional philosophical disinterest in pregnancy by putting 'the body that births' at the heart of its agenda,[3] but has routinely excluded and marginalized pregnancies that end in miscarriage or stillbirth. So I began to wonder what would happen if we tried to conceptually disconnect 'pregnancy' from 'birth' by rethinking pregnancy from the perspective of miscarriage.

A while after starting this project, I experienced a very early miscarriage myself, a couple of years after my first child was born. In my case, it was a briefly unsettling, but not life-altering, event, and in fact I didn't count it as a 'proper' miscarriage at all. It certainly didn't seem appropriate to include it in this book, as I felt that doing so would be laying claim to an experience I had not *really* been through. But I came to see that this logic revealed an unconscious subscription to the increasingly predominant representation of miscarriage as 'the loss of a baby' that will produce grief and trauma. This framing does give many people a vital sense of social recognition and validation; but it also has the effect of sidelining miscarriages that are not experienced this way, thus erasing the huge variability and ambiguity of miscarriage as an embodied phenomenon. So I have opted to include my brush with miscarriage here after all, but I want to emphasize that this is intended in the spirit of feminist candour, and not to qualify my interest in the subject. Indeed, one of the core arguments in the book is that miscarriage must be treated as a feminist issue that concerns us all, not only those personally affected by it.[4] And though I have focused primarily on miscarriage rather than stillbirth, my ultimate hope is that this book will contribute to the 'full-spectrum' understanding of pregnancy, which seeks to break down pregnancy hierarchies and presumed divisions – between pregnancy, miscarriage, stillbirth, live birth and abortion – in the interest of building inclusive intersectional alliances in the struggle for reproductive justice and freedom.

Introduction

Pregnancy is a complex bodily phenomenon with multiple possible meanings and endings. Yet so often, pregnancy is deemed significant solely because of the baby it is expected to produce.[1] Think, for example, of the 'Baby on board!' badges that Transport for London provides for pregnant people to wear while travelling.[2] The message to fellow travellers to offer up their seats is centred upon the imagined 'baby' who is figured as a passenger in its own right. This is what gives the call for consideration and care its emotional appeal, surpassing the needs of the one who is pregnant at that time and place.

Figure 1 'Baby on board!' badge image, Transport for London, 2022.[3]

To be sure, many pregnant people do relate to their foetuses as their babies or children, engaging in material and social practices that interpellate them as such. And many who wear the 'Baby on board!' badges embrace their pregnancies being represented in this way. But as feminists have long argued, the externally imposed logic that treats foetuses as already separate beings with interests, even rights, of their own, comes with serious consequences for pregnant people when their well-being is rendered secondary or merely instrumental, particularly those whose lives are already socially devalued by systemic racism, ableism and poverty. At best, it frames the pregnant person in sentimentalized terms as a 'carrier' or 'holder' of the future, and at worst, as a dangerous subject who jeopardizes that future and requires levels of regulation, discipline and intervention which in other situations would be considered a gross breach of bodily integrity. Another consequence is that pregnancies which do not lead to the birth of a living baby – due to abortion, miscarriage or stillbirth – are cast outside the world of normative pregnancy altogether, and consistently shrouded in shame, stigma, silence or suspicion. Abortion is much more prominent as a feminist issue than miscarriage and stillbirth, as anti-abortion politics constitute such a blatantly oppressive attempt to control women's bodies and reproductive lives. But attitudes towards miscarriage and stillbirth are similarly shaped by conventional ideas about productivity, femininity, maternity and social value. When pregnancy is presumed to be all about birth and babies, a pregnancy that ends without a live birth can appear only as a failure, or a waste of time – indeed, as not proper to pregnancy at all.

The aim of this book is to extricate pregnancy from its over-association with birth and futurity via a feminist philosophy of miscarriage. The core argument is that bringing miscarriage to the foreground – against its usual positioning as an aberration or an afterthought – can do important work in disentangling pregnancy from birth as its normative futural horizon, because the imagined future of 'the child' is extinguished quite literally, and usually unexpectedly. When pregnancy ends with 'no baby to show for it' (Cancellaro 2001: 163), we are compelled to reckon not only with the damaging effects of discourses that promote birth as pregnancy's 'natural' and 'normal' endpoint, but also with the intractable realities of contingency and ambiguity that are concealed by such discourses. We are forced to consider what pregnancy might amount to besides the production of a child.

Putting miscarriage experiences front and centre, therefore, is valuable to feminist philosophy and politics, not only because such experiences are so often marginalized and misunderstood, but also because they can illuminate important aspects of pregnancy that exceed its gestational function, as we consider more fully what pregnancy can mean, and the different ways it can play out. In other words, when we pay attention to miscarriage, we are not just learning things about miscarriage – we are learning things about pregnancy, and the imaginaries, temporalities and power structures that shape it as symbol and as lived experience. Each chapter of the book takes up a theme that is commonly articulated within personal accounts of miscarriage – a sense of failure; of being out of control yet nevertheless to blame; of being immersed in ambiguity and confusion; of being 'stuck in limbo' or out of time; of resentment and anger as well as solidarity and empathy – and asks what these experiences reveal about the dominant socio-cultural discourses of pregnancy, as well as exploring the alternative understandings that emerge in such times of dislocation and uncertainty.

Centralizing miscarriage, moreover, is a method designed to fully politicize it as a feminist issue. Miscarriage has been thoroughly *depoliticized* through being framed as simply 'nature's way', and as a personal problem that has no wider social significance.[4] In contrast, *politicizing* miscarriage entails critically examining how experiences of miscarriage are embedded within gendered power relations and imaginaries that produce feelings of failure, inadequacy, guilt and shame as *socio-cultural phenomena*, rather than simply private emotions to be managed by the individual (Ahmed 2004: 8–9). It also involves interrogating the profound inequalities that render some pregnancies more socially valued and materially supported than others. This inequality means not only that the overall rate of miscarriage and stillbirth is higher among women of colour and poor women, for example, but also that while the miscarriages of the privileged may be increasingly treated as a grievable and tragic loss, others are all too often dismissed as 'for the best' or vilified as the result of 'poor lifestyle choices', even criminal neglect. Yet to approach miscarriage as a political issue is also to affirm that these power structures are both 'contested and contestable' (Kafer

2013: 9), and that more liberatory discourses and equitable conditions are urgently possible.

The rest of this Introduction focuses on scene-setting and ground-clearing. It firstly sketches out the problematic that *Pregnancy Without Birth* sets itself against: the normative values and temporalities of 'foetal motherhood' (Berlant 1994) and 'reproductive futurism' (Edelman 2004) and their socio-cultural manifestations in both the UK and the US. It then turns to feminist philosophies of pregnancy, maternity and natality (e.g. Young [1984] 2005; Irigaray 1985a; Kristeva 1986; Cavarero 1995; Battersby 1998; Guenther 2006; Stone 2011), affirming the forceful challenge this body of work has made to patriarchal models of pregnancy as incubation, yet also highlighting the tendency within feminist philosophy to conflate pregnancy with maternity, and to overdetermine the meaning of pregnancy through assumptions of birth and the postnatal future. Accordingly, I suggest, it is feminist philosophies of abortion and miscarriage that offer most potential for shattering the ideological edifices of 'foetal motherhood' and 'reproductive futurism', and for defining pregnancy as a fundamentally ambiguous and contingent situation[5] – particularly miscarriage which so obviously frustrates teleological models of pregnancy as naturally destined for birth as well as neoliberal models of pregnancy as an object of control determined by individual choice.[6] What is the value, meaning or significance of a pregnancy that ends without a choice or a child?

Finally, the Introduction explains the book's transdisciplinary methodology, and makes some terminological clarifications pertaining to 'miscarriage', 'stillbirth', 'pregnancy loss', 'pregnant people' and 'pregnant women'.

Foetal motherhood and reproductive futurism

Every year in the UK and the US, millions of people become pregnant. The majority of pregnancies result in live births, but a significant number end differently, through abortion, miscarriage or stillbirth.[7] Current estimates, for example, suggest that 10–20 per cent of known pregnancies end in miscarriage.[8] Pregnancy statistics are contestable and imprecise,[9] but they do signify the variety of possible outcomes as well as the intersecting factors that condition pregnancy as a lived situation, including gender, class, race, age, religion, sexuality, citizenship, language, housing, income, education, employment, physical capacity, mental health, social networks, intimate relationships and reproductive histories. The diverse and dynamic realities of pregnancy, however, are consistently swallowed up by a suite of homogeneous representations that reduce the pregnant person to one who is 'carrying' or 'expecting', even to a 'maternal environment' that must be optimized. As Kelly Oliver argues, 'the pregnant body' is highly visible as a cipher, or a metaphor for other types of transformation, but the subjective experiences of pregnant people themselves are consistently rendered marginal or invisible (2012: 207).

Various iterations of this kind of argument have been made by feminists over the past four decades, especially in relation to the impact of ultrasound scanning technology, and the appearance of the fetishized 'public fetus' as a ubiquitous image in mass culture and politics (e.g. Petchesky 1987; Franklin 1991; Hartouni 1992; Berlant 1994; Harraway 1997; Morgan and Michaels 1999; Dubow 2011; Gentile 2014; Mills 2014). The 'teleological construction of the foetus', as Sarah Franklin explains, inscribes the time of pregnancy as a singular trajectory of linear progress aligned to the foetus's expected biological development (1991: 197–200). The *lived time* of the pregnant person is thereby collapsed into the *gestational time* of the foetus, as the standardized temporal markers and milestones – the successive weeks, months and trimesters – serve as a one-way 'countdown' to birth (Scuro 2017: 234; see also Beynon-Jones 2016). Foetocentric pregnancy narratives also take on a proleptic structure when the foetus is treated as a separate 'baby-person' already, even a citizen bearing rights (Katz Rothman 1986). As a result, the present situation of pregnancy becomes subordinated to the projected future – be that the hopeful future symbolized by the foetus-as-child, or the catastrophic future that 'motivates action and meaning-making in the present' through the management of risk (Gentile 2014: 291). Pregnant time, then, is not only represented as developmental and progressive but also as a time of containment: a time that both holds the future in the present yet simultaneously serves as a potential block to its realization.

Lauren Berlant coined the term 'fetal motherhood' to capture the way that the foetus is presented in advance as a separate individual, and the pregnant person as 'already a mother embarked on a life trajectory of mothering' (1994: 148). According to this logic, the pregnant person is expected to 'act like a mother' to the foetus, but at the same time is effectively made a 'child to the fetus', through the de-legitimation of their agency and identity as they become 'more minor and less politically represented than the fetus' (1994: 147; see also Bordo 1993; Ruddick 2007; Baird 2008).[10] More recently, Jennifer Scuro has proposed the term 'childbearing teleology' to refer to 'the scripts and rituals that underwrite socio-political, gendered, and embodied expectations about pregnancy', domesticating the possible phenomenal content of pregnant embodiment by validating only its productive aspects, and presuming pregnancy to be 'all directed for the sake of a child produced' (2017: 189). Childbearing teleology is exercised through a 'medical and cultural complex of guidance and instruction' (2017: 189) – for instance, in popular pregnancy books where the foetus 'talks' to the imagined pregnant reader:

> When I first opened The Healthy Pregnancy Book … I was startled by an image … There on the second page was a gray, delicately shaded pencil illustration of a baby nestled cosily in a womb, its arms and legs crossed. A thought bubble emanated from the baby, carrying a firm message: 'Mama take good care of yourself so I can grow better'. I was only eight weeks pregnant (my fetus was kidney-bean size …), and yet here was this fully formed baby admonishing me for mistakes I was already making. 'Do you really want to eat that'? the baby asked incredulously on page 54.
>
> (Garbes 2018: 19)

The model of pregnancy as 'foetal motherhood' can generate significant levels of social approval for those who fulfil the 'happy-glowing-pregnant-lady myth' and are seen to behave appropriately (Faulkner 2012: 336). As Maggie Nelson writes in *The Argonauts*: 'You are holding the future; one must be kind to the future (or at least a certain image of the future, which I apparently appeared able to deliver …)' (2015: 90).[11] But pregnancy can also be the source of acute social shaming and censure in the case of those whose reproductivity is deemed a threat to social or national futures (Davis 1981; Roberts 1997; Deutscher 2016; Ross et al. 2017; Millar 2018). The figure of the 'pregnant teen', for example, or the 'pregnant immigrant', are ubiquitous symbols of demonized reproduction, along with pregnant bodies of all ages marked by disability, conspicuous queerness, racialized otherness or a whiteness 'contaminated by poverty' (Tyler 2008: 30). 'Stratified reproduction' is a concept widely used within feminist theory to describe the 'power relations by which some categories of people are empowered to nurture and reproduce, while others are disempowered' (Ginsberg and Rapp 1995: 3; see also Colen 1986). Such stratifications have a long history of state programmes of forced/coerced sterilization, abortion and contraception, as well as punitive welfare systems designed to prevent the 'wrong' kind of reproduction. Dorothy Roberts, for example, examines cases in the 1980s and 90s of Black pregnant women in the US who tested positive for drugs being given the 'choice' of abortion or prison (1997: 181).[12] Or as Lisa Guenther documents, between 2006 and 2010, nearly 150 women were unlawfully sterilized in California prisons – a practice defended by prison medical staff as a 'service to taxpayers', and even to the women themselves, as a way of preventing the birth of 'unwanted children' (2016: 217).[13]

Contemporary discourses of what Kelly Ray Knight describes as 'soft eugenics' (2015: 210) are couched in the language of 'dysfunctional communities', 'problem families' (Millar 2018: 231) or 'anti-socials' (Salem 2018; Shilliam 2018). But as Laura Briggs argues, the logic of public benefits and state-mandated private benefits in the US is 'precisely eugenic', when, as a matter of law and regulation, 'insurers pay for the poor to get birth control and the rich to get IVF' (2017: 108).[14] At the same time, there has been a significant rise in arrests and prosecutions of women under laws such as 'child endangerment' or 'fetal homicide' in cases of criminalized miscarriage/stillbirth. Lynn Paltrow and Jeanne Flavin report that in the US between 1973 and 2005, 413 recorded arrests and forced interventions were made, and those targeted were overwhelmingly low-income (71 per cent) and disproportionately women of colour (59 per cent) (2013: 311; see also Callahan and Knight 1993).[15] Since then, the National Advocates for Pregnant Women have recorded 1,254 more such cases in the US between 2006 and 2020 (NAPW 2021a). In the UK, criminal punishment and forced interventions are much rarer, though there have been some troubling high-profile instances. In 2012, for example, Essex social services obtained a court order to enforce a C-section on a pregnant woman suffering from bipolar disorder without her consent, and subsequently sent her back to her country of residence and put the baby up for adoption (Hamilton 2013).[16]

It may seem contradictory that the same groups of people whose reproduction is marked as deviant are more likely to be punished or subjected to state intervention when their pregnancies are deemed 'at risk', or end without a live birth. But this apparent contradiction only lays bare how the professed concern for 'the child' functions as a smokescreen or 'cover story' for wider political agendas and exercises of control (Briggs 2017: 71).[17] Indeed, the groups most subjected to heightened surveillance and forced interventions, as Laura Woliver points out, overall continue to experience the highest levels of miscarriage, stillbirth and pregnancy-related death (2008).[18] One large study conducted in 2013, for example, shows that the rate of miscarriage for Black women in the US is around 57 per cent higher overall and 93 per cent higher after week 10 of pregnancy than the rate for white women (Mukherjee et al. 2013; see also Chatterjee and Davis 2017).[19] In the UK, statistics published in 2020 show that like in the US, where Black women die from pregnancy- or childbirth-related causes at three to four times the rate of white women, 'there remains a more than fourfold difference in maternal mortality rates amongst women from Black ethnic backgrounds and an almost twofold difference amongst women from Asian ethnic backgrounds compared to white women' (MBRRACE UK 2020: iii).[20] And a report published in November 2021 by the UK National Maternity and Perinatal Audit estimates that 24 per cent of stillbirths, 19 per cent of preterm births and 31 per cent of foetal growth restriction (FGR) cases are attributable to socio-economic and racial inequality. It projects that 'half of stillbirths (53.5 per cent) and seven in ten FGR cases (71.7 per cent) among South Asian women living in the most deprived fifth of neighbourhoods in England could be avoidable if they had the same risks as white women in the most affluent fifth', and that 'this was similarly the case for nearly two-thirds of stillbirths (63.7 per cent) and half of FGR cases (55 per cent) among Black women from the most deprived neighbourhoods' (Gregory 2021).[21]

There are strong points of resonance between feminist critiques of 'stratified reproduction' and regimes of 'foetal motherhood' and

Lee Edelman's influential indictment of 'reproductive futurism' and its central figure: the imaginary 'Child' to which heteronormative politics defers as a symbol of innocence to be protected. Though it is usually presumed 'self-evident' that any kind of progressive politics is ultimately oriented towards the future and 'fighting for the children' (2004: 2), Edelman's analysis in *No Future* demonstrates how sentimentalized representations of the imaginary future 'Child' in fact serve to consolidate the social injustices of the status quo: by holding us 'in thrall' to 'a future continually deferred by time itself' (2004: 30), while vilifying those positioned outside or against the heteronormative fantasy of 'the future' staked upon linear developmental time and reproductive continuity. Edelman's own focus is the figure of the queer man or the 'sinthomosexual' as 'non-reproducer'; and pregnant people, indeed women in general, barely feature in *No Future*. Critics including Alison Kafer and Jose Esteban Muñoz have also highlighted how the text overlooks the ableism and racism inherent to reproductive futurism, as the figure of the 'Child' of the future is so consistently coded as 'always already white ... healthy and nondisabled' (Kafer 2013: 32–3; Muñoz 2009: 95). But despite these limitations, Edelman's analysis of the symbolism and political function of the 'Child' can augment feminist interrogations of 'foetal motherhood' and its damaging effects upon pregnant people (and actual children) in the present. 'The pregnant woman', as Penelope Deutscher contends, 'can certainly be added to [Edelman's] account of those held hostage ... to reproductive futurism' (2016: 51). Extending the argument, Deutscher proposes that the fantasy of the 'Child' also stimulates fantasies of the 'Pregnant Woman' as its counterpart, who can appear in the guise of the 'Good Mother' who will deliver the future that the imaginary 'Child' is made to stand for, or the 'Bad Mother' who jeopardizes this future's materialization. 'The Child of the Future', she writes, 'is associated with this concurrent imaginary pregnant mother, whether her role is highly visible, fetishized, or invisible in the teleology of the Child's value' (2016: 51).

To counter what might seem to be an excessively gloomy portrait of contemporary pregnancy, it is important to acknowledge the multiple ways in which normative models of 'foetal motherhood' and 'reproductive futurism' are challenged, undermined and simply ignored. Various feminist analyses of gestational surrogacy, for example, highlight ways that this practice can decouple pregnancy from naturalized motherhood

in the political and popular imagination, thus expanding understandings
of kin-making practices (see e.g. Teman 2010; Jacobson 2016; Lewis
2019). We might also think of the increasing public visibility of trans and
nonbinary pregnancy, particularly 'the spectacle of the pregnant man
and the potential challenge it poses to heterosexual, binary gendered
notions of reproduction' (Toze 2018: 203; see also Halberstam 2010).[22]
At the same time, however, scholarship on surrogacy and multi-
gendered pregnancy also demonstrates how resilient the model of
pregnancy as a 'straight line' from conception to birth can be, and
moreover, the patriarchal understanding of the pregnant body as
'host' to an imagined future child that is already granted conceptual
autonomy. Yasmine Ergas, for example, argues that recent discourse
and jurisprudence on commercial surrogacy routinely ignores the lived
experience and situation of pregnant surrogates, and has reinforced
the idea of pregnancy as a production process or 'service' whose value
and significance lies solely in the expected child as 'product' (2017:
110–12). Pregnant surrogates may not be enlisted as 'mother' to the
foetus, but they are nevertheless consistently rendered subordinate to
its projected future as well as the interests of the intending parents,
particularly when there is a serious imbalance of power and wealth (see
e.g. Pande 2014; Vora 2015).[23]

Further, whilst the symbolism of masculine or nonbinary pregnancy
transgresses gender norms, the sensationalism that has surrounded the
phenomenon of 'the pregnant man' suggests that male pregnancy is still
far 'outside the frame of social recognition', even 'socially unthinkable'
(Toze 2018: 204). Indeed, Michael Toze points to concern that has
been expressed within some trans male/masculine communities
about the potentially negative effect of trans pregnancy upon social
validation: 'how can anyone take us seriously as men, if some of us
get pregnant?' (2018: 204). Much more research is needed into the
ways that pregnancy, abortion, miscarriage, stillbirth and live birth are
experienced by those who do not occupy a conventionally feminine
hetero cis-normative social position and identity.[24] But there are signs
that gendered notions of the pregnant body as unruly and the pregnant
mind as irrational – and hence in need of paternalistic regulation and
intervention – do carry over into the treatment of pregnant people who are
not women. For instance, the headline-attracting pregnancy of Thomas
Beatie in the US in 2008 was the subject of much disapproving public

'concern' that the foetus might be negatively affected by testosterone use – he was condescendingly instructed by an obstetrician via a television network that it was 'really important' that he did not take any testosterone during the pregnancy – and that the future child would be 'confused' later in life about their parental situation (Barkham 2008; see also Grigorovich 2014).

So while it is crucial to highlight and engage with all the ways that non-normative practices, discourses and imagery continue to subvert dominant ideals and generate alternatives, the insistent promotion of normative pregnancy remains a major problem for feminists to struggle against. Cultural inscriptions of the docile pregnant body seem as forceful as ever, as pregnant people are instructed how to sleep, eat, walk and even think during pregnancy (Brooks-Gardner 2003); and in legal and medical contexts, pregnant people have been treated 'more and more … as sites for fetal growth, or worse yet, barriers to fetal care' (Katz Rothman 1986: 264). The persistence of the sacrificial narrative is well illustrated in the latest edition of the widely read pregnancy manual *What to Expect When You're Expecting*, which suggests that while this edition has not altered its references to 'traditional family relationships', the reader themselves can simply 'mentally edit out' any term or phrase that does not match their own set-up and 'replace it with one that's right for you and your loving family' (Murkhoff 2017: 19). The author is thus confident that there is no need to make significant changes to the text – that even if the reader 'mentally' switches the central terms around, the narration of the 'pregnancy journey' can stay essentially the same.

Feminist philosophies of pregnancy and maternity

Contemporary representations of 'the foetus' as an individual being in its own right depend significantly upon the foetal imagery provided by ultrasound technology, which may give the impression that such depictions are a recent phenomenon. Yet from a feminist philosophical perspective, the 'foetal narratives' that circulate through vectors such as commercial pregnancy guidebooks, national healthcare pamphlets and the speech of politicians can be viewed as the latest iteration of a much older problematic. Imogen Tyler, for example, argues that the historical canon of Western philosophy has operated on the basis of exactly the same disavowal of pregnant subjectivity and embodiment as the foetal narratives we encounter today. Indeed, she writes, 'the foetus is, simply put, the most recent reincarnation of the figure of the philosopher' (2000: 300) – an atomized masculinized subject entirely disconnected from the bodily relations and labour that sustain him.

This idea has been central to the work of Luce Irigaray and Julia Kristeva, for example, who write of pregnant embodiment as the forgotten originary site of subjectivity and corporeal existence.[25] 'Mother-matter', claims Irigaray, makes possible the individuals which populate the Western symbolic order and cultural imaginary, and yet is essentially unthinkable within their terms (1985a: 162).[26] The pregnant body cannot conform to masculine principles of individuality, non-contradiction and singular temporality. It exists, as Tyler puts it, as a 'question' within a 'philosophical landscape of stable forms' (2000: 292). Yet it also poses a threat to this metaphysical system and the fantasy of self-sufficiency and 'coming-from-nothing' (Stone 2007: 181), because it exposes the fragilities of patriarchal individualism and its dependence upon that which it would erase. Political anxieties over pregnant bodies can thus be said to incorporate philosophical anxieties over the very boundaries of 'self' and 'other', 'mind' and 'matter', as the figure of the pregnant person represents 'the ever-present possibility of sliding back into the corporeal abyss from which [we] were formed' (Grosz 1994: 198; see also Shildrick 2001: 31).

Since feminist philosophy has become consolidated as a scholarly field, pregnant embodiment has frequently been construed as a paradigmatic phenomenon of 'multiple embodiment' that offers a route out of patriarchal metaphysics and individualist politics by revealing our intercorporeal intertwinement more generally. Feminist philosophers have also been concerned to restore subjectivity to pregnancy and reframe the pregnant person as 'the site of her proceedings' (Kristeva 1986: 237) rather than a 'container' for foetal development. Against the medical model of pregnancy as a 'state of the developing fetus' or an objective 'condition' to be treated, and against the economic model that calibrates value according to what will be produced or 'delivered', feminists have sought to 'give voice' to the pregnant subject and attest to that 'wild oxymoron – a pregnant person who thinks' (Young [1984] 2005; Nelson 2015: 91). They have promoted a way of thinking about pregnancy not as a production process and instead as a unique way of being in the world. Feminist philosophy, of course, is not a homogeneous bloc. Some feminists do propagate a model of the autonomous bounded self (pregnant or otherwise), while others disagree over the extent to which the pregnant subject should be considered 'undone' by the blurred boundaries of pregnant embodiment. In Kristeva's account, for instance, pregnancy is a 'place of splitting' where the pregnant subject finds herself alienated from her own flesh in a kind of delirium (Kristeva 1986: 238). If a pregnant person does retain a sense of bodily integrity and unified identity, Kristeva proposes, this is due to a kind of false or 'closed' consciousness that comes with the habitual thinking of the self as 'one' (see also Ziarek 1999).[27] Elizabeth Grosz, however, argues that Kristeva's account of the pregnant body accepts too quickly the 'overtaking of women's corporeality and identity by a foreign body, an alien intruder' (1990: 162); and Lisa Guenther similarly suggests that the very possibility of alienation in pregnancy 'suggests there is always already a difference between mother and child even in the very midst of ambiguity' (2006: 26).[28] But though there are certainly differences and disagreements, feminist philosophy offers up a host of powerful resources for countering the treatment of the foetus as an already separate individuated being and the pregnant person as an 'identity machine for others, producing children in the name of the future' (Berlant 1994: 147).

Having said this, however, feminist philosophy of pregnancy has consistently been criticized for making universalizing assumptions about the experience of 'the pregnant subject' – an inheritance from both the psychoanalytic and phenomenological traditions from which it has drawn. As in so many other areas of feminist enquiry, white middle-class women's experiences have been universalized via claims about how 'the pregnant subject experiences herself' or under-examined ideas of a 'typical' pregnancy (Mullin 2005: 45). For instance, while the effects of capitalist ideologies of productivity upon imaginaries of pregnancy, reproduction and kinship are not lost on Irigaray (1985b), the effects of racial logics and power structures are never grappled with in her work (Ziarek 2010: 210).[29] Further, as Caroline Lundquist points out, for the pregnant subject who never positively accepts her pregnancy, the sense of 'splitting subjectivity' described by Kristeva and others can be 'radically unlike the experiential mother-child differentiation of chosen pregnancy … a chiasm not of two subjects, but rather of a subject and some unwanted or menacing object, some less than human, perhaps monstrous creature, or the embodiment of the aggressor, in pregnancies resulting from rape' (2008: 145).

There has also been a lack of recognition that the right and capacity to become pregnant and have children has been systematically obstructed or denied to disabled and economically/racially subordinated groups. The 'reproductive justice' framework developed by Black feminists in the 1990s emphasizes that the right to reproduce, and 'to parent the children we have in safe and sustainable communities', must be defended as much as the right *not* to be pregnant and give birth; and since then, as Loretta Ross outlines, it 'has impressively built bridges between activists and the academy to stimulate thousands of scholarly articles' (2017: 286). But white feminist philosophy has on the whole focused more on the political project of 'resist[ing] compulsory maternity at the expense of fighting anti-natalism' (Jones et al. 2014). Another issue is that while opposing compulsory maternity, feminist philosophical writings on pregnancy have nevertheless tended to treat 'the pregnant body' and 'the maternal body' as interchangeable terms.[30] This equation of pregnancy and maternity, as Jane Lymer argues, ends up 'maternalizing' all pregnancy experiences including abortion, which gets coded as an 'opting out' of maternity even as it is defended as an essential recourse (2016: 20). Adriana Cavarero, for example, describes the 'full power both to generate and not to generate' as a 'maternal power' (1995: 64).[31]

What is particularly pertinent to the concerns of this book is the related tendency within feminist philosophy to overdetermine the meaning of pregnancy in light of birth and the postnatal future it is imagined to generate.[32] Guenther, for example, suggests that for the pregnant subject who decides to stay pregnant, pregnancy is characterized primarily by the force of the anticipated but unknowable future of the child which 'makes the woman a mother' (2006: 3).[33] To be clear, Guenther insists that the time of pregnancy and the time of gestation must be understood as distinct, though intertwined, thereby articulating a powerful philosophical refutation of the 'foetal motherhood' ideology: 'It is precisely not as a vessel that the maternal body is maternal; the relation between mother and child is not ... a relation of containment but of inspiration by an Other' (2006: 101). The futural force Guenther evokes, moreover, is disruptive, elusive and discontinuous with the present, and therefore emphatically different to the teleological future of 'reproductive futurism'. 'The future of the child to whom the pregnant woman will someday give birth', she writes, 'does not quite belong to her, even if it does implicate her in a future of responsibility ...' (2006: 100). Nevertheless, though insightful and innovative in so many ways, Guenther's analysis here does seem to imply that the temporality of the pregnant person is structured by the future of the child above all else, even as that future is theorized as open and unpredictable.

This accent on the future or futurity is common across feminist philosophy, which can have the effect of sidelining all those aspects of pregnancy that have little or nothing to do with imagined futures or parent–child relations (Mullin 2005: 36). It also leaves us uncertain about how to interpret the significance of a miscarried pregnancy whereby a maternal 'future of responsibility' is foreclosed. As Oliver points out, the imagined futurity of pregnant embodiment 'may just highlight the "empty promise" of a future that, for whatever reason – and there are many – does not lead to childbirth' (2010: 773).[34] To make this kind of critique is not to repudiate the future-oriented features of pregnancy: the reckoning with possible postpregnancy futures; the planning and preparing; the affective intensities of anticipation, expectation, speculation, hope and longing, as well as anxiety, fear or dread. It is also not to deny the fact that attachment to a newborn infant often 'flows out' of attachment to the foetus during pregnancy (Stone 2007: 168).[35] My argument, rather, is that pregnancy has been so thoroughly assimilated to birth, maternity and futurity that there is analytical and political value in trying to disaggregate these terms and consider pregnancy as an embodied situation in its own right – through a conceptual suspension or 'bracketing' of the presumption of birth and postnatal relations.[36]

This is not to say that pregnancy should be understood as an entirely self-enclosed phenomenon; and indeed, it is extremely difficult, perhaps impossible, to completely disassociate pregnancy from birth and maternity, especially when terms like 'prenatal care' (rather than 'pregnancy care') or 'maternity jeans' (rather than 'pregnancy jeans') anchor pregnancy so firmly to birth and maternity in everyday discourse.

But it does bear emphasizing that being pregnant is not necessarily equivalent to 'having a baby' or being 'with child', and that 'the relational result of gestation is not always "motherhood"' (Lewis 2018: 309). The connections between pregnancy, birth and maternity are certainly not arbitrary, but they *are* contingent, uncertain and variable – a reality that often gets lost within representations of them as interchangeable or as 'moments on an experiential continuum' (LaChance Adams and Lundquist 2013: 21). This book therefore argues for a more thoroughgoing extrication of pregnancy from maternity, futurity and birth in a bid to break the spell of 'foetal motherhood' and 'reproductive futurism', and to give an account of pregnancy as a lived situation that is much more than simply a precondition or build-up to something else.

Rethinking pregnancy through abortion and miscarriage

Above I have said that birth, maternity and the future of the imagined child have overdetermined the meaning of pregnancy within feminist philosophy, but that is not quite true. Feminist philosophers have in fact devoted a lot of attention to pregnancies that do not produce a child, but under the heading of 'abortion' rather than 'pregnancy'. To learn and think about pregnancy, we might not automatically think that the best place to turn is abortion, but feminist writing on abortion provides a lot of insight into the highly variable experiences of pregnancy as a lived situation, precisely because the presumption is that pregnancy might well be terminated. Of course, pregnant people imagine different possible futures when considering abortion. But feminist writing on abortion also pays close attention to the 'here and now' of pregnancy: how it feels to the one who is pregnant and the kinds of circumstances and relations that are entailed.

I have in mind here phenomenological accounts of abortion that place the lived experience of the pregnant person at the centre of their analyses. This contrasts with the dominant analytic approach within abortion ethics, which adopts a rights-based framework and positions the pregnant person and the foetus as separate individuals, even as adversaries, with rights that need to be weighed against each other. For instance, rights-based arguments often proceed by way of analogy, where the relation between the pregnant person and foetus is represented by a relation between two adults, often strangers. Perhaps the most famous example is Judith Jarvis Thomson's thought experiment where a woman wakes to discover that an ailing violinist has been plugged into her circulatory system, and she must decide whether to allow him to remain plugged in for the nine months necessary for him to survive (1971:14). Though Thomson's essay is a defence of the right to abortion, what is written out of analogies like these is the bodily reality of pregnancy – a situation marked by 'a particular, and particularly thoroughgoing, kind of physical intertwinement' (Little 1999: 296). A foetus is not 'contracting with the woman for the use of her body,' as Catriona Mackenzie contends, and a pregnant person's body is not their 'property' (1992: 151). Rather, our bodies are our 'mode of being-in-the-world', and as such, 'a fetus is a being whose existence and welfare are biologically and morally inseparable from the woman in whose body it develops' (1992: 136; see also Sherwin 1991).

Philosophers like Little or MacKenzie who take a phenomenological approach therefore focus upon the 'extraordinary physical enmeshment' of pregnant embodiment as a basis for ethical understandings of abortion as an 'ethics of intimacy'. Like Young, Kristeva and others, they demonstrate not only the absurdity of treating foetuses as separate individuals with rights and interests of their own, but also how pregnant people are 'given over' in pregnancy in ways they can never fully control. Yet what makes this body of work on 'abortion' distinct from much feminist philosophical writing on 'pregnancy' is the attention paid to the enormous variety of ways that pregnant people conceptualize and relate to the foetuses that are sustained by, and intertwined with, their bodies: 'It can be a wonderful intermingling; it can also be an invasive occupation in which the self feels subsumed' (Little 1999: 303). Moreover, there is a strong concern to detach pregnancy from maternity and presumed parenthood. As Little writes, for example:

> Some women feel from the start that they are in a special personal relationship with the growing fetus. They conceptualize themselves as a mother, thickly construed, in relationship with an entity that is 'their child', whatever the further metaphysical details ... For others,

the sense of relationship grows, as most personal relationships do, slowly: the pregnancy begins as mere biological relationship but, as the day-to-day preoccupations of decisions involving the welfare of another ... accumulate ... she finds herself in a personal relationship. For other women, the relationship is never one of motherhood thickly construed: she is simply in biological relationship with a germinating human organism. For still others, the sense of relationship shifts throughout pregnancy: a conception of motherhood is tried on, then dispatched, or arrives fully formed out of the blue.

(1999: 310)

Phenomenological philosophies of abortion thereby promote an understanding of pregnancy as a highly variable relational phenomenon that should be taken seriously in itself, regardless of its ultimate outcome. Nonetheless, it can be difficult to fully extricate pregnancy from teleological frameworks of meaning when the topic is 'abortion', because so often within discussions around abortion, it is the decision about whether to terminate that pulls ultimate focus. The *telos* of childbirth is thus effectively replaced by 'the decision' or 'the choice' as that which endows pregnancy with purpose and direction. So if a pregnancy ends in childbirth, this is seen as the culmination of the choice to continue, and if it ends in abortion, this can likewise be regarded as the realization of choice. In contrast, pregnancies that end through miscarriage or stillbirth are less easily recuperated within a teleological framework of meaning, because the involuntary 'spontaneous' ending of a pregnancy is less likely to be regarded as its culmination, or rightful ending, that retrospectively determines how a pregnancy should be understood.

Teleological narratives of pregnancy do certainly inform how miscarried pregnancies get framed: as pregnancies that have fallen short of their 'normal' trajectory or 'natural' purpose, and have failed to deliver their expected 'product' (to be discussed in Chapter 1); or as pregnancies that were 'never meant to be'. Likewise, narratives of pregnancy as a matter of individual choice shape the cultural meanings of miscarriage through negation: when the miscarrying person is portrayed as passive and 'powerless' through the removal or absence of choice (to be discussed in Chapters 2 and 5). But my proposal here is that reflection on the nonchosen nature of miscarriage brings into view the fundamental contingency of *all* pregnancies, whatever choices have been possible, even when the choices made align with the eventual outcome. After all, aborted pregnancies, just like child-producing pregnancies, could always have ended otherwise (Lind 2017: 148).[37]

Accordingly, the guiding idea of *Pregnancy Without Birth* is that miscarriage should not be treated as an anomaly, or a 'sub-category' within the philosophy of pregnancy, but rather as a 'possibility proper to all pregnant embodiment' (Scuro 2017: 204). This can have a transformative effect because, as Scuro similarly argues, 'if the phenomenon of pregnant embodiment is already bound to the possibility of miscarriage', then we can begin to free up pregnancy from its 'assumed and expected possibilities of child production' (2017: 204). And in so doing, we overturn the persistent idea that 'productive' birth-giving pregnancy is the only kind of pregnancy that really counts (Mullin 2005: 1). This approach can be understood as congruent with scholarship that seeks to *queer* pregnancy, whereby pregnancy is extricated from the stronghold of 'reproductive futurism' and appears instead as an unpredictable mode of embodiment that exceeds and 'skews' the narrow linear visions that would subsume it as symbol and lived experience (Andrzejewski 2018; see also Mamo 2007; Park 2013; Gibson 2014; Summers 2014; Brown 2019).

A challenge for this project, though, is that miscarriage has been 'shockingly under-theorized' from a philosophical and political perspective (Cahill et al. 2015b). A considerable amount of research has been conducted in the fields of psychology and nursing since the 1960s that explores grief, anxiety and depression;[38] and recent texts by feminist psychotherapists discuss how to reframe miscarriage as a transformative experience that can enable emotional growth and self-knowledge (Epstein-Gilboa 2017; Bueno 2019; Zucker 2021). There is also a growing body of research articles, monographs and edited collections within feminist sociology and anthropology,[39] which demonstrate how social context and cultural norms 'dramatically impact the experience and management of miscarriage' (Kilshaw et al. 2017: 2), while also attesting to the wide variation of subjective responses that may be socially and culturally conditioned but are never uniformly determined. Studies based within the US and the UK, for example, show that while for some losing a pregnancy can be a highly traumatic experience as the loss of 'their baby' or 'their child,' for others, the event is of much less significance or has a different meaning (see e.g. Letherby 1993, 165–6; or Frost et al. 2007). But in terms of philosophical and political theory, there has been scant attention beyond a passing mention until the past decade or so, in which dedicated analyses have begun to appear (see e.g. Parsons 2010; Cahill et al. 2015a; Browne 2017, 2018, 2022; Scuro 2017; Deveau and Lind 2017). As feminist writer Alexandra Kimball recounts:

> I wandered around our living room and looked at my bookshelves, the rows of Cixous and Butler and de Beauvoir, and realized that feminism had nothing to say to me. Here, lined up left to right, was sexual assault, abortion, childbirth, body image: but nothing about miscarriage ….
>
> (2015)

This relative silence can be attributed to the concern that 'if one were to acknowledge that there was something of value lost, something worth grieving in a miscarriage,' one would be ceding ground to the anti-abortion movement (Layne 1997: 305). The claim that pro-choice feminism straightforwardly dismisses the foetus as a 'bunch of cells' is, as Ann Cahill argues, something of a caricature. Yet it cannot be denied that the continued assault on women's reproductive lives renders 'any attempt at subtlety politically dangerous' (2015: 48). Just as 'speaking as an aborting body … from within abortion can feel impossible' (Doyle 2009: 25), speaking from 'within miscarriage' can feel equally so. Nonetheless, it is imperative that miscarriage is fully embraced as a feminist issue across all disciplinary, advocacy and activist contexts, given how profoundly attitudes towards miscarriage are shaped by patriarchal power structures – including the anti-abortion lobby – and socio-economic, ableist and racialized inequalities.

The rise of what anthropologist Linda Layne describes as the mainstream 'pregnancy loss movement' in the US and the UK (2003) (to be discussed in Chapter 3), clearly attests to the need for public engagement and support networks that enable 'ritual affirmation of a shared experience' (Hardy and Kukla 2015: 114). Yet this movement of 'women's self-help' (Layne 2003: 55) has built up predominantly around the lived experiences of straight white middle-class non-disabled women, resulting in the endemic marginalization of those located outside the realm of cis–het relationships and culturally dominant identity groups (Peel and Cain 2012; see also Gibney and Yang 2019). Further, as Sarah Hardy and Quill Kukla argue, the tropes and symbols which proliferate across pregnancy loss literature, blogs and websites can have 'very formulaic ways of inscribing maternal and "child" identity – as angels with birthdates, for instance – and it is not clear that there is social room for other ways of conceiving the identity, or lack thereof, of a miscarried fetus' (2015: 124). Indeed, while some strands of the pregnancy loss movement are explicitly pro-choice, plenty of groups and individuals are rather quiet on the matter, and others are actively anti-abortion. Feminist philosophy, therefore, needs to marshal its wealth of conceptual resources to construct those alternatives, and push back against assumptions that supporting abortion and miscarriage are incompatible, even opposed, political projects.

Transdisciplinary methodology

The approach I take in this book is 'transdisciplinary': a term that denotes 'a movement across existing fields' and 'locates the source of transdisciplinary dynamics pragmatically in a process of problem-solving related, ultimately, to problems of experience in everyday life' (Osborne 2015: 16).[40] The book draws not only on feminist phenomenological philosophy but also critical disability/crip theory, queer theory and feminist scholarship on the politics of reproduction, as well as existing literature on miscarriage within sociology, anthropology, psychology and beyond. Each of the chapters proceeds by taking up a theme that is frequently articulated within what I term 'miscarriage stories' – 'I felt like a failure', for example, or 'I was stuck in limbo' – as a provocation to feminist philosophy. Accounts of personal experience are thereby treated not as transparent or self-evident empirical 'data' but rather as posing questions and problems to be critically examined (Scott 1991; Ahmed 2004; Oksala 2014).[41]

The miscarriage stories I draw upon are situated within the US and the UK, and include first-person accounts as well as reported experiences disclosed through qualitative interview-based research. I have made extensive use of collections such as *Interrogating Pregnancy Loss: Feminist Writings on Abortion, Miscarriage and Stillbirth* (Deveau and

Lind 2017) and *What God Is Honored Here? Writings on Miscarriage and Infant Loss by and for Native Women and Women of Color* (Gibney and Yang 2019). My research has also incorporated memoirs by literary writers, personal reflections in newspapers, magazines and blogs, and many conversations I have had in seminars, reading groups and writing groups while living in both the UK and the US over the past few years. It must be noted that sociological scholarship on the lived experiences of miscarriage in the US and the UK has to date been focused – like the 'pregnancy loss movement' itself – largely upon white cis–het middle-class non-disabled women (Van 2001; Cosgrove 2004). Studies that consider a wider range of experiences and perspectives, however, have been appearing more regularly (see e.g. Wojnar 2009; Peel and Cain 2012; Eichenbaum 2012; Kilshaw and Borg 2020); and in my research I have sought to 'recuperate the narrative gap' (Gibney and Yang 2019: 5) by including writings produced outside the academy as well as advocacy publications that feature qualitative interview material – like *Battling Over Birth: Black Women's Birthing Justice* (Chinyere Oparah et al. 2018) – to ensure a fuller range of perspectives and positions are considered.

Engaging with this broad range of miscarriage stories makes abundantly clear the extent to which socio-economic factors affect how miscarriage is differentially treated and experienced. The accounts of women of colour, for example, regularly document dismissive, and indeed openly hostile, treatment by health workers as a form of 'obstetric racism' (Davis 2019; Chinyere Oparah et al. 2018; Gibney and Yang 2019); and those of LGBTQ+ people consistently emphasize the heterosexism of health professionals and mainstream pregnancy discourses, which can amplify feelings of isolation (Luce 2010; Craven and Peel 2014). Personal stories also demonstrate that an individual's experience of miscarriage will depend upon their embeddedness within particular cultural, religious or spiritual interpretative frameworks, their unique reproductive history (which may include difficulties conceiving, or previous pregnancies, abortions, miscarriages and births), and the quality of their intimate relationships and social networks.[42]

In terms of wider context too, there are significant historical, socio-economic and political differences between the US and the UK to take into account, including their respective healthcare systems. For instance, though the UK's National Health Service is currently being subjected to a governmental campaign of chronic underfunding and privatization by stealth,[43] at present, medical treatment for miscarriage is free for the majority of people in the UK (the new NHS charging regime, introduced in 2015 as part of the 'hostile environment', renders some migrants 'chargeable' for pregnancy-related care, which may include treatment for miscarriage and stillbirth).[44] In comparison, one estimate from 2015 is that on average, uninsured women in the US pay between $4,000 and $9,000 for medical treatment of miscarriage, while insured women pay out-of-pocket expenses of between $250 and $1,200, depending upon their co-payments and deductibles (Grose 2015). Other key points of contextual difference include the centrality of abortion to US politics compared to the UK (where it remains, for now, a relatively marginal 'backbench' political issue), and the greater restrictions upon, and threat to, abortion rights and access in the US,[45] as well as the rising criminalization of miscarriage and stillbirth in states like Indiana and Oklahoma.[46]

At the same time, however, there are several experiential themes – like feelings of failure and guilt – that recur again and again throughout the wide-ranging material I have drawn upon, and which serve as the starting point for each of the book's chapters. It must be emphasized that such feelings are not experienced by everyone – miscarriage can generate an increased trust in one's body, for example, or a sense of emotional strength – and when they are, they are not felt or articulated in the same way. But they do resonate as tropes across miscarriage stories even as different individuals are immersed within different national contexts and social worlds, subjected to differing social pressures, and have differing levels and kinds of social and economic capital. As such, the book attempts the difficult balancing act of attending to affinities, connections and continuities across difference, injustice and inequality, hoping to illuminate points for solidarity along the way.[47]

In terms of the philosophical persuasion of *Pregnancy Without Birth*, it takes inspiration from those whose work can be described as 'critical phenomenology' such as Gail Weiss (1998, 1999), Rosalyn Diprose (2002), Sara Ahmed (2006) and Lisa Guenther (2013a, 2019). These feminist philosophers deploy generic phenomenological concepts such as 'intercorporeality' to foreground the transcendentally intersubjective conditions of subjective experience and the relationality of personhood, while also examining how contingent historical and social structures like heteronormativity, patriarchy and white supremacy shape our embodied subjectivities in constitutive 'quasi-transcendental' ways (Guenther 2019: 12; see also Salamon 2018).[48] As Guenther explains, this requires reaching beyond the confines of the classical phenomenological canon, drawing on a range of empirical and theoretical sources to understand and expose how these structures operate as 'ways of seeing' and 'ways of making the world' (2019: 12). In so doing, she proposes, critical phenomenology opens up space for 'new and liberatory possibilities for meaningful experience and existence', and can thus be understood as 'both a way of doing philosophy and a way of approaching political activism' (2019: 15).

This book seeks to participate in this critical phenomenological project by putting everyday taken-for-granted assumptions about 'normal' or 'natural' pregnancy up for critical scrutiny, while at the same time exploring and promoting alternative feminist understandings. To this end, as outlined above, I have adopted an eclectic transdisciplinary approach; but I have made one significant exclusion via the methodological decision not to engage in any detailed exegesis of omnipresent philosopher men such as Maurice Merleau-Ponty, Emmanuel Levinas, Jacques Derrida, Michel Foucault and so on. This is partly because there is already a rich body of feminist work that enters into productive dialogue with these thinkers (see e.g. Weiss 1999; Diprose 2002; Guenther 2006; Bornemark and Smith 2016; Deutscher 2016; Lymer 2016); but also because I want to resist organizing feminist work around male authority figures, which can imply that feminists are simply 'interpreting' or 'extending' the work of men when they are often doing something quite different and original. The aim is thus to circumvent what Bonnie Mann refers to as philosophy's 'reverence problem' (2018: 42) and put the intellectual labour, ingenuity and creativity of women and gender nonconforming people front and centre.

Problematic terminology

One of the biggest challenges of this project has been language. First off, the terminology used to designate 'the foetus' takes us into highly vexed and unsettling territory, partly because of the high political stakes, and also because we are dealing with particularly liminal states of existence. In relation to specific pregnancies, moreover, the choice of term depends upon how a pregnancy is experienced and lived by the person who is pregnant and those close to them (Han 2018; Kilshaw 2020). For some, 'foetus' can seem too clinical or medical – 'did anyone ever paint the "fetus room" or knit sweaters for a "fetus"?' (Katz Rothman 1986: 107) – and the linguistic switch from 'baby' to 'foetus' that often occurs in medical settings during miscarriage (as discussed in Chapter 3), can be experienced as a serious form of social hypocrisy and betrayal. Yet to others, the language of 'baby' or 'child' performs an ontological over-projection that attributes too much too soon: for instance, when corporate pregnancy websites and even the NHS refer to 'your baby' when the blastocyst has barely implanted in the uterine wall. This book deploys 'foetus' as a minimal general term recognizing that foetuses can accrue further meanings as 'baby' or 'child', and that foetuses inhabit multiple layers of reality that cannot be easily captured by any one concept or figure of speech.[49]

Another complicated issue has been how to designate the involuntary 'spontaneous' ending of a pregnancy without a live birth. In the first instance, there is the uncertain boundary between 'miscarriage' and 'stillbirth'. The UK National Health Service defines 'miscarriage' as 'the loss of a pregnancy during the first 23 weeks', and a stillbirth as 'when a baby is born dead after 24 completed weeks of pregnancy';[50] but in the US, the point of distinction is more often twenty weeks. The terms themselves are also widely despised for being cold, insensitive and brimming with problematic implications. The word 'miscarriage', for instance, indicates that the proper outcome of a process has not materialized, as in a 'miscarriage of justice'. Indeed the 'mis' may seem to imply 'not only that something is wrong but you have an active role in making it so' (Garbes 2016); and 'carriage' arguably conjures up the image of the pregnant person as a 'carrier' or 'vessel' that feminists so vehemently reject. 'Pregnancy loss', therefore, is often used as an alternative within academia as well as pregnancy loss support communities – a wide-ranging term that can cover the cessation of a pregnancy however many weeks it lasted, as well as instances where a pregnancy has been voluntarily terminated but loss is felt.[51] However, as Erica Millar demonstrates (and as will be discussed in Chapters 3 and 5), the language of 'loss' is coming to overdetermine the representation of both miscarriage and abortion in politically problematic ways, because it implies that there is always loss when a pregnancy ends, even if the miscarrying/unpregnant person themselves does not see it that way (2016, 2018). The term 'pregnancy loss' also does not necessarily move us away from the idea of personal responsibility. As Alison Reiheld puts it, 'A lost pregnancy must have been lost by someone ... Such attempts to comfort are all too easily converted into a devastating subject-verb-object: "I lost the pregnancy" or "I lost the baby"' (2015: 15).

There is no existing term, then, that is not problematic. In this book, the priority is to avoid universalizing experiential presumptions regarding what miscarriage means or how it feels to those who go through it, and so after much deliberation – and abandoned attempts at neologisms – I have opted to use the colloquial term 'miscarriage' as arguably the more experientially neutral term, while being acutely aware of its inadequacy. The focus is on what is generally understood to be 'miscarriage' rather than 'stillbirth'; and there are important aspects of stillbirth that render it distinct and require dedicated analysis, such as it being rarer than miscarriage,[52] the publicly visible signs of pregnancy at the later stages (in most cases) that make it 'common knowledge', and the process of giving birth itself. But many of the arguments made in the book are germane to the involuntary cessation of pregnancy without a live birth at whatever stage; and though conflating miscarriage and stillbirth can feel very hurtful to some, research suggests feelings of loss are not necessarily influenced by the length of gestation despite temporal presumptions that 'later means worse' (Lovell 1983; Cosgrove 2004). I also want to flag here the linguistic challenge of referring to a person going through a miscarriage or stillbirth who is at once 'pregnant and not pregnant', or who has been pregnant but has not given birth and thus is not considered 'postpartum' (Silbergleid 2017). To refer to such states of being I use the terms 'miscarrying' or 'unpregnant' person, while again recognizing their potentially discomfiting nature.[53]

Finally, it must be noted that the designation of those who are/have been pregnant also raises issues, as speaking in generic terms of 'pregnant women' can be taken as exclusionary of pregnant men or those who are gender nonbinary or nonconforming. More inclusive gender-neutral terms like 'pregnant people' are increasingly being adopted, and impatience has been expressed in relation to feminists who persist in referring to 'pregnant women' as a generic collective, or 'the pregnant woman' as an abstract singular (see e.g. Lewis

2019: 24–5). Yet moving to gender-neutral language is by no means a simple fix. In the first instance, as Laura Briggs points out, the language of 'pregnant people' and 'non-pregnant people' has a history of reactionary usage: for instance, by those who seek to deny protections against pregnancy discrimination in the workplace by insisting it is not a form of illegal sex/gender discrimination (2017: 5). Moreover, the use of gender-neutral language can feel somewhat obfuscatory when pregnancy is hardly a gender-neutral affair. Just as the capacity for pregnancy has consistently been linked to femaleness and womanhood within the binary sex/gender model, normative and misogynist ideas about femaleness and womanhood – such as feminine self-sacrifice, the unruliness of female flesh or the untrustworthiness of women's testimony and conduct – have in turn determined social expectations and the regulation of pregnancy. So while de-naturalizing the circular link between 'pregnancy' and 'women' is essential to the project of transforming dominant imaginaries of pregnancy and overturning the patriarchal, heteronormative, cisnormative government of reproduction, it does not necessarily make sense to speak of pregnancy in exclusively gender-neutral terms, or to abandon 'pregnant women' altogether as an analytical category. This is especially true when the intention is to examine how struggles for control of pregnancy and reproduction impact particularly upon people understood to be women and girls, though as Toze argues, 'feminist critiques of the regulation of female bodies can be expanded to offer a mechanism for analysing the ways in which trans masculine bodies are also regulated' (2018: 205).

With such considerations in mind, this book does use gendered terminology like 'pregnant women' when referring to gendered discourses and regimes of pregnancy that explicitly or implicitly evoke and impact upon pregnant women qua women. For instance, if I am evoking hegemonic representations of 'the pregnant woman' or the 'mum-to-be', I echo this gendered language to reflect a social and cultural reality. As Millar argues, the dominant modes of representing pregnancy, abortion and miscarriage 'invariably assume "woman" as the subject', and the claim that cultural representations of pregnancy are 'gendered feminine' does not equate to a claim that 'only women experience pregnancy' (2018: 27). When quoting, I also leave in authors' original language. However, when the use of gender-specific terminology is not vital to the point being made, the book uses more capacious and inclusive terms like 'pregnant people' in a bid to expand the conceptual frame. To those who argue that this gesture 'erases women',[54] I would suggest embracing the strategic benefits of the emphasis on 'people'. After all, as the feminist slogan goes, 'women are people too!'

Book overview

Chapter 1 – Failure – interrogates the normative biological imaginaries that condition subjective experiences of miscarriage as the reproductive body 'failing' in its 'most natural function'. It draws on feminist and critical disability/crip theory, as well as philosophy of biology, to explore how essentialist logics of 'organic purposefulness' and 'womb teleology' operate along gendered, racialized and ableist lines to construct 'successful' pregnancy as the ultimate marker of feminine identity and 'use value'. It also examines how 'normal' and 'natural' have come to serve as value-laden ideals that destine us all for failure in some way or other. Contrary to the view that miscarriage must be 'normalized' and 'naturalized', therefore, this chapter argues instead for an eradication of 'natural' and 'normal' as measures for pregnancy of any kind.

Chapter 2 – Control – turns towards questions of subjective agency, offering a phenomenological response to commonly expressed feelings of being passive or powerless in the event of miscarriage, yet at the same time responsible and blameworthy. How can this apparent contradiction be navigated? At first glance, it appears we are stuck in an impossible double bind: if we insist that miscarriage simply 'happens' to the one who experiences it, this seems to confirm patriarchal views of pregnant people as 'bodies-to-be-managed' rather than active subjects of their own pregnancy; but when we claim 'control of our own bodies', this is easily co-opted by the neoliberal model of pregnancy as a 'project' determined by a pregnant individual's lifestyle choices. To offer a way out of this pernicious binary, the chapter draws on feminist philosophies of 'intercorporeality' to promote a non-individualist concept of agency as a relational capacity for shaping and responding to a transformative bodily situation, which may or may not conform to one's will. This enables us to recognize miscarrying/unpregnant people as fully agential subjects, I argue, while also dismantling pregnancy hierarchies that render 'successful' pregnancies a laudable individual achievement, and anything else a site of guilt, judgement and blame.

Chapter 3 – Ambiguity – extends the 'intercorporeal' understanding of pregnancy to explore the uncertainties and incongruities that often run through miscarriage stories when it comes to conceptualizing the status of the foetus and what exactly may have been lost. From the intercorporeal perspective, the material and conceptual complexities of miscarriage stem from the fundamentally ambiguous nature of pregnancy and are thus ineliminable. Yet the increasingly prevalent 'proleptic' model of pregnancy – which represents the foetus as an individuated 'baby-person' already – leaves us ill-equipped to deal with them. On the one hand, the proleptic model produces a hypocritical form of social betrayal in the event of miscarriage, whereby celebration of 'the baby' gives way to awkwardness, avoidance or silence. But it has also given rise to a compensatory and universalizing redescription of miscarriage as 'baby loss' which covers over the ambiguity of pregnancy and miscarriage and the multiple ways these phenomena are experienced – thus coinciding with anti-abortion logics and imaginaries. Accordingly, the chapter calls for a more critical and transformative approach to the politics of silence around miscarriage, which works to expose the hypocrisies of dominant pregnancy culture, while also building greater social tolerance of ambiguity as something to be affirmed rather than resolved or eliminated. Silence, then, appears not as a void but as a generative pause in the proleptic narrative, reimmersing us in the ambiguity that was there all along.

Chapter 4 – Suspension – considers the sense of a 'lost future', or being 'stuck in limbo', that is frequently described by those who undergo miscarriage. It begins by examining these temporal experiences in relation to the model of pregnant time as 'liminal': a transitional time between the past status of 'not-mother' and the future status of 'mother' following birth. Though this model does affirm the ambiguous nature of pregnancy (unlike the proleptic model), it nevertheless presents ambiguity as a temporary phase to be ultimately overcome. As such, it ends up depicting miscarriage in rather conventional terms as an incomplete rite of passage, and the miscarrying/unpregnant person as 'left behind' or 'stuck' in a liminality that was never supposed to be permanent. As an alternative, I draw in this chapter on feminist/queer theory to shatter the presumed opposition between pregnant time (as a forward time) and miscarriage time (as a stuck time) by rethinking *both* through the lens of 'suspended time'. By 'suspending the future to encounter the present', I seek to highlight some of the continuities between overlooked present-oriented temporalities of pregnancy and miscarriage, such as 'catching up to what is already happening' and 'growing sideways', arguing that if pregnant time is not represented in exclusively future-oriented terms as *being-towards-birth*, miscarriage need not be understood as wasted time, or as pregnancy's undoing.

Chapter 5 – Solidarity – turns finally to expressions of anger and resentment, as well as empathy and solidarity, within miscarriage stories, to explore how political solidarity could be further extended across 'miscarriage', 'pregnancy' and 'abortion' as sites of experience and struggle. To demonstrate the urgency of this political project, the chapter highlights the increasingly punitive treatment of miscarriage and stillbirth in the US, as hundreds of women – overwhelmingly poor and disproportionately of colour – have been arrested, prosecuted and incarcerated for allegedly causing their miscarriages/stillbirths through drug use, or for disguising illegal 'self-abortion' as miscarriage/stillbirth. Though it may seem that this rising criminalization of miscarriage necessitates a protective response that insists on its 'innocence', I argue instead for a feminist refusal of 'divide and rule' politics that would have us defend 'innocent' miscarriage at the expense of 'guilty' abortion or 'irresponsible' pregnancy. As an alternative approach, the chapter points to the rising 'full-spectrum' doula movement in the US – which offers non-judgemental support and care to all pregnant people whether their pregnancy ends in birth, abortion, miscarriage, stillbirth or adoption – as an inspiring practical example of feminist solidarity that paves the way for coordinated struggle at a broader level.

Chapter 1
Failure

I felt like a failure … I felt cheated by my own body.[1]

I felt I had failed as a woman … there was a sense of shame that my body could not bring into being this most ordinary of human realities.[2]

One of the most customary responses to miscarriage is that it is 'normal' and 'natural'. Indeed it is often said that a miscarrying body is successfully doing its job: 'The body is wise. It recognizes a pregnancy that could never be carried to term' (Garbes 2018: 82). Yet at the same time, it is striking how often personal accounts of miscarriage articulate feelings of bodily failure. As anthropologist Linda Layne demonstrates, miscarriage is regularly experienced as an 'unthinkable deviation from the natural, normal, biological and social progression that pregnancies are expected to entail' (2003: 175).[3] Even Michelle Obama describes a sense of inadequacy and 'personal failure' that set in when her first pregnancy ended in miscarriage (2018: 187–8).

This widespread experience of miscarriage as failure can be attributed, in part, to being situated within a socio-economic system in which neoliberal values of 'maximum productivity' and 'personal responsibility' circumscribe so many aspects of contemporary life. As will be discussed in the following chapter, the promotion of 'optimal' pregnancy lifestyles becomes deeply internalized, such that many people not only monitor their every move during pregnancy, but also blame themselves when a pregnancy does not turn out as willed or expected. In this chapter, however, the focus is less upon disciplinary mechanisms and intentional behaviour – what a person does or doesn't *do* – and more upon ideas about 'natural' and 'normal' bodily functioning. What do feelings of failure in the event of miscarriage reveal about dominant notions of the 'natural' and the 'normal', particularly in relation to that fabled entity 'the female body' and the production of normative womanhood?

Before proceeding, I should clarify that I am taking for granted here that 'nature', 'culture' and 'society' are mutually constitutive (Kukla 2009: vii).[4] Medical technologies and interventions are perhaps the most obvious examples of how bodies can be manipulated and reconstructed, but social norms, structures and environments also have a major impact on how organs, cells and bones behave, such as carcinogenic working conditions or the 'weathering effect' of structural racism (Geronimus 1992). Cultural value systems, likewise, play a vital role in determining how different kinds of bodies are judged and treated, and hence what bodies are able to be and do.[5] From a phenomenological perspective, we can be said to 'have' bodies in that we have a 'body image', or indeed multiple overlapping 'body images' that we scrutinize and objectify, and are objectified by others (Weiss 1999). Yet embodiment is simultaneously characterized by an 'internal differentiation' whereby 'I must have this body while at the same time being this body' (Jansen and Wehrle 2018: 38). Corporeal meanings and standards are therefore 'not only constitutive of the images we have of our bodies, but also have a more direct impact on our experiences, for example, on how we move, eat, sleep, and behave; on how we sense, feel, and perceive the world; and how we relate to ourselves and others' (Jansen and Wehrle 2018: 38).

The objective of this chapter, accordingly, is to interrogate the biological imaginaries that produce gendered experiences of a miscarrying/unpregnant body as having 'failed' in fulfilling its 'most natural function'. Of course, miscarriage can engender a wide range of feelings, including a sense of relief that the body has taken an 'executive decision' (Garbes 2018: 84), or an increased sense of trust in one's body and oneself: 'I thank my body for knowing what to do, and I appreciate myself for listening to my body' (Lee-Ortiz 2019: 167). But I am interested here in the ways that miscarrying/unpregnant bodies are so often experienced as failing bodies in relation to what is deemed the 'higher' function of reproduction – the end towards which 'able' and 'normal' bodies, especially women's bodies, are imagined to 'naturally' tend.

To explore this, the chapter firstly considers how women's validity has been 'tangled up with reproductive functionality' (Scuro 2017: 200) as a foundational feature of gendered, racialized and ableist biological essentialism, tracing logics of 'organic purposefulness' and 'womb teleology' as they cut across intersecting and unequal social positions. It then goes on to assess 'the female body' as a biomedical object of

Figure 2 Image taken from 'Miscarriage or Abortion? (Or, #shoutingmyabortion in a Graphic Novel' by Jennifer Scuro, included as part one of *The Pregnancy [does not equal] Childbearing Project: A Phenomenology of Miscarriage* (2017)).[6]

analysis, drawing on contemporary philosophy of biology and critical disability/crip theory to understand how 'normal' and 'natural' function as optimal ideals even as they purport to be neutral descriptors. The chapter thereby demonstrates how feminized bodies are '*set up to fail*', as they are idealized as 'givers of life' as well as being measured against an impossible ideal of what is 'normal' and 'natural' that puts them 'in constant need of correction' (Scuro 2017: 240).

Organic purposefulness and womb teleology

A pervasive image of the 'able', 'healthy' and 'happy' organic body is a teleological one in which parts work together for the sake or good of the whole. The concept of *telos* can be translated as 'end', 'goal' or 'purpose' – the 'for-the-sake-of-which' things exist or happen – and is most famously elaborated within the 'natural philosophy' of Aristotle. In texts such as *Generation of Animals* and *Parts of Animals*, Aristotle proposes that biological processes operate according to a teleological order, at the level of organs and behaviours, as well as organisms as a whole which are 'understood functionally as aiming towards certain ends' (Bianchi 2014: 2). Not all features of nature participate in a *telos* or final cause, Aristotle claims, and as such are 'necessary' merely in the simple sense that particular physical or biological conditions make them so.[7] Yet such biological necessity is ultimately subordinate to teleological necessity, and what is *good* accords with its natural *telos*: the 'things which Nature employs are determined by necessity but at the same time, for the sake of some purpose, some final cause' (1953: 559). Throughout *Generation of Animals*, for instance, Aristotle makes references to the 'workmanship' of 'Nature'[8] alongside claims that 'Nature' seeks 'completion and finality' (1953: 7).[9]

If understood as a mysterious 'inner force' or metaphysical principle, Aristotle's teleological notion of natural 'purpose' finds few adherents within contemporary academic philosophy or biology (Ariew 2002: 7; Hoffe 2003: 89). But the residual effects of the Aristotelean worldview are nonetheless evident today in the persistent endowment of bodily function and productivity with some sort of naturalized moral value (Scuro 2017: 190). What is 'natural' or 'good', in this mode of thinking, is what fulfils its function in producing the expected or desired outcome – the implication being that the proper operation and temporality of the body is purposive or end-directed. Sara Ahmed describes this as an ideology of 'organic purposefulness' that can be traced to the classical Aristotelian worldview but also runs through various strands of modern European philosophy (Ahmed 2014). Take, for instance, this quotation that she draws from seventeenth-century philosopher Blaise Pascal, as he conjures up an imaginary organic body to serve as an analogy for the social body and the general will:

> Let us imagine a body full of thinking members ... If the foot and the hands had a will of their own, they could only be in their order in submitting their particular will to the primary will which governs the whole body. Apart from that, they are in disorder and mischief; but in willing only the good of the body, they accomplish their own good.
>
> (cited in Ahmed 2014: 99)

For Ahmed, Pascal's words here not only demonstrate the co-production of the 'organic body' and the 'social body' as imagined entities, but also how deeply *moralized* these imaginaries are. 'The idea that parts are sympathetic', she writes, 'not only *describes* how parts relate to each other, but also *prescribes* what parts must do for other parts, and for the body of which they are a part' (2014: 101). The logic of 'organic purposefulness' declares that parts 'must be willing to do what they are assumed to be for': 'feet walk, brain know, hand grasp, stomach digest, genitals procreate!' (2014: 101). Or, if they cannot, they must at least be 'willing if not able' or 'willing to be able', as per Robert McRuer's concept of 'compulsory able-bodiedness' (Ahmed 2014: 109; McRuer 2006). Imaginaries of the social body as an organic, purposeful whole can prop up a variety of political ideologies that are more or less hierarchical or egalitarian (Ahmed 2014: 103).[10] But what Ahmed is pointing to is a part–whole logic common to different versions of the 'social body' or 'body politic', which confers a duty upon the part and thus operates as 'a moral as well as a discursive frame'. It is a logic of imperative cooperation that does inherently tend towards hierarchy in some form, argues Ahmed, because if the social is imagined as a body with parts, then 'some bodies more than others' tend to be cast as the brains, while others must function as the limbs, the feet, the hands, and so on. 'What you are assumed to be for', she proposes, 'can then become what you are good for, even all that you are good for' (2014: 108).[11]

Nowhere is this more evident than in essentialist imaginaries of 'the female body', given how consistently women have been defined by reproductive function under patriarchal sex/gender regimes as their 'natural purpose', with the womb rendered a kind of synecdoche for womanhood or femaleness *per se* (Yuval-Davis 1997: 29). "Woman?', writes Simone de Beauvoir, 'Very simple, say the fanciers of simple formulas: she is a womb, an ovary ...' ([1949]1997: 35). Or as Lauren Berlant argues, 'When the meaning of a person is reduced to a body part, the identity fragment figures as a sign of incomplete personhood' (1994: 155). But it is not just having a womb that becomes the dominant marker of womanhood or femaleness within gender essentialism. It must be a womb that produces a baby as its supposed proper function:

> If women exist as wombs, as child makers, then they inherit the reproductive will, as that which if thwarted or blocked, causes illness and damage ... The barren womb not only does not deliver its own will to reproduce but compromises the health or wellbeing of the whole body. A willing womb would be one that lives in expectation of becoming fruitful.
>
> (Ahmed 2014: 119)

To illustrate, Ahmed turns to a favourite feminist example: the historical attribution of hysteria to the 'wandering womb' (Ahmed 2014: 118). The most notorious account of the 'wandering womb' can be found in Plato's *Timaeus*: 'There exists inside the womb ... a living being with an appetite for child-making, and so if it remains unreproductive long past puberty, it gets irritated and fretful. It takes to wandering all round the body, and generating all sorts of ailments, including fatal problems ...' (cited in Ahmed 2014, 118; see also Shildrick 1997; Cornell 2002; Villarmea 2020). But though this can be read as a quaint historical quirk from an Ancient era, the imputation to the womb of teleological purpose is not simply a relic. Scuro demonstrates this by citing a present-day 'pro-life philosopher' who proposes a 'womb teleology', baldly stating that '[the] fact of the uterus existing for the unborn child also tells us something about women: they are to be mothers' (2017: 190). And such teleological presumptions are not limited to the patriarchal Right. Contemporary depictions of the womb tend not to portray it as 'wandering off course' when it is not gestating a foetus, but they do consistently evoke it in figurative terms as an empty space, waiting to be filled up (Shildrick 1997: 36–44).

We need to recognize, moreover, how 'womb teleologies' are inflected by histories of race, class, nation, disability and the logics of 'stratified reproduction' (Colen 1986; Ginsburg and Rapp 1995). In *Feminist Queer Crip,* for example, Alison Kafer argues that disability both complicates and enables the reduction of women to their supposed reproductive capacities (2013: 56). On the one hand, because disabled women are consistently cast outside of sexuality and reproduction, this prevents them from being reduced to their reproductive organs as a 'sign of their personhood', as it is assumed that such body parts will not work or will not be needed. Hence these parts can be removed or altered through medical procedures 'without any problem', as in the case of 'Ashley X' that Kafer analyses – a girl diagnosed with static encephalopathy whose womb and breast buds were removed when she was aged 6 to ensure that her body did not go through puberty and become developmentally 'out of sync' with her mind.[12] Yet at the same time, Kafer suggests, anxieties over the fertility of disabled girls or women as threatening and in need of containment '[reveal] the extent to which the female body is always and only framed as reproductive' (2013). Moreover, when the reproductive organs of disabled girls or women are treated as irrelevant and unnecessary, this only testifies to 'the persistence of a reproductive use-value understanding' of women's bodies. If 'the only purpose of these body parts is reproductive, if reproduction is not in one's future, then these parts can be shed without ethical concern' (2013; see also Asch and Stubblefield 2010; Stein 2010).

The racialized dimensions of 'womb teleologies' are also inextricable from gendered essentialism given the extent to which the 'health' and reproduction of the 'social body' has been imagined and managed in racial as well as ableist terms. Françoise Vergès demonstrates in *The Wombs of Women* (2020), for instance, how the bodies of Black women have been used as 'so many tools' to serve the interests of capital and the state in ways that render them both commodifiable and expendable at the same time (2020: 2).[13] On the one hand, the structural capture of Black women's wombs[14] has long been integral to the functioning of racial capitalism as 'generators of human capital' that reproduce an enslaved or exploitable labour force (2020: 53).[15] But on the other hand, the bodies of Black women and other women of colour have been framed as a hyper-reproductive *threat* to the social body, and accordingly targeted by eugenic or neo-eugenic forms of 'population management' (2020: 54–62; see also Roberts 1997, Ross and Solinger 2017).[16] And in response to these legacies of capture, exploitation and persecution, various Black cultural or nationalist movements have promoted biological reproduction as a 'racial imperative' and means of overcoming white supremacism and collective survival (Yuval-Davis 1995; Mitchell 2004; Ceballo et al. 2015), thereby making yet another attempt to 'own Black women's wombs' (Gumbs 2016: 21). Loretta Ross highlights a particularly pernicious example of this in the anti-abortion movement of the Black religious Right in the US which equates Black abortion with Black genocide – a rhetorical move that functions as a way of 're-enslaving Black women by making us breeders for someone else's cause' (2008; see also Nelson 2003; Weinbaum 2004; Guenther 2013b; Denbow 2016).[17]

Individual pregnancies, it must be emphasized, are always unique, and shaped not only by intersecting histories and structures of oppression but also by transformative forces of resistance and re-signification. No single theoretical paradigm, therefore, can serve as the metanarrative with exhaustive explanatory power. Yet something feminist and reproductive justice theorists have abundantly demonstrated is the extent to which pregnancy-as-childbearing has been established as the primary generator of women's 'use value' and locus of identity across a wide range of unequal subject positions. While pregnancy undeniably serves as a key site of racial, ableist and class division, what cuts across the dividing lines is the essentialist presumption that the work of reproduction belongs more properly to women, as women are prescribed a particular role in reproducing the revered biological family line as well as ensuring 'either the survival, or destruction, of the body politic' (Millar 2018: 222).

This is not to say that all women are equally oppressed by 'womb teleologies' or logics of 'organic purposefulness' though in different ways, given that some are supported and rewarded for reproduction, while others are punished and despised for it. It is also vital to recognize how ideas about masculinity and manhood are determined by ideas about reproductive capacity or 'virility' that differ according to racial and national identity, dis/ability and class position. But the core point is that the biological process of reproduction is more commonly 'gendered feminine' (Millar 2018: 227). This is why discourses of 'problem' pregnancies like 'teen pregnancies' or 'immigrant pregnancies' are targeted at particular groups of girls and women rather than boys and men – like when the British National Party (BNP) warns of 'colonisation via the womb' rather than, say, the testes (Millar 2018: 222; see also Brown and Ferree 2005). It is also what makes the pregnant man so 'unthinkable' (Toze 2018) and nonbinary, nonfeminine and queer pregnant people so marginalized. As Margrit Shildrick has put it:

> At the most reductive level, women have been seen as little more than baby machines; and even when the derogatory valuation has been put aside, it does seem to express a self-evident truth that the reproductive role is more properly that of the woman ... That the reproductive body stands for something essentially female, and that to be valorised as a life-giver just is to be valorised as a woman, has been taken as a biological given.[18]
>
> (1997: 22)

I have begun by assembling feminist critiques of 'organic purposefulness' and 'womb teleology' because this body of work goes a long way to accounting for the sense of failure experienced by so many women in the event of miscarriage, even those who consciously reject this ideology: 'It will be hard ... not to listen to the internal accusations of incompetency. Your body has failed at this most natural of functions' (O'Farrell 2017: 100); 'I feel that I have let my entire family down' (Nakamura Lin 2019: 137); 'I disappointed everyone' (Valmidiano 2019: 230). The 'unwilling' womb, as Ahmed explains it, has been seen not only to fail the individual feminized body of which it is a part, but moreover, the ultimate goal of reproducing the 'family line', the nation, or indeed the species, as women's presumed reproductive capacities have been so thoroughly co-opted to serve patriarchal, nationalist and capitalist interests as 'bearers of future children for the community' (Bueno 2019: 100). Consequently, miscarrying/unpregnant women's bodies have been socially and culturally marked as incomplete and inadequate, such that miscarriage frequently undermines women's sense of self-worth and gendered identity, right across the hierarchies of stratified reproduction. For instance, Rosario Ceballo and colleagues illustrate how internalized stereotypes about the hyperfertility of women of colour mean that personal distress in the event of infertility or miscarriage may be 'heightened for women of color because of their own and others' expectations of them as the kind of people who have babies rather than those who have trouble becoming pregnant' and producing children: 'the media represents us as popping out babies left and right ... so I didn't think there was a problem with us' (2015: 505; see also Ceballo 1999; Szkupinski-Quiroga 2002).[19] Zsusza Berend claims that surrogates too can be especially vulnerable to feelings of failure because of high levels of confidence in their childbearing capacity (2012: 93).

Conversely, if to fail *as a woman* is to not be 'successfully' pregnant, then what are the implications of a 'failed pregnancy' for those who are not women or not subject to the usual gendered expectations? While being pregnant generally serves to *confirm* or shore up female/feminine gender identity, the opposite occurs in relation to masculinity or maleness which is so often *undone* by pregnancy. For example, Paisley Currah and Damien Riggs both contend that pregnant men are repeatedly subjected to being 'de-transitioned' by others or met with 'stupefied resistance'; and medical assessment procedures too have often presumed that a 'true' trans man would have no desire to become pregnant (Currah 2008: 331; Riggs 2013; see also Toze 2018).[20] Scholarly research into miscarriage is currently skewed towards the experiences of nondisabled cis–het white women, but the extent to which such women experience their miscarriages as failure reveals a lot about the deep and enduring link between 'productive' pregnancy and ideals of 'natural' or 'true' womanhood, while also raising interesting and important questions in relation to differently gendered pregnancies. For instance: How do gendered ideas about reproductive failure intersect with the 'official trans narrative' of the trans body as already 'wrong' and 'failing' (skelton 2017: 133)? And if a womb is located within a non-feminized body, is it still assigned a reproductive *telos*? Are wombs imbued with 'organic purposefulness' regardless of gender?

To further consider these latter questions, the next part of the chapter will examine the 'common-sense' assumption that at the level of 'pure biology' (away from philosophical flights of fancy or patriarchal ideology), bodies and body parts simply do have 'proper functions', however those bodies are culturally constructed or politically organized. Consider, for example, this piece about breastfeeding by a popular feminist writer and journalist:

> Breasts have only one functional purpose: to make food for our offspring … breasts exist for babies first – any adult enjoyment or appreciation is secondary. Breasts can only fulfil their true calling through pregnancy. If they've never produced milk, they simply haven't reached full biological maturity.
>
> (Garbes 2018: 142)

Elsewhere in the essay, the author insists that breasts can still play a part in a 'happy and fulfilling life' whether they lactate or not, and vehemently rejects essentialist ideologies of compulsory maternity (Garbes 2018: 142). But the language of 'maturity' and 'true calling' does suggest an underlying subscription to the logic of 'organic purposefulness' and 'use value' presented as 'the science' behind the ideological maelstrom – the bare 'facts of the matter' beyond dispute. Accordingly, the next section will turn to discussions in the philosophy of biology and critical disability/crip theory in order to interrogate this kind of claim by developing a more fine-grained understanding of notions of 'function' and 'purpose', 'natural' and 'normal', as they pertain to pregnant/unpregnant bodies as biomedical objects of analysis. Is the idea of 'function' inherently wedded to teleological ideas of 'purpose'? To what extent are notions of 'natural' or 'normal' function tied to gendered ideals of how a body should be, what it should do and what it is for?

The 'normal', the 'natural' and the normative

As stated above, the notion of a *telos* immanent to natural entities is broadly dismissed within contemporary biology, when understood as some kind of mysterious metaphysical force. That said, biology is unique within the natural sciences in its deployment of what many do recognize to be generically teleological language of 'purposes', 'functions' or 'ends' in relation to organisms (Ariew 2002: 7). As philosopher of biology Michael Ruse puts it, while 'no-one one would ask what "purpose" or "end" the planet Mars serves', or speak of hydrogen combining with oxygen 'in order to' make water, it is perfectly common to ask questions about the 'function' or 'purpose' of an organic entity – that is, to ask what a heart or womb is *for* and not just what does it *do* (2002: 33). Ruse and others defend the legitimacy of the teleological 'in order to', or 'for the sake of which', on both intuitive and heuristic grounds, claiming that such language enables biologists to ask questions that lead to significant insights into how such systems and organisms operate. The idea here is that organisms intuitively invite teleological thinking about life, survival and reproduction in a way that rocks or gases do not, and that they should be considered above all as 'directively organised' or self-regulating systems (2002: 55; see also Boorse 1977; Ayala 1999).[21]

In opposition, however, are philosophers who contend that teleological function statements can and should be eliminated as far as possible within biology as a natural science. Attributing the function of pumping blood to the heart, gestation to the womb or lactation to the breast, for example, can be understood as merely a 'shorthand description of certain attributes of the heart' or womb or breast. Accordingly, teleological explanations can be simply reformulated as causal-mechanistic explanations (Allen et al. 1998: 4, see also Ariew et al. 2002: 1). From this perspective, the notion of 'function' can thus be retained or 'rescued' by sharply distinguishing between teleological explanation understood as *purposive*, and functional explanation as an aspect of *causal or system analysis*. If we follow this line of thought, it is certainly possible to speak of bodily functions without summoning ideas about 'organic purposefulness' or 'proper' functions. So we could legitimately say that a function of the heart is to pump blood, of the womb to gestate, or of the breast to lactate, but not that hearts exist *in order to* pump blood, that breasts exist *in order to* lactate or that wombs exist *in order to* gestate, as such latter statements constitute teleological claims about why a body part exists and what it is *for* (Ariew et al. 2002: 2).[22] Nonetheless, even if 'function' can be differentiated from stronger teleological notions of 'purpose' or '*proper* function', we are still faced with the question of what it means to say that a body part has a function if it does not or cannot perform that specified function. What of a breast that does not or cannot lactate? Or a womb that does not or cannot gestate, or begins to gestate but then stops? Can such body parts still be said to function 'normally' or 'naturally'?

A commonly cited account of biological 'normality' can be found in philosopher Christopher Boorse's 1977 article 'Health as a Theoretical Concept'. In this article, Boorse defines the 'normal function' of a body part as 'a statistically typical contribution by it' to the individual survival and reproduction of an organism within a biological 'reference class' – specifically, an age class or binary sex class (1977: 555).[23] Boorse claims that his theory can be captured by the phrase 'the normal is the natural', defining what is 'natural' as 'typical species-design', or in more detail, 'the typical hierarchy of interlocking functional systems that supports the life of organisms of that type' (1977: 557).[24] Boorse does recognize that the models of 'typical species-design' he refers to are a 'series of ideal types of organism'. But he insists that 'the idealization is of course statistical, not moral or aesthetic or normative in any other way', and hence that his account is purely empirical and 'value-free' (1977: 555). Though the ideal 'normal' type may not exactly resemble any species member – 'any frog', for instance, is 'bound to be atypical in some respect' – the ideal should nevertheless serve as the basis for judgements of what is healthy despite the endemic reality of variation (1977: 555). So according to Boorse, a body or body part can be declared 'healthy' if it demonstrates the 'readiness' or 'ability to perform all typical physiological functions with at least typical efficiency' (1977: 555), while 'diseases' are 'deviations from the species biological design' (1977: 543) and involve 'interferences with normal functioning' (1977: 559).

From the Boorsian perspective, then, can a body that 'miscarries' pass the test for 'normal species-typical functioning'? Boorse does not specifically refer to miscarriage in his influential article but his comments on 'infertility' can give us some indication. On the one hand, he claims that 'pure reproductive success' cannot be the sole criterion for 'health' because 'parents hardly become healthier with each successive child' (1977: 548). Indeed, he says that reproduction upsets the equilibrium of an individual organism (1977: 550). Nevertheless, Boorse does presume 'sterility' to be a 'disease'[25] because 'individual reproductive competence' is a key component of 'species-design' (even though it may not necessarily cause harm or discomfort to an individual who is so embodied).[26] As Htut Maung explains, a body that repeatedly does not conceive and is deemed 'infertile' would clearly not pass the Boorsian test for 'normal functioning' because it involves the 'failure of an internal biological part to perform its statistically typical contribution towards achieving the organism's goal of reproduction at a statistically typical level of efficiency for the relevant reference class'– in this case 'women' (2018: 47). On this logic, *recurrent* miscarriage as a form of 'impaired fecundity' (Crawford et al 2017)[27] would also fail the test for 'normal functioning'. Yet Boorse's theory does allow for some 'variation within the normal' and hence some level of 'dysfunction', as long as it does not fall 'more than a certain distance below the population mean' (Boorse 1977: 595). So a singular miscarriage could be taken to fall within 'the normal' if not preceded by too many previous miscarriages, and if followed by 'successful' pregnancy. And indeed, this is how it is regarded within the UK National Health Service at present, which only treats miscarriage as a medical health problem to be investigated and potentially treated once it has occurred three times in a row.[28]

Boorse's account of 'normal function' thus provides a criterion for classifying singular miscarriage as 'theoretically normal' (in the sense of not falling too far below the 'statistical typical contribution to reproduction'), as well as having 'the practical normality of requiring no medical attention' beyond immediate medical management if required (Boorse 1977: 549). Yet I have taken this detour via Boorse not to endorse this argument for miscarriage's 'normality' and 'naturalness' – at least when it is a singular event – but rather, because it enables further insight into why common reassurances about the 'normality' and 'naturalness' of miscarriage may in fact be cold comfort to those who miscarry. In the first instance, this is because Boorse's model provides an exemplary demonstration of how evolutionary concepts of species reproduction get used as an index of 'health', 'naturalness' and 'normality' at the level of individual bodies, such that not reproducing appears to have significance at a truly epic scale. Moreover, as critical disability/crip theorists have thoroughly established, the Boorsian account reveals how 'natural' and 'normal' have come to operate above all as *ideal types*, even though Boorse's use of 'typical' might seem to imply merely common, usual or frequent (Amundson 2000: 35; see also Garland-Thomson 1997; Tremain 2010). It is 'by comparing X with its reference class Y', Boorse contends, 'that one distinguishes the way X does function from the way it ought to' (1977: 562). Even if a certain level of 'dysfunction' is deemed to fall within the 'normal' range, the judgement of 'normality' always depends on measuring a particular body or body part against the ideal type for the 'reference class' that actual bodies in all their functional variation rarely match up to precisely, as he himself admits. Variation is always variation *from* the 'norm'.

So while the Boorsian model purports to be value-neutral, the equation of 'typicality' with 'normality' carries an implicitly evaluative 'normative taint'. As Ron Amundson points out in 'Against Normal Function' (2000), this becomes particularly apparent when we consider that the binary opposite term 'abnormal' must then designate anything other than typical (2000: 34). After all, abnormality is rarely used to label a mode of functioning deemed to be *superior* to the typical, frequent or average mode, as when disabled bodies are defined as 'abnormal' (2000: 35). Further, argues Amundson, if we considered merely the *level* of functional performance, rather than the *mode*, 'the disadvantages of disability would not seem so natural and inevitable' because 'high levels of function are possible for very atypical people when they use atypical modes of functioning' (2000: 35).[29] From this perspective, then, it is the concept of 'normal' rather than the concept of 'function' that is the problem (Hacking 1990). Though the word 'normal' is supposed to stand 'indifferently for what is typical, the unenthusiastic objective average', writes Ian Hacking, it uses 'a power as old as Aristotle to bridge the fact/value distinction, whispering in your ear that what is normal is also all right' (Hacking 1990: 160; see also Davis 1995).[30]

Within critical disability/crip theory, the comprehensive rejection of the Boorsian account of normality is part of a broader critique of biomedical constructions of the 'normal' body that define 'the way the body "should be"' and hence create intense pressure to strive to approximate the ideal (Hacking 1990: 164; Davis 1995: 5: see also McRuer 2006; Tremain 2010; Kafer 2013). To return to Ahmed's formulation: one must at least be 'willing if not able' or 'willing to be able' (Ahmed 2014: 109). To critique biomedicine in this way does not equate to generalizing claims about medical institutions, professionals and bodies of knowledge being 'all the same', nor a dogmatic rejection of medical intervention. Instead, as Kafer explains, 'rather than taking medical intervention for granted, [this approach] recognizes ... that medical representations, diagnoses, and treatments of bodily variation are imbued with ideological biases about what constitutes normalcy and deviance' (2013: 6). 'Normality' or 'normalcy', therefore, must be understood not merely as descriptive or empirical categories that refer simply to statistical typicality, as the Boorsian account would have it. Rather, these concepts as generally understood and deployed today bear 'an inherent relation to an optimum' (Jansen and Wehrle 2018: 39). The body images presented in biomedical textbooks, medical pamphlets or pregnancy guidebooks, for example, are of 'a normative body rather than exact copies of any particular bodies' (Poovey 1995: 79; see also Kafer 2013: 7). This is what Boorse refers to as a 'composite portrait' that may not 'exactly resemble any species member' but nevertheless serves as the standard-bearer for the 'normal', 'natural' and 'healthy' body (1977: 557).[31]

Paradoxically, however, the so-called 'natural/normal' body always remains to be realized precisely because it is a normative ideal – an *achievement* that requires constant maintenance and modification to hold off the ever-present threat of deviation from what Boorse calls the 'natural' standard of the 'reference class'. In such cases of deviation, as Shildrick points out, 'it is the unmodified body which is seen as unnatural' and in need of corrective interventions (2001: 55), like, for instance, the removal of ovarian cysts, or a 'cervical stitch'. The 'normal' or 'natural' body is thereby materialized through a set of interventions and 'reiterative practices that speak to the instability of the singular standard' (2001: 55). In other words, the fact that so much effort goes into achieving the 'natural' and the 'normal' is what reveals their constructedness – a paradox that is made particularly apparent in the case of 'the female body'. Though women and girls have been represented in Western cultural and philosophical imaginaries as 'closer to nature' due to their supposed capacity for menstruation, pregnancy, birth and lactation, at the same time, biomedical discourses have presented women's bodies as more in need of intervention and external management compared to the masculine norm, precisely because of such capacities that render them permeable, 'leaky' and 'out of control' (Shildrick 2001: 31; see also Grosz 1994; Parker and Pausé 2018). As Kathryn Pauly Morgan once put it, 'the female body' has routinely been treated as 'a "difficult" assemblage of organs and processes, some of which may be malfunctioning' (1989: 74).

Within discourses on infertility produced by the National Health Service in the UK, for example, while 'recognition of men's biological involvement may be stressed and their social involvement normalised', it is above all 'women's bodies that are manipulable' and located as the main site of the problem (Shildrick 1997: 24). This is perhaps even more true of miscarriage, which is so often presumed to be entirely a 'women's issue', in biological terms at least. The NHS webpage on 'diagnosis' of miscarriage, for instance, refers to a potential scan that can be done following 'recurrent' miscarriage to 'check the structure of your womb for any abnormalities' or for signs of a 'weakened cervix', as well as blood tests; but there is no mention of any tests for the sperm provider.[32] Biomedical discourse, moreover, incorporates a range of value-laden terms that imply 'deviant resistance to motherhood', such as 'hostile mucus', 'irritable uterus', 'insufficient placenta' and 'incompetent cervix', marking out those who experience pregnancy complications, infertility, miscarriage and stillbirth as 'unnatural and unfeminine' (Throsby 2004: 65).[33]

Building on this analysis, Khiara Bridges argues that poor pregnant women of colour are produced as possessors of particularly 'unruly bodies' as they are conceptualized as a 'high risk population', such that poverty itself becomes medicalized as an extra layer of pathology that high-tech intervention can remedy (2008: 16). Michael Toze also suggests that gendered notions of the 'unruly' pregnant body affect the treatment of trans men who are or could be pregnant. He observes, for example, that NHS 2013 protocol of recommending sterilization for trans masculine people taking testosterone, '"just in case" of a relatively unproven risk' of uterine problems (like endometrial hyperplasia or cancer), is at odds with the usual institutional belief that surgery for trans people should be a 'last resort', arguing that this inconsistency derives not only from the presumption that trans people 'will not – or should not – become pregnant', but also from the long-standing perception of anatomy deemed 'female' as inherently risky and in need of 'fixing' (2018: 201).

De-naturalizing and de-normalizing pregnancy

Platitudes that miscarriage is 'normal' are generally intended as a gesture towards commonness (you're not alone), and that it is 'natural' as a form of reassurance (it's not your fault). But feminist and critical disability/crip theory helps us see how such reassurances are undercut by the entanglement between the statistical sense of 'normal' (how bodies frequently function) and the normative sense of 'normal' (how bodies *ought* to function). Consequently, while miscarriage may be glossed as a 'normal' and 'natural' part of reproductive life, it is in fact the 'successful' or 'optimal' pregnancy that sets the implicit and 'profoundly narrow standard of normalcy' against which pregnancies in all their variation are measured (Frederick 2017: 92). So when a body does not or cannot 'meet the desired outcomes and expectations in a way that resonates as natural and normal', it is unsurprising if that body is experienced as abnormal, deficient or failing (Scuro 2017: 183).

Feminist scholars of reproduction have also thoroughly demonstrated how the ideal model of the 'normal' and 'natural' pregnancy has been formulated through a series of technological transformations that have done much more than give nature a 'helping hand' (Stanworth 1987; Franklin 1995; Lewis 2019). Lara Freidenfelds and Linda Layne, for example, both argue that the contemporary Western 'myth of the perfect pregnancy' (Freidenfelds 2020) is premised largely upon notions of medical and technological progress that create unrealistically high expectations about the ability to control reproduction, have 'perfect experiences' and produce 'perfect babies' (Layne 2003; Freidenfelds 2020). Yet this is the very same myth that fetishizes the 'natural' pregnancy – because in its most optimal mode the 'perfect pregnancy' proceeds apparently with no intervention at all[34] – via racist and colonial tropes which exoticize pregnancies that occur within non-Western environments as 'simpler', 'primitive' and 'instinctive', and hence as examples from which 'we' can learn.[35]

Normative ideas of the 'natural' are thereby embroiled in various ways with technologically mediated understandings of what a body can (and should) do, as well as gendered and racialized ideas about what is 'closer to nature'. And these ideas not only shape constructs of the 'natural pregnancy', but also notions of 'natural' or 'expectant miscarriage' as a process of simply 'letting nature take its course' rather than having a D&C procedure, for instance, or taking medication. Within contexts of reproductive normativity in which what is 'natural' is held up as what is *best*, 'medical management' may feel like an 'unnatural' and less 'authentic' kind of experience: 'The following week I took more tablets. All I could think was how my body was letting me down again; I couldn't even get miscarriage right after already failing at pregnancy' (Miscarriage

Association 2021). Depictions of 'natural miscarriage' as an unmediated biological phenomenon – as something that 'just happens to you' – also do those who go through it a serious disservice, because they obscure the coping techniques and effort that go into handling this painful and frequently drawn-out process. As Sophie Lewis points out in relation to 'natural pregnancy' and 'natural birth', such processes are hardly free from intervention when they are constituted by 'a regimen full of carefully stylized … hacks and artifices, a suite of mental and physical conditioning that may be billed as "intuitive" but which nevertheless take time and skill to master' (Lewis 2019: 6; see also Mansfield 2008: 1093).

My aim here, to be clear, is not to imply that a desire for reduced intervention is necessarily wedded to fetishized notions of the 'natural', or to repudiate the work of feminist healthcare movements that have pushed back against patriarchal and racist management of pregnancy under the sign of 'de-medicalization'.[36] It is rather to repeat and amplify the feminist call for the idealized myth of 'normal' or 'natural' pregnancy to be 'evacuate[d] from the conversation', along with 'the myth of a normal or natural human body untouched by the scientific shibboleth we call "technology"' (Lewis 2017: 205; see also Firestone [1970] 1999; Stanworth 1987: 34).[37] There is certainly a seductive power to the performance of 'normal' and 'natural', particularly in contexts in which there are diminished avenues for women to cultivate a sense of self-worth, value and success.[38] It may also be true that those pregnancies which conform least to the optimal standards set by what Angela Frederick describes as 'the normalcy project' are most damaged by them (2017). But the discourses that create such divisive pregnancy hierarchies are not simply a 'minority problem'. To borrow the words of Ladelle McWhorter, they 'create the conditions under which all of us live; they structure the situation within which each of us comes to terms with ourselves and creates a way of life' (2005: xv). Critical reflection on experiences of miscarriage as bodily failure can therefore bring to light the multiple ways that pregnant people are 'set up to fail' (Scuro 2017: 183) as a rallying point for feminist solidarity and pushback. After all, a sense of failure is not exclusively experienced by people whose pregnancies do not produce a living baby, but also by many who conceive, or do not conceive, via IVF, who do not fulfill norms of 'glowing' pregnant femininity, or who do not have an unmedicated vaginal birth. Adrienne Rich, for instance, writes that 'Sometimes I felt that my three unconscious deliveries were yet another sign of my half-suspected inadequacy as a woman; the "real" mothers were those who had been "awake through it all"' ([1976]1992: 176).

Quill Kukla has argued that 'something very strange and problematic happens to our critical and theoretical stance when we focus our analytic attention on the minority of cases where the "normal" narrative *goes wrong*' (2005: 100). Doing so, they contend, gives us a 'biased picture of the social reality of pregnancy' because most pregnancies are 'normal, healthy, embraced pregnancies'. Moreover, it 'implicitly presume[s] that healthy, accepted, normal pregnancies are somehow immune from the constitutive power of rhetoric, ideology and politics … that they form an innocent or "natural" terrain where no ethical and rhetorical interrogation is required' (2005: 100). But focusing analytic attention on cases where the 'normal' narrative *goes wrong* need not, in my view, entail a presumption that pregnancies classed as 'normal' are somehow free from what Kukla describes as the normative 'technics of pregnancy'. On the contrary, because pregnancies that fall short of the normative ideal most clearly expose the instability of that ideal, foregrounding such pregnancies – rather than positioning them as an afterthought or a 'sub-topic' – will surely only facilitate the critical interrogation of those 'normal' pregnancies that Kukla so brilliantly de-naturalizes and politicizes.

This strategy of starting from miscarriage, in some ways, is congruent with popular campaigns to 'normalize' miscarriage – like #IHadaMiscarriage[39] or #misCOURAGE[40] – that seek to bring in miscarriage from the margins by emphasizing its relative commonness and challenging its 'taboo' status through sharing stories and increasing awareness. But the core point I am making is that efforts to destigmatize miscarriage will only be effective as part of a much more ambitious project to develop a 'full-inclusion' model of pregnancy that does not 'assume a centre' to which all variations are peripheral (Long 2018: 9). The idea, then, is not so much to 'normalize' or 'naturalize' miscarriage as to insist that there is no such thing as a 'normal' or 'natural' pregnancy.

The stakes of doing so are certainly high when ideas about what is 'normal' and 'natural' play such a central role in the classification of health, illness, disease and pathology, and hence in determining what medical research is done, and the kind of medical treatment to which pregnant/nonpregnant/unpregnant people have access. For instance, discussions over what qualifies as 'infertility' or 'impaired fecundity', and whether such conditions should be classed as 'diseases' or not, have become integral to debates over the ethics and politics of state-funded or insurance-covered fertility treatment (Becker and Nachtigall 1992; Greil et al. 2011; Htut Maung 2018).[41] From a pragmatic point of view, then, there may seem to be a good case for miscarriage to be categorized as 'abnormal' or 'pathological' if this is the condition for accessing sought-after medical investigation and treatment. After all, plenty of people do express frustration when miscarriage is dismissed as a 'normal' and 'natural' part of reproductive life and thereby deprioritized on research agendas or not taken seriously in clinical settings.

But even if it were decided that 'medicalization' of miscarriage is desirable (if it would enable people to access investigative treatment prior to the 'three in a row' rule, for example, or lead to increased funding for medical research),[42] there is no need for categories of 'natural', 'normal' and 'abnormal', to play a legitimating role in this process. Various bioethicists, for example, have offered up evaluative frameworks based upon notions of 'harm', 'suffering' or 'collective well-being' as a means of deciding what the tools of medicine should be used for – frameworks that do not depend upon a supposedly 'natural' or 'normal' standard against which we can all be measured (Kukla 2014). Jiri Vácha has argued, for example, that the concept of 'species normality' could be replaced by a non-comparative, non-statistical and non-ideal concept like 'responsiveness'. So rather than gauging whether an individual conforms to an ideal 'species design', medical judgement would assess the congruence between the actual level of functioning of an individual and that deemed necessary for their well-being 'without regard to the quality or quantity of the morphology and function which the statistical norm would wish to prescribe for [them]' (1978: 826).

Feminist challenges to constructs of 'normal' and 'natural' pregnancy, therefore, are by no means fanciful or divorced from practical concerns. Concepts of 'natural' and 'normal' are not a 'merely' philosophical matter: they shape the material, social and cultural conditions of a pregnancy and therefore its lived reality. Yet language can be changed, concepts reconstituted and metaphors abandoned. Linguistic or conceptual shifts are not sufficient in themselves without socio-economic structural transformation, and indeed, in isolation function as distraction or 'window dressing'. But as part of such processes of transformation, linguistic change can make a material difference.[43] The rising acceptance and usage of the language of the neurodiversity movement, for example, demonstrates that public understandings can slowly shift, and that the 'incompetent cervix' and the 'normal birth' need not be permanent fixtures of the ob–gyn lexicon. And while being predictably ridiculed in the right-wing press, the efforts by medical institutions such as the British Medical Association and the Midwives Alliance of North America[44] to shift towards gender neutral or 'gender additive' terms such as 'pregnant people' serve not only as an inclusive gesture designed to challenge the erasure of trans and nonbinary pregnant people and enable more adequate healthcare, record-keeping and research (see e.g. Hines et al. 2021), but further, as a way of shaking loose the gendered expectations and presumptions about proper femininity and 'normal/natural' womanhood that have stuck so firmly to pregnancy.

Beyond the institutional level, moreover, the rejection of 'normal' and 'natural' as regulative ideals can open up multiple ways of understanding and living 'non-normative morphology not as failure of form but another way of being' (Shildrick 2001: 50). As Ahmed writes, 'corporeal diversity, how we come to inhabit different kinds of bodies, with differing capacities and incapacities, rhythms and tendencies, would be understood as a call to open up a world that has assumed a certain kind of body as a norm' (2014: 51).[45] Jack Halberstam, moreover, has talked about failure as a 'queer art', arguing that failure to meet conventional heteronormative standards of success can reveal and exploit 'the unpredictability of ideology and its indeterminate qualities' (2011: 88). When it comes to miscarriage, however, the affirmative tone of much of this strand of academic theorizing feels somewhat unsuitable, given that unwanted miscarriage is commonly experienced as painful and distressing – as 'one's body doing that which one most wants one's body not to do' (Clark Miller 2015: 145). As Kafer and others argue, though it is vital to refuse normative body ideals and affirm corporeal variation, this must not become a kind of body positivity mandate. It is important to 'make room for people to acknowledge – even mourn – a change in form or function' or an incapacity that causes suffering, while also acknowledging that such changes and incapacities 'cannot be understood apart from the context in which they occur' (Kafer 2013: 6; see also Samuels 2017).

In conclusion, then, part of 'doing justice to the richness of our bodily differences' (Weiss 1999: 67) must involve paying proper theoretical attention to that unsettling and confounding experience of being 'let down' or 'failed' by one's body. My main aim in this chapter has been to investigate how gendered, racialized and ableist narratives of the 'natural' or 'normal' pregnancy ideologically condition personal feelings of failure: 'You are *not* a success. You are *not* pregnant' (Baker 2019: 84). But experiences of what Harriet Cooper describes as 'internalized oppression' are complex and varied (2020). As I emphasized at the beginning, not everyone does feel this way: just as gender is embodied and lived in multiple variations, so too are pregnancy and miscarriage, and we are never straightforwardly 'produced' through pregiven power relationships and social discourses (Sufrin 2017: 23). And those who do articulate a sense of failure do so in subtly different ways. So in the next chapter, I want to consider more carefully the 'failed pregnancy' as an experience *of*, *with* and *as* a body, particularly in relation to the question of agency. How can we understand ourselves to be subjects with agency when our bodies act against our will? In what ways are we, as embodied beings, participants in pregnancy and miscarriage? And how does miscarriage disturb individualist myths of control?

Chapter 2
Control

I felt, with some certainty, it must have been my fault.[1]

They psyche us all out to think that all this stuff was in our control ... and it never was.[2]

The previous chapter explored feelings of failure, which are often infused with a sense of powerlessness in being unable to do anything to prevent miscarriage from occurring, or indeed, a sense of bodily betrayal: *it was my body, not me*. Yet it is also common for people who experience miscarriage to describe feelings of self-blame and guilt that pertain not so much to the functioning of the body, but to their actions and behaviour: *I must have done something to cause this.*[3] Medical professionals and discourses may reassure that miscarriage is just 'nature taking its course', but as Layne points out, 'this contradicts all the morally laden messages [pregnant people] have receieved throughout the pregnancy regarding their personal responsibility for the well-being of their child' (2003: 19; see also Chinyere Oparah et al. 2018: 44). In this contemporary era of the highly regulated pregnancy, pregnant people are under serious pressure to control themselves and make 'good choices', at a time when they often experience their bodies as particularly out of control. The neoliberal doctrine of individual responsibility and self-control, Layne argues, thus produces something of a 'double bind' for those whose pregnancies end in miscarriage: 'Either women accept responsibility for the pregnancy loss and blame themselves ... or they must admit that the loss was a bodily event over which they had no control' (2003: 19), which can be a highly unsettling and disempowering thought within such an ideological climate.

This chapter explores how this kind of 'double bind' has been navigated within feminist philosophy, as feminists have sought to dismantle the patriarchal framing of pregnant bodies as passive 'containers' that must be acted *upon,* while also resisting the neoliberal model of pregnancy as a 'project' whose fate is determined by a pregnant individual's lifestyle choices. Though it can appear as a kind of Catch-22 – either we are *out of control* and hence must be controlled, or *in control* and thus blameable – my aim here is to show that the apparent 'double bind' is in fact a false binary, and to chart a way out. The chapter begins by setting out the conceptual dichotomies – transcendence vs. immanence, active vs. passive – that have underpinned the reduction of pregnancy to a passive biological condition within Western philosophy; and then proceeds to examine how feminist phenomenologists have overturned them. At first, I revisit the pivotal argument developed by Iris Marion Young ([1984] 2005), and built upon by others, that a pregnant subject may not directly control the gestational process but is nevertheless actively involved in their pregnancy as both a 'source and participant'. This body of work provides valuable conceptual tools for refuting the patriarchal model of pregnancy as an 'objective condition' that has nothing to do with subjective agency; but it has tended to focus exclusively on positively accepted 'successful' pregnancies. This methodological division implies that pregnancy does in fact eradicate a pregnant person's agency when it does not go to plan.

Rejecting this implication, I turn to a different strand of feminist phenomenology that begins not with the first-person standpoint of the pregnant individual, but with the existential fact of intercorporeality. Drawing especially on work by Rosalyn Diprose (2002) and Ann Cahill (2015), I show how the intercorporeal model of pregnancy opens up an expansive non-individualist concept of agency as a relational capacity for shaping and responding to a transformative bodily situation, which may or may not conform to one's will.[4] This is important, I argue, because it upends the disempowering representation of miscarriage as an event characterized by a passive loss of agency, inviting instead an examination of all the ways that miscarrying/unpregnant people do act, do make decisions and do shape their situation, even if it was not something they chose or intended. Finally, I consider more closely the political implications of the intercorporeal paradigm, outlining the strategic need for a de-individualization of pregnancy *contra* the dominant neoliberal model of pregnancy as a 'project'. By emphasizing that pregnancy extends beyond the individual and is never fully controllable, philosophies of intercorporeality enable us to break down pregnancy hierarchies that render 'successful' pregnancies an individual achievement, and anything else a matter of shameful, even culpable, inadequacy.

'Life's passive instrument'

Feminized bodies, as established in Chapter1, have been systematically defined by and reduced to reproductive functionality as a lynchpin of gendered, racialized and ableist biological essentialism. Key to this biological reductivism has been the representation of pregnancy itself as a purely biological phenomenon that has nothing to do with agency or conscious becoming, particularly the pregnancies of those classified by the logics of racial capitalism as 'breeders' rather than 'mothers' (Davis 1981). Within Western patriarchal philosophy, pregnancy has consistently been taken for granted as a precondition of existence but deprived of existential significance itself.[5] Jean-Paul Sartre, for example, acknowledges that 'I am not the foundation of my being', but argues that this very fact should compel an individual to assume their own foundation, as if they had chosen it for themselves ([1943] 2003: 22). Moreover, insofar as pregnancy has been dismissed as a purely biological process, it has also been represented as a passive phenomenon of incubation – as within Aristotle's legendary rendering of the pregnant body as a feminine container for the reception of active masculine seed.[6] According to this patriarchal 'flowerpot' model, women may be defined by or reduced to their supposed capacity for pregnancy – 'she is a womb, an ovary' (Beauvoir [1949]1997: 35) – but pregnancy is in fact represented as having little to do with women as embodied subjects at all, because it encourages a view of pregnant bodies as simply a 'resource for foetal growth', and of gestation as 'something that happens inside, but separate from, a woman's body' (Lymer 2016: 22). Women are expected to produce the baby, but pregnancy itself is not regarded as properly 'productive' or 'creative'. Indeed, when pregnancy has been equated with generativity and creative activity within the philosophical canon, it has typically been in a metaphorical sense, in relation to the philosopher man who is 'pregnant' with his ideas (Mullin 2005; Sandford 2008).

It is not only philosopher men who have reduced actual pregnancy to pure biology, however. There is also a current within feminist philosophy that replicates the reductive notion of pregnancy as biological 'species-work', though rather than simply taking it for granted, the concern here is how women can be liberated from its ensnarement.[7] Simone de Beauvoir most famously gives an existentialist account of pregnancy as an ordeal that chains 'the second sex' to the immanent 'life of the species', impeding the capacity of the pregnant individual to engage in conscious, purposive projects and hence their path to 'transcendence' of the given.[8] In Beauvoir's analysis, pregnancy does not conform to the structure of a freely chosen project because it is a passive mode of being-for-others. Pregnancy, birth-giving and breastfeeding are thereby designated in *The Second Sex* as 'natural functions', not '*activities*' ([1949] 1997: 94), and those who perform such functions as passive instruments of continuity rather than active creators of the future ([1949] 1997: 94–6). While, for Beauvoir, 'creative production conforms to the will of the producer', reproduction 'happens despite the one whom it nevertheless requires' (Guenther 2006: 20). To produce is to make something new and inject 'creativity into time', whereas to reproduce is 'to make more of the same, thereby binding the future to the present and past' (Guenther 2006: 21).

Pregnancy, in Beauvoir's estimation, therefore cannot be classed as a form of transcendent 'activity' or even productive 'work'; rather, it is 'labour' in the sense of producing matter required for material existence and continuation of the species.[9] Though pregnancy is often deployed as a metaphor for futurity and may seem to signify a kind of 'transcendence, a stirring toward the future … it remains a gross and present reality' (Beauvoir [1949]1997: 513). Beauvoir acknowledges that a pregnant person may themselves find a kind of dignity or value in their capacity to gestate: 'they seek eagerly to sacrifice their liberty of action to the functioning of their flesh: it seems to them that their existence is tranquilly justified in the passive fecundity of their bodies'

([1949]1997: 513). But she contends that this 'feeling that she is a human being in herself, a value' is only an illusion:

> Ensnared by nature, the pregnant woman is plant and animal, a store-house of colloids, an incubator, an egg; she … makes young people titter contemptuously because she is a human being, a conscious and free individual, who has become life's passive instrument. Ordinarily life is but a condition of existence; in gestation it appears as creative; but that is a strange kind of creation which is accomplished in a contingent and passive manner … For she does not really make the baby, it makes itself within her … It is beyond her power to influence what in the end will be the true nature of the being who is developing in her womb.
>
> ([1949]1997: 512–14)

If we subscribe to this existentialist model of pregnancy as a burden and block to meaningful, creative existence, then miscarriage appears as biology giving the miscarrying subject a 'free pass'. Indeed, in previous historical periods in both the US and the UK, the 'free pass' has been one of the dominant social meanings of miscarriage, in that it has provided women with a physical break within a rapid succession of pregnancies, and alleviated the financial or emotional drain of raising numerous children.[10] And plenty of people today experience miscarriage as a 'lucky escape' or a 'near miss' for a variety of reasons. Yet a philosophical conceptualization of miscarriage as a 'free pass' could hardly serve a liberatory feminist politics when it simply repeats the reduction of pregnancy to mere biology, and reissues the masculinist metric for liberated agential subjectivity, apparently free from the weight of embodiment and relations with others. After all, Beauvoir herself says that it is 'Man' who 'regards the body of woman as a hindrance, a prison, weighed down by everything peculiar to it' ([1949]1997: 15), and acknowledges that the lived experience of pregnancy is hugely variable: 'the facts of biology take on the values that the existent bestows upon them' ([1949]1997: 69). Beauvoir's position is thus characteristically ambivalent, shifting between her visceral denigration of pregnancy and her suggestion that if pregnancy is regarded or experienced as biological entrapment, this is more down to gendered social structures and value systems than anything integral to bodily capacities or 'natural' role-differentiation within reproduction. Ultimately she affirms that the lived experience of pregnancy depends upon the pregnant person's 'total situation and her reaction to it' which is 'highly variable' ([1949]1997: 526) – ranging from 'revolt' or 'resignation' to 'satisfaction or enthusiasm' ([1949]1997: 510).[11]

'Active subjects of their own gestation'

Over the past half century, rethinking and revaluing pregnancy has become a central aim for feminists working in the existential and phenomenological philosophical traditions. In the first instance, feminist philosophers have affirmed the capacity of pregnant people to be effective actors during their pregnancies, refuting presumptions that they will be rendered useless by 'pregnancy brain', uncontrollable emotions or insatiable cravings and idiosyncrasies of the body. But they have also explored how pregnancy itself may be taken up as a creative, purposive process. This is not 'purpose' in the essentialist teleological sense of existing for-the-sake-of producing children; but rather, in the existentialist sense of directedness and intentionality, imbuing pregnancy with significance and meaning, and defying the presumed opposition between 'immanence' and 'transcendence'. As Imogen Tyler writes, 'it's time to make a pregnant self, to reclaim pregnancy as a transient subjectivity by reframing pregnant women as the active subjects of their own gestation' (2000: 292).

A major point of reference in this body of work is Iris Marion Young's classic essay 'Pregnant Embodiment: Subjectivity and Alienation' written in 1984, which offers a phenomenological account of pregnant embodiment and takes as its paradigm the 'positively accepted' pregnancy where the individual has 'been able to take up their situation as their own' (Young [1984] 2005: 47). Young does acknowledge that pregnancy can be reckoned with in various ways, and that 'for the vast majority of women in the world today, and even for many women in this privileged and liberal society [the US], pregnancy is not an experience they choose'. But in this essay, the assumption is that focusing on positively accepted pregnancies – which can be 'experienced for [their] own sake, noticed, and savored' ([1984] 2005: 47) – is the most effective way of overturning the patriarchal view of pregnancy as a process that simply 'happens' to the one who is pregnant.

At the heart of Young's phenomenological analysis is a major challenge to the common idea within phenomenology that when one's body no longer sinks into the habitual background of everyday life, and emerges instead as an object of concern, this is necessarily an alienating experience that impedes a subject's habitual 'operative intentionality', and hence their capacity for 'act intentionality' or conscious self-direction.[12] The most common phenomenological example of such 'estrangement' is when one becomes ill or injured, though Young argues in essays like 'Throwing Like a Girl' that patriarchal gender norms produce a form of alienation that girls and women must contend with as a routine fact of feminine existence ([1980] 2005). As Jansen and Wehrle explain it, 'The more a woman *has* a body (worrying over what the body should do and what it should look like), the less a woman can just *be* a body (aiming at the world and what she wants to do in it)' (2018: 42). In the case of pregnancy, however, Young contends that an unusual level of focus on one's body does not necessarily result in a state of 'alienated objectification' in which 'I am not my body and my body imprisons me' ([1984] 2005: 51). Pregnancy may well make us more aware of our bodies than we habitually would be, she argues, yet this body-awareness can be experienced in the 'aesthetic mode', whereby 'we can become aware of ourselves as body and take an interest in its sensations and limitations for their own sake, experiencing them as a fullness rather than as a lack' ([1984] 2005: 51). Attending to one's pregnant body, therefore, can be understood as an empowering mode of 'innocent narcissism' as the pregnant subject takes pleasure in discovering new things about their body, perhaps even experiencing a temporary reprieve from conventional expectations of attractiveness, availability and girlishness ([1984] 2005: 47).[13] Pregnancy, Young writes, 'roots me to the earth, makes me conscious of the physicality of my body not as an object but as the material weight that I am in movement' ([1984] 2005: 53).

This account of pregnant body-awareness and comportment forms the basis of Young's argument that pregnancy should be understood as a form of subjective becoming, and not an objective 'condition'. From the point of view of others, she argues, pregnancy may appear primarily as a time of 'waiting and watching' – as though 'this new life were flying in from another planet' – but pregnancy as lived experience has a temporality of 'movement, growth, and change':

> The pregnant woman experiences herself as a source and participant in a creative process. Though she does not plan or direct it, neither does it merely wash over her; rather, she is this process, this change. Time stretches out, moments and days take on a depth because she experiences more changes in herself, her body. Each day, each week, she looks at herself for signs of transformation.
>
> ([1984] 2005: 54)

The essay, however, actually has a dual strategy: not only does it challenge the 'flowerpot' model of pregnancy, but also the more general conception of the agential self within Western philosophy as a bounded, self-contained entity that is necessarily stymied or undone by the vicissitudes of the body. The integrity of the pregnant body, Young acknowledges, is indeed undermined by the 'externality of the inside' as the body gestates an embryo/foetus that is both part of and separate from it. It is also interrupted by the break in continuity between the habitual body and the changing pregnant body 'at this moment' ([1984] 2005: 50). This does not mean, though, that the pregnant subject no longer operates as an effective subject in the world. 'Reflection on the experience of pregnant subjectivity', she argues, reveals a body subjectivity that is 'animated by a double intentionality: my subjectivity splits between awareness of myself as body and awareness of my aims and projects' ([1984] 2005: 51). Other feminist philosophers and theorists have since built upon Young's phenomenological account, arguing that as well as understanding the pregnant subject as a 'source and participant' in a generative bodily process, we should recognize the physical and emotional adjustments that pregnant people make, alongside changes in their cultural, social, economic and personal lives, as an active and intentional form of 'pregnancy work' (Neiterman 2012: 374). Amy Mullin, for example, argues it is important to realize that pregnant people are 'not merely spectators to the physical changes they experience and seek not merely to change their self-understandings … but also to change their situations, for instance, making changes at work and in relationships' (2005: 50).

But is this body of literature able to account for embodied agency in relation to pregnancies that do not 'grow and change' as desired or expected? After all, Young has deliberately focused upon positively accepted pregnancies in which everything is going well. And this methodological cordoning-off is in fact necessary to her argument that subjective 'splitting' does not constitute a weakening or eradication of the pregnant person's agency. The pregnant body, in Young's account, is not the 'habitual body' that fades into the background and enables an easeful mode of existence; and it is not what Beauvoir terms the 'I can' body that is the 'instrument of the will' (Heinämaa 2003: 131). But nor is it experienced as a debilitating alien 'otherness' because it happens to be doing what the imagined pregnant subject wants it to do. This is what enables her to experience the sensations and limitations of her body as 'a fullness rather than as a lack'. But in unwanted miscarriage, the miscarrying body may seem to simply invalidate positive acceptance of a pregnancy, as well as any 'pregnancy work' that might have been undertaken – appearing not as the creative, generative body whose power is empowering, but the troublesome, traitorous body whose power is overpowering.

Accordingly, we might infer that for Young, miscarriage of a desired or positively accepted pregnancy would indeed put us in a state of 'alienated objectification', where the miscarrying body materializes as 'a painful otherness preventing me from accomplishing my goals' (Young [1984] 2005: 51). This is what Caroline Lundquist, for instance, suggests in relation to unwilling or rejected pregnancies, where 'the splitting of bodily subjectivity seems more akin to the splitting of the transcendent from the immanent flesh described by existential phenomenologists' (2008: 146). But would this framing not simply revert to the patriarchal positioning of unruly feminized bodies thwarting existential possibilities for becoming? Does Mullin's claim that pregnant people are 'not merely spectators to the physical changes they experience' not apply equally to those who are unwillingly, ambivalently or complicatedly pregnant, or those whose pregnancies end unexpectedly in miscarriage?

To be sure, miscarriage stories do often convey an experience of disconnection and disidentification that might aptly be captured by the concept of 'alienated objectification': 'I feel so betrayed by [my body]. It feels like it can't possibly belong to me, or it wouldn't have strayed so far from what I want so badly ... It's like I'm a stranger in my own skin' (Zucker 2021: 105). But could this kind of performative disidentification itself be understood as an exercise of agency: a way of actively reconstructing or shoring up an identity that has been shaken to the core by miscarriage? Do alienation and objectification have to be taken as signs of a lack of agency? In many experiential accounts of surrogacy, for example, a constructed sense of subjective separation from the pregnant body is described as essential for maintaining a liveable pregnancy; and this kind of constructed separation might also enable the preservation of agential identity through miscarriage: *it was my body, not me*. The work of critical disability/crip theorists like Susan Wendell, Alison Kafer and Cristina Crosby is also relevant here, who each argue that the act of distancing or othering oneself from the pain, miseries or limitations of one's body should not be simply dismissed as an effect of ableist ideology or erroneous mind/body dualism, because it can be an important psychological survival strategy and mode of self-validation (Wendell 1997; Kafer 2013: 6; Crosby 2016).[14]

On the other hand, however, if we take seriously the predominant feminist view of the self as thoroughly embodied, then insisting that a miscarrying person has 'nothing to do with their miscarriage' seems to belie the embodied reality of this very physical process. Indeed, as Sarah Clark Miller argues, the acknowledgement that 'there was nothing you could have done' might bring relief to many, but it is also 'a potentially disempowering realization' (2015: 151). Articulations of self-blame in the wake of miscarriage – *I must have caused this* – can thus be interpreted as assertions of agency as much as statements that separate the 'self' from the miscarriage, because they reveal a desire 'to imagine oneself as more than a passive recipient of a biological action that one desperately does not want to happen' (2015: 149). After all, the embodied self can be recognized as the 'means' of the miscarriage if not the intentional actor (2015: 153), and thus as fundamentally *involved* in the miscarriage as a 'source' to use Young's terms, even if this bodily process is unwanted and understood as destructive rather than creative. Claims like 'it must have been my fault', therefore, should not be viewed as simply mistaken or irrational. Rather, they can be read as attempts to assert agency using the inadequate conceptual tools available. Looking at it this way, the problem is not that agency is annihilated by miscarriage; it is that miscarriage reveals the inadequacies of the dominant individualist understandings of agency as the ability to assert control, or 'to act in the world so as to achieve one's self-determined ends' (Clark Miller 2015: 145):

> It hadn't been my fault. The fertilized egg decided on its own to disintegrate. But wasn't it *my* egg? Did not the egg belong to *my* body? ... *I blight it – My body blights it – It blighted – I – My body – It – Blight – What – Whom – By whom – Am I my body and is this not part of me?*
>
> (Valmidiano 2019: 226; 235)

The point of this analysis is not to imply that we can identify a right way or wrong way to experience and conceptualize one's body during and following miscarriage, or that some responses should be deemed more or less appropriate, more or less 'feminist' than others. From an experiential standpoint, there are various ways of mediating extrinsic and intrinsic perspectives on our bodies using the conceptual resources and interpretative repertoires available, and there should be no normative presumptions regarding how people come to terms with their embodiment within the 'profoundly gendered context of reproductive normativity' (Throsby 2004: 188). From a theoretical standpoint, however, it is important for a feminist philosophy and politics of miscarriage to promote a more adequate account of agency, because it is the question of agency that can make the negotiation of embodied identity in the event of miscarriage so vexed and troubling. Such an account needs to go further than Young's essay, demonstrating that agency is not simply annihilated or rendered impotent when our bodies do not do what we want them to do. Instead of asking only how willingly pregnant agency is possible, then, what if we started by asking how *unwillingly unpregnant* agency is possible? What if we have agency not despite the involuntary 'power of the body to act' (Mullin 2005: 39) but because of it?

'A task not of their choosing'

However planned, wanted, accepted or nurtured a pregnancy might be, there is truth in Beauvoir's claim that gestation is 'a strange kind of creation which is accomplished in a contingent and passive manner'

([1949]1997: 513). For Beauvoir, as we have seen, this ineluctable passivity is what excludes pregnancy from the realm of transcendent becoming; and in light of the persistent subordination of the feminine on account of its association with passivity, it may seem an unlikely thing for feminists to embrace. However, various feminist philosophers have indeed foregrounded and embraced passivity as a vital starting point for opening up a non-individualist way of thinking about pregnancy. Most obviously, the gestating foetus is an entity that is passively dependent upon the pregnant body for its continuing existence. Yet as Lisa Guenther argues, the pregnant person can also be understood as passive in this situation, because once pregnant, the body 'involuntarily gives of itself ... Short of terminating her pregnancy altogether, [the pregnant person] cannot limit or arrest her bodily exchange with the fetus', nor have much impact upon how the process develops (2006: 99–100). Accordingly, a mutual passivity characterizes the situation of pregnancy as 'giving and being given intermingle' (2006: 3).

This mutual interdependence is at the heart of the 'intercorporeal' model of pregnancy developed by Guenther and others, which moves beyond the first-person standpoint of the individual pregnant subject 'experiencing herself' and into the territory of 'generative phenomenology' – a strand of phenomenology which examines how subjective experience and intersubjective sociality are made possible in the first place by the affectivity between bodies (Dolezal 2015; see also Bornemark and Smith 2016).[15] The 'intercorporeal' model is premised upon a strong notion of relationality as *sub*-personal rather than *inter*-personal, the idea being that we are constituted in our very individuality through our corporeal permeability and openness to being affected (Stone 2010: 360–1).[16] As Ann Cahill explains it, while the self is so often 'represented and even celebrated as self-made, self-contained, and self-moving', and sociality itself as 'the result of decisions made by independent agents', there is in fact no intentional subject that is separate from, or prior to, the constitutive relations through which it is formed, no identity that can come into being 'except through relations with other bodies and other beings' (2015: 50–1). So it is not that we are singular individual beings who then enter into relations; rather, we are only singular individual beings *because* of intercorporeal relationality. 'Corporeal identity', in the words of Rosalyn Diprose, 'is never singular, always ambiguous, neither simply subject nor object … the "alienation" of corporeality grounds rather than follows after the constitution of the self' (2002: 54).

Diprose develops a distinct and influential understanding of intercorporeality as 'corporeal generosity' which she defines as

> [A]n openness to others that not only precedes and establishes communal relations but constitutes the self as open to otherness. Primordially, generosity is … the being-given to others that undercuts any self-contained ego, that undercuts self-possession … that constitutes the self as affective and being affected, that constitutes social relations and that which is given in relation.
>
> (2002: 5–6)

In Diprose's terminology, the fundamental 'generosity' of intercorporeal existence is not governed by conscious choice, intention, reflection or deliberation, and 'corporeal gifts' are not circulated within an economy of exchange between sovereign individuals. Rather, corporeal generosity operates at the level of pre-reflective sensibility and is 'where agency, perception, affectivity and, combining all of these, identity, are born' (2002: 69). Being out of control of one's body is therefore not to be understood as an exceptional situation that thwarts individual agency or compromises the self, because it is never the case that 'I first exist in control of my body and then decide to give my body away'. On the contrary, 'it is because my body is given to others and vice versa that I exist as a social being' and it is only through other bodies that possibilities for agential becoming, for making meaning and decisions, are 'opened in any substantial way' (2002: 72).

Various feminist philosophers have drawn on Diprose's work to rethink pregnancy as an intercorporeal phenomenon of complicated interdependence, rather than an object of individual will or intention. Myra Hird, for instance, offers up a materialist take on 'corporeal generosity', arguing that Diprose's account implies 'gifting' goes beyond 'inter-human' interactions and refers to 'the giving and receiving of matter itself' (2007: 3). In Hird's account, we are engaged 'in nearly limitless processes of gifting' (2007: 11) including the circulation of microbes like bacteria, which defy the autonomy and individuality of any living organism. So pregnancy is not hailed as an exceptional case of bodily merging, but rather as an exemplary site of experience which reveals intercorporeal enmeshment as a condition of existence more generally. The 'mundane and extraordinary exchanges of physical matter' that occur during pregnancy, as Hird puts it, represent a 'particularly potent site of corporeal generosity' (2007: 12). The foetus absorbs oxygen, antibodies, bacteria, minerals, proteins, vitamins, salts, hormonal secretions alongside derivatives of noxious substances, in turn expelling waste and carbon dioxide back into the pregnant body's circulation system and producing biochemical and metabolic changes, heart rate acceleration, hormonal variations and altered immunity. The vital organs of that pregnant body shift to make room as the gestation proceeds and makes itself felt in various ways including nausea, changing contours, breathlessness, sleeplessness, exhaustion and sometimes life-threatening conditions such as high blood pressure and preeclampsia. Cells traffic in both directions during pregnancy – a phenomenon known as 'microchimerism' – as foetal bodies and pregnant bodies 'co-produce' one another at the genetic and epigenetic level (see also Lewis 2019).

Cahill is another philosopher inspired by Diprose, who argues that through the lens of corporeal generosity, 'the pregnant body shows up as simultaneously receiving and giving corporeality' (2015: 52). In Cahill's account, significant emphasis is placed on the fact that the relation between pregnant body and foetal body is not symmetrical because the dependence of the foetus on the pregnant body is primary: for many months, it would not survive separately from the pregnant body, while the pregnant person does not similarly depend upon the continuing existence of the foetus for their own life (though foetal demise *in utero* can put the pregnant person at risk). Nevertheless, the pregnant person is also undergoing an exposure to a foetal body which produces a transformation of their own body. Like Guenther and Hird, then, Cahill argues that pregnancy can be understood as a 'co-constituting' phenomenon because 'once it has begun, the relation between the fetus and the pregnant person continues apace, the two bodies affecting each other immediately and significantly' (2015: 55; see also Raphael-Leff 2016: 162–3). Moreover, in cases where there is conscious awareness of pregnancy, this ambiguous corporeal reconstitution brings multiple possibilities for subjective reconstitution, depending upon the unique situation of the pregnant person in question (Cahill 2015: 52). Both the pregnant person and foetus are thereby 'profoundly implicated in each other's existence' (Cahill 2015: 53), albeit in different ways:[17]

> The person who realizes she is pregnant has no choice but to undergo a transformation, required by her bodily relationship with an embryo/fetus, in her embodied subjectivity. That the transformation is required does not mean that it is predictable or determined. Transformation could take the form of denial: a pregnant person who has learned that she is pregnant may aspire to live as if she were not pregnant. But this very state of denial, and the energy that it demands, emanates from a relationship with the fetus.
>
> (2015: 53)

To a wider feminist audience, the language of 'generosity' in these philosophical texts may be rather jarring when pregnancy has so often been framed in highly romanticized terms as the ultimate feminine act of giving oneself up to others. Can this term really be shorn of its traditional connotations? And does it imply that a miscarrying body which is no longer sustaining a living embryo/foetus is less 'generous' than a gestating pregnant body?[18] But the intercorporeal model of pregnancy need not rise or fall with the language of generosity. The key terms, in my view, are interdependence, co-constitution and affectivity – which can be defined as 'the capacity to be moved rather than simply the reception of an effect' (Gago 2020: 195). These terms establish the openness of intertwined bodies to being affected, and affecting in turn, as the fundamental condition of pregnant agency: 'It is because bodies are open onto others, rather than being distinct, that we can act, have an identity, and remain open to change' (Diprose 2002: 69). This theoretical model accounts, in the first instance, for the experience pregnant people may have of being a 'participant in a creative process', as Young describes it, which they affect but are also affected by, in ways they often cannot control. But it can also incorporate the affectivity of miscarriage and the ways it is shaped by the miscarrying/unpregnant subject as an affected/affecting agent: the decisions that are made, the identity work that is undertaken, the relationships, life plans and time frames that are rethought and renegotiated.

So when we take intercorporeality as our theoretical starting point, there is no need to isolate positively accepted 'successful' pregnancies from unwilling or ambivalent pregnancies, or from pregnancies that end in miscarriage. As Cahill argues, just like the pregnancy with which it overlaps, miscarriage produces an ambiguous set of possibilities for 'subjective reconstitution', depending on the specific circumstances in which it unfolds:

> Regardless of its origins, and even if the pregnancy was planned to be terminated, the relation was co-constituting ... This is not to say that there are no relevant distinctions to be made among different cases of miscarriage: surely, the experience of miscarrying a pregnancy that was the result of a sexual assault is drastically different from the experience of miscarrying a pregnancy that had been longed for by all involved. But ... both pregnant women in the examples just described will face a similar challenge: how to once again pick up a task not of their choosing, a task that may come across as a gift, a reprieve, a challenge, or an imposition, but in any case a task that they did not set for themselves.
>
> (2015: 56)

Feminist philosophies of intercorporeality can therefore provide an important levelling force: on the one hand, by providing a relational account of affective agency that applies to all pregnancies, however they are experienced and however they end; and on the other hand, by underscoring the ultimately contingent nature of any pregnancy, including those that seem to be the most carefully controlled. Within normative pregnancy culture, 'the baby' is usually spoken of as a given (Nakamura Lin 2019: 140), and 'the possibility for loss that accompanies every pregnancy' is thereby 'glossed over, "taken care of", managed' (Scuro 2017: 202). Accordingly, the 'ontological fact that *all pregnancies are open to miscarriage*' (Scuro 2017: xii) may only come into direct awareness in the event of an actual miscarriage, in cases when medical professionals have identified 'complications', or when miscarriage or stillbirth have been previously experienced. Yet while Young contends that from the standpoint of the pregnant subject, 'pregnancy has a temporality of movement, growth, and change', in contrast to the external perception of pregnancy as a time of 'waiting and watching' ([1984]2005: 53), many first-person pregnancy stories do speak of 'watching and waiting', 'seeing what happens' or of finding it difficult to think about or hear stories of miscarriage because it feels 'too close to home' (Mullin 2005: 38–9; Pugliese 2016: 72–3; Neiterman and Fox 2017; Nakamura Lin 2019: 140), even when all is proceeding as desired and expected. Drawing on the intercorporeal model, we can see in such statements a kind of existential attunement to contingency or felt sense of dependence upon the foetal body, whose continuing development and future birth cannot be guaranteed.

To emphasize that all pregnancies are existentially 'open to miscarriage' is not to deny that some people's pregnancies are in reality more 'open to miscarriage' than others. Black women and other women of colour in the US and the UK, for example, experience miscarriage and stillbirth at disproportionately higher rates than white women – a fact that can be a source of acute anxiety and stress (Chinyere Oparah et al. 2018: 111). The point, rather, is to insist on the fundamental contingency of pregnancy, which gets covered over by narratives of pregnancy 'success' and is at once an existential and sociopolitical matter. In Diprose's account, for instance, intercorporeality or 'corporeal generosity' does not operate separately from structures of economic, racialized, gendered and ableist inequality. Indeed, it is the profound ambiguity of 'corporeal generosity' that creates the possibility of exploitation, violation, harm and neglect, as much as it makes possible love and care. The 'ambiguity of body interlacing', Diprose writes, is 'not temporally prior to or separate from the processes of socio-legal determination that would reduce ambiguity and so close off possibilities for existence' (2002: 56). Privileged bodies thrive and acquire social value through the appropriation and forcing of 'corporeal gifts' from subordinated bodies – for example, through forced or exploited labour and sexual violence – which in turn are depleted and destroyed by these extractions. Political processes, inequalities and imaginaries thus 'have our bodies' and are 'in our bodies' (2002: 174), shoring up privileged ways of being, as well as diminishing and constraining others. In this way, miscarriage as existential possibility gets converted into miscarriage as unequal reality via a political system that supports and values some embodied lives more than others.

Ultimately, then, feminist philosophies of intercorporeality engender a wider view of pregnancy, stretching beyond the individual pregnant subject to encompass the multiple social relations and power structures that shape how a pregnancy plays out, as well as the phenomenological conditions of pregnancy as an existential situation. 'The model of the autonomous, self-contained individual', as Cahill argues, 'can make little sense of miscarriage' (2015: 54), or indeed, of pregnancy more generally. From a strategic perspective, however, the move to de-individualize pregnancy may appear somewhat counter-intuitive, given the extent to which pregnant people continue to be infantilized and treated as 'bodies under guardianship or tutelage' (Gago 2020: 222) – particularly those within oppressed social classes who routinely have their agency denied or ignored, or are treated like 'disobedient children' (Chinyere Oparah et al. 2018: 47). The apparent 'double bind' once again comes to the fore. If we argue that a pregnant subject does not and cannot fully control their pregnancy, do we not risk giving credence to patriarchal claims that *they must be controlled*? So even if we *know* we are never fully in control of ourselves, would it nevertheless make political sense to speak and act as if we are, or at least could be?

De-individualizing pregnancy

Concerns about women's lack of control and decision-making power in encounters with obstetrical medicine have been central to feminist campaigns around reproductive health, freedom and justice from the 1970s onwards. But it is vital to recognize the extent to which feminist calls for empowerment and control have been co-opted by the neoliberal construction of the 'conscientious' and 'active' pregnancy as an individual 'body project', where the body is understood as a personal resource to be managed and maximized, as well as a symbol which conveys messages about a person's self-identity and status (Shilling 1993: 4).[19] As Rosalind Petchesky put it over three decades ago, the principle of 'individuality and control over one's own body' so easily becomes 'perverted into what is truly bourgeois individualism' (1980: 671). A perfect contemporary example of this can be found in the report produced by the 2016 UK National Maternity Review – 'Improving Outcomes of Maternity Services in England' – in which the pregnant person is depicted as a 'savvy consumer' in a pregnancy marketplace who wants to 'be in control of their care', even managing the NHS budget allocated to them. The report is quick to point out, moreover, that 'with this control comes a responsibility' for ensuring their own 'personal health and fitness' as 'integral to safe and fulfilling childbearing'.[20]

This individualist model of pregnancy as a 'body project' for the pregnant consumer is also promoted by segments of the pregnancy 'wellness' industry – via blogs, websites and pregnancy manuals that establish a host of normalized cues and 'elaborate prefabricated regimens of bodily control' (Kukla 2005: 130). Pregnant people, argues Elena Neiterman, 'are expected to "do" pregnancy, actively performing socially established practices that signify the status of the body as pregnant', as well as consuming a wealth of products such as pregnancy yoga classes and pregnancy pillows to demonstrate due diligence and commitment to optimal well-being (2012: 373).[21] Affluent individuals are obviously able to conform most fully to these pregnancy ideals and patterns of consumption; but these dominant norms of pregnancy 'set the standard against which even those with the fewest resources are judged' (Freidenfelds 2020: 9). Indeed, Neiterman suggests that observable lifestyle changes are often taken on especially diligently by those who face stigmas of 'deviant' pregnancy, like pregnant teens determined to demonstrate to others and themselves that they 'could be a good mother' (2012: 388). As the next chapter will discuss, even 'forging an individualized bond' with one's foetus has 'become a special kind of project for the pregnant woman – one that is understood to be an important part of a conscientious pregnancy' (Kukla 2005: 112).

The presumed dichotomy between passivity and activity, as Kukla argues, thus 'does not function neatly in the case of pregnancy' (2005: 135) – not only in the existential sense, as I have outlined above, but also in sociopolitical terms pertaining to the 'highly complex set of interdependencies and mutually constitutive relationships' between personal responsibility and public accountability. Though pregnancy is treated as something that ought to be designed and monitored in accordance with public standards – for instance, standardized guidelines and schedules are set for 'normal' weight gain at different stages of pregnancy – it is the pregnant individual who is instructed and expected to take on the project:

> She is the one who must discipline her own body and practices and who must "purify her womb" ... she needs not only to understand the public standards of self-discipline and bodily regulation by which her

pregnancy is to be designed but also to feel personally responsible for meeting those standards.

(Kukla 2005: 128)

It must be acknowledged that the restrictions and rules of pregnancy can be reassuring, in that they offer a semblance of control over what otherwise can feel random or chaotic (Garbes 2016: 45). But for so many pregnant people, these 'exhaustive, demanding and precise scripts of self-regulation' produce 'impossible stress norms' and an oppressive environment of public judgement (Kukla 2005: 130; Briggs 2017: 10). The pregnancies of those who are disabled, poor and presumed 'high risk' are particularly closely policed; though more privileged women also find their bodies and behaviour scrutinized by the 'never-resting public eye' to an extent they will rarely experience at other times in their lives (Neiterman 2012: 374; see also Longhurst 1999; Bridges 2011; Frederick 2017).

The contemporary neoliberal model of pregnancy as an individual 'body project' is thus anathema not only to Beauvoir's existentialist notion of the creative 'project' as a practice of freedom, but also to what pioneering feminists like Adrienne Rich had in mind when they spoke of making 'strong connections between knowledge of our bodies, the capacity to make our own sexual and reproductive decisions, and the more general empowering of women' (Rich 1992: iii). On the *What to Expect* website, for example, an article titled 'What to Eat for Lunch During Pregnancy' goes so far as to claim that 'women who eat well while they're expecting can minimize a host of pregnancy symptoms, including morning sickness and mood swings, and are more likely to deliver on time and have a speedier postpartum recovery. Now that's definitely easy to stomach!' (Picard 2021). Assuming adequate nutrition is an individual choice (rather than a matter of social distribution), these kinds of pronouncements mean that contemporary pregnancies are structured to a troubling extent by excessive self-discipline, self-recrimination and regret aversion, as pregnant people imagine a future of miscarriage, stillbirth or birth complications in which they look back and castigate themselves for not doing their pregnancy in the right way – for not making 'healthy lunchtime choices' or not sleeping in the right position. This is all too easily dismissed as a form of pregnant hysteria, but it clearly reveals the underside of the idea that pregnancy is something that can be optimized and controlled through individual behaviour and lifestyle choices: *If it all goes wrong, surely that behaviour and those choices will be to blame*?

To pursue this line of argument is not to deny that the image of pregnant people as passive 'containers' or 'flowerpots' remains a powerful cultural trope. But the long history of this model of pregnancy as a passive state of being intersects with another long history of women being blamed as soon as pregnancy *goes wrong*, not only for their actions or behaviours during pregnancy but even the power of their minds.[22] Indeed, in *The Second Sex*, having categorized the pregnant woman as 'life's passive instrument', Beauvoir herself proceeds to attribute 'disorders of pregnancy' to a mixture of misdirected desire and anxiety on the part of the pregnant woman, proclaiming that 'almost all spontaneous miscarriages are of psychic origin' ([1949]1997: 516). The greatest burden of this misogynistic practice of women-blaming today is borne by women of colour and poor women who are most likely to be treated with suspicion and blamed, even prosecuted and imprisoned, when things go wrong. Transphobia and fatphobia also fuel speculations about why miscarriage has occurred. As Emily Lind argues, 'the fat body is imagined to be the consequence of poor choices' and hence is a 'symbol of failure' (2017: 142–3); or as j wallace skelton recounts: 'My mother wants to know if I miscarried because of the testosterone … I hear blame' (2017: 133). But even those who match up to all the normative ideals of the 'good pregnant mother' often speak of a '"whirlpool' of self-blame' when their pregnancies do not go as intended or expected (Reagan 2003: 364). And as there is usually no clear or satisfying medical reason given for miscarriage, at least in the first twelve weeks, there is a wide-open space to be filled by self-scrutiny and self-blame, and scrutiny and blame by others:

> While I understand that guilt is a useless emotion and there's nothing that I did (or didn't) do … it's still the first place my mind goes. (Borok 2019: 35)
>
> All I could think was, 'This is my fault. If only I had gone to triage and not let that nurse on the phone make me think I was a hypochondriac. If only I had taken more naps, or not taken the class, or not tried to walk to the pool. If I had known about membranes. If only I had done some small or large or insignificant thing differently.' (Squires 2019: 217)

All this amounts to a compelling case for promoting a non-individualist model of pregnancy as a transformative intercorporeal situation that requires multiple layers of support and networks of care, but can never be fully predicted or controlled.[23] De-individualizing pregnancy, to be clear, does not mean decentring the pregnant person or downgrading their agency. The point, rather, is to frame the woman- or person-centred model of care in strongly relational rather than responsibilizing terms. The pregnant person then appears as an 'active, though not entirely autonomous, agent within the relation that is pregnancy' (Cahill 2015: 57), instead of being set up as project manager of the pregnancy that is their 'own'. I will take this argument up again in Chapter 5 in relation to the rising criminalization of miscarriage and stillbirth in the US, and the politics of abortion in 'the era of "choice"' (Millar 2018). But in the next chapter, I want to further consider the status of the foetus within cultural narratives and lived experiences of pregnancy and miscarriage. Cahill suggests that from the intercorporeal perspective, miscarriage appears 'not as the loss that an individual suffers of some thing (a fetus, a baby, the imminent promise of parenthood)', but as the 'unexpected cessation of co-constitution' (2015: 54). But it is still important to consider the different ways that foetuses are conceptualized and imagined, *in utero* as well as during and following miscarriage. For instance, how can subjective understandings of miscarriage as 'the loss of a baby' be validated without the fundamental ambiguity, variability and materiality of pregnancy being erased or eclipsed? How can grief and loss be articulated and acknowledged without fuelling anti-abortion logics and imaginaries?

Chapter 3
Ambiguity

I feel as though I've lost a child, I do ... I mean people sort of say, you know, as they said in the hospital, it probably never even formed, but there was something there ...[1]

I was lost in an inchoate, confused state mirroring what had happened inside my body ...[2]

A deep sense of uncertainty often pervades miscarriage stories, as many people struggle to make sense of what has happened, and what the 'appropriate' reaction should be. Sociological studies also document wide variation in terms of how people articulate what might have been lost, from a 'small seed' to a 'baby' or 'child' (Frost et al. 2007: 1012), and highlight the tensions that emerge between physical experiences of passing blood clots, fragments of tissue, gestational sacs or intact foetuses, and conceptualizations of miscarriage as the loss of a 'baby' or 'child', or a fantasy of 'what might have been' (see e.g. Cosgrove et al. 2004; Murphy and Philpin 2010).

According to the intercorporeal account of pregnancy set out in the previous chapter, such uncertainty and variation is to be expected and affirmed, because pregnancy is a fundamentally ambiguous situation. The pregnant person and foetus may be 'profoundly implicated in each other's existence', but this existential entanglement opens up multiple possibilities for corporeal, relational and subjective reconstitution (Cahill 2015: 53). So there could never be a definitive answer to questions about what a miscarried embryo/foetus 'is' or 'was', or how a miscarrying/unpregnant person and those close to them should feel and respond. 'Because "the" pregnant body is actually pregnant bodies', as Brittany Leach argues, 'the ontological status of the fetus is not fixed by biology, society, or even the law', but is determined by pregnant subjects' lived experiences within specific social and discursive contexts (2020: 143).[3] Moreover, the same foetus can inhabit many levels of reality – as matter, image, fantasy – at different times, or all at once, as foetuses are located in different material, visual and psychic spaces: 'in bodies (both pregnant and miscarrying) … in plastic containers, on dissection mats, as sonogram images, as pictures on smart phones' (Kilshaw 2017a: 4).[4]

Within normative pregnancy culture, however, this ontological ambiguity, multiplicity and complexity is consistently disavowed,[5] as foetuses are represented in proleptic terms as separate 'baby-persons' already, and expropriated from the pregnant bodies that sustain and intertwine with them. The future is thus 'brought into the now' (Dinshaw 2015: 40) when two imagined figures of the future – the 'mother and baby' – are superimposed on to the present, such that they come to stand in for pregnant embodiment as such. A core argument of this chapter is that this proleptic disavowal leaves us ill-equipped to deal with the conceptual complexities and messy materialities of miscarriage. On the one hand, the culture of proleptic pregnancy produces a hypocritical form of social betrayal when miscarriage occurs, whereby social certitude and celebration of 'the baby' suddenly give way to awkwardness, avoidance, squeamishness and silence. But it has also given rise to an increasingly dominant compensatory representation of miscarriage as 'the loss of a baby' who must be mourned. To many who have experienced miscarriage, this definition may come as a welcome form of social recognition; but the universalizing language of 'baby loss' marginalizes any miscarriage that is not understood or lived in this way. Moreover, in constructing 'the baby' as a separate individual being, discourses of 'baby loss' and 'foecentric grief' (Millar 2018) overlap with (and in some cases have directly borrowed from) the symbolic repertoires of the anti-abortion movement, which are deeply invested in denying the ambiguity of pregnancy.

In response, this chapter seeks a more critical and transformative approach to 'breaking the silence', by asking what we might actually learn from the silences and awkwardness engendered by miscarriage. Instead of regarding silence as a void to be filled up by compensatory social scripts and cultural forms, I suggest, it can be viewed as a generative pause: an opening in which to work through and sit with the complex realities of pregnant embodiment that pregnant/miscarrying/unpregnant people themselves inhabit and negotiate as a matter of everyday existence. So rather than trying to resolve the meanings of miscarriage and the uncertain status of the foetus, miscarriage should be approached instead as an 'encounter with ambiguity', which in turn prompts a relearning of pregnancy itself as fundamentally ambiguous.

Proleptic pregnancy and social betrayal

Since the 1980s, a number of feminist scholars have analyzed the increasingly proleptic nature of contemporary pregnancy and the rise of the 'public foetus' within popular and political culture.[6] From a range of cross-disciplinary perspectives, these studies chart how the 'public foetus' has emerged on to the national and international stage as a 'tiny, fully formed person who only requires further incubation in a maternal body in order to emerge as the autonomous subject that it already "is" in nascent form' (Guenther 2006: 146; see also Sofia 1984). The damaging impact of this image of the foetus as a 'baby-person', with interests of its own, is most obvious when it is deployed as an anti-abortion tactic, or as a tool in the criminalization of miscarriage and stillbirth: 'fetus gets Facebook page, mother gets thrown in jail' (Dinshaw 2015: 42). This will be examined in the final chapter of the book. But there is also a lighter 'cuddlier' version of the proleptic foetus that warrants critical investigation. It appears within a wide range of quotidian pregnancy scenes – from consumer advertising and social media to antenatal clinics – and significantly shapes the ways in which pregnant people and their social circles 'call the foetus into personhood' as a material, social and imaginative practice (Lindeman 2015).

For instance, visual images of pregnancy that foreground the foetus, and render the pregnant body invisible, convey a 'visual message of

Figure 3 'Mommy. Can't wait to meet you' mug, sold by UbuntuDesigns4U via Etsy online.[7]

apparent autonomy' that suggests 'a being to be related *to* rather than one that is an integral part of a pregnant person's body' (Bueno 2019: 31). This conceptual and visual separation of the foetus is also secured by the importation of future characteristics into the present, in order to make the foetus appear more 'baby-like' or 'person-like'. The 'pregnancy bible' *What to Expect,* for example, refers to the 'adorable face' of 'your baby' at week 6 of pregnancy, and to 'your tiny dancer' at week 9 (Murkhoff 2017).

Taking a historical view, both Linda Layne and Lara Freidenfelds chart how various forces and factors have interwoven to '[move] up the time and pace' with which pregnant people begin to 'socially construct the personhood of a wished-for child' (Layne 2003: 17; Freidenfelds 2020).[8] These include the ascent of the 'public foetus' in tandem with technological developments in biomedicine – such as the earlier establishment of pregnancy through tests, the routine use of ultrasound imaging and the earlier assignment of gender – and the commercial targeting of newly pregnant people to spend on pregnancy products and 'buy for the baby'. As Freidenfelds writes:

Two months into pregnancy, at a stage when women in the not-so-distant past would have been just beginning to trust their suspicions and intuitions that they might be pregnant, and waiting cautiously for the confirmation provided by a second missed menstrual period, women in America today have often already spent weeks celebrating, caring for, and growing attached to their expected children.[9]

(2020: 2)

Even within the most medicalized clinical environments, pregnant people are regularly 'encouraged to form an attachment, not with the foetus as part of themselves, but with the separate baby-person it will become' or indeed is imagined to already *be* (Katz Rothman 1986: 115). Ruth Cain, for example, describes waiting in an NHS antenatal clinic for an ultrasound scan and seeing a poster of 'a cartoon foetus complete with wiggly umbilical cord, shouting to *"mum": "if you want a photo of me, tell the technician before you leave!"'* (Peel and Cain 2012: 83). Ultrasound technicians themselves frequently grant foetuses physical and social abilities such as 'waving' or 'smiling', and might even address the foetus itself – for example, 'accusing it of being "shy" or "modest" when its genitals prove hard to see' (Kukla 2005: 114; see also Barnes 2015). Layne notes that during IVF treatment, embryos may be personified by prospective parents prior to being implanted, and follicles too are sometimes endowed with personal characteristics (2003: 83–4). In the online 'fertility community', embryos sometimes get referred to as '#embies' and frozen embryos as '#snowbabies' or '#frosties', and 'even the odd "#cellfie", an image of life at a few cells old, makes its way online' (Bueno 2019: 52–3).

'Proleptic pregnancy' is thereby configured through various means and channels as a process of 'catching up to itself' as the due date approaches (Lindemann 2015: 84). But in the event of miscarriage, the proleptic pregnancy never does catch up to itself, and the easy and positive social energy that has circulated around 'the baby' and propelled the pregnancy along may dissipate fairly dramatically.[10] Feminist sociological and anthropological research has repeatedly demonstrated how the social constitution of the foetus as a 'baby' can falter or be revoked altogether when a pregnancy ends in miscarriage or stillbirth (Layne 2003: 17).[11] As Alice Lovell writes in a 1983 article calling for urgent changes to the treatment of miscarriage and stillbirth in medical settings:

From the start, health professionals talked about the 'baby' and referred to her as 'mother' … However, from the moment it was discovered that the baby was lost, there was an abrupt cut-off in the identity construction process. Denial of the baby's existence was expressed in word and deed. There was an instant unravelling of a woman's lived experience and rapid de-construction of her motherhood ... She had lost her baby. When this was followed by denial of its life and death, she was even robbed of her loss ... She was expected to forget her baby and a chunk of her life, and submit passively to having her motherhood role stripped.

(1983: 760)

In their 1990 collection *Miscarriage,* Ann Oakley and colleagues similarly highlight discursive practices of re-medicalization within the clinical arena: 'Listen to the next conversation during a normal scan: "There's the baby's head. See his leg there". Should that baby die in utero, though, they hide behind "fetus" or "embryo" or "16-week pregnancy"' (1990:11).

It must be appreciated that clinical codes of conduct today have become much more sensitive, especially in relation to late miscarriage and stillbirth (Bueno 2019: 16). Many hospitals now have designated staff such as bereavement midwives, and while previously the foetus/baby was 'usually whisked away' with 'indecent haste' (Lovell 1983: 755), it is now standard practice for parents to be asked if they would like to see or hold the foetal body if that is a possibility, have foot or handprints or a photograph taken, and to be consulted about disposal or organizing a ceremony. Penelope Deutscher proposes the term 'ontological tact' to characterize the ways in which 'a consensual making and unmaking of the fetus takes place between women or parents and health professionals in conformity with the woman's or parents' choices'. In some cases, they might 'desire to get rid of a dead fetus as soon as possible ... to see the fetus as mere matter with no relationship to an anticipated future, and medical protocol can support that perception'; while in others, 'the tactful medical expert might well expect to humanize the fetus, to remove it with a different ceremony, in a "slower" temporality' (2016: 171; see also Rapp 1999: 82–3).[12]

Yet Deutscher also emphasizes that these forms of 'clinically inflected ontological tact' are not equally available to all due to economic and socio-cultural inequalities (Deutscher 2016: 172) – a claim supported by research undertaken in both the UK and the US. Paulina Van, for example, suggests that because Black women experience pregnancy and infant losses at higher rates than white women, their experiences of loss are more likely to be normalized or trivialized by health professionals, especially in light of the 'strong Black woman' archetype which fosters expectations that Black women are 'tough' and 'can handle anything' (2001: 230–1; 239). And despite 'best practice' guidance and protocols now in place, NHS hospitals in the UK frequently lack the adequate resources to ensure appropriate care, and there is serious variability in accessibility and standards. Long waits, lack of specialist training, inappropriate physical spaces and hurried encounters mean that social and racialized privilege does not necessarily insulate against insensitive treatment: 'The doctors were talking in technical terms and suggested that my baby was just some sort of "growth". But to me, it was my baby' (Bueno 2019: 49).

This kind of ontological demotion also continues to occur within social encounters outside of clinical contexts. Here, the rolling back is enacted not so much through recourse to medical terminology, but rather, through the proliferation of awkwardness, avoidance and silence. In some instances, this may be down to social embarrassment at having 'jumped the gun'; and indeed, those who experience miscarriage themselves sometimes speak of feeling 'embarrassed for getting excited before the loss' (BBC 2020b). But social awkwardness and discomfort around miscarriage also derive from its 'death salience' within a culture that avoids confronting the materiality of death, and indeed anything corporeally unpleasant (Ariès 1974; Reiheld 2015: 12; Chinyere Oparah et al. 2018: 42), which is intensified by the misogynistic fear and denigration of feminized bodies in particular, for their 'unruliness', 'leakiness' and lack of clear boundaries (Shildrick 2001). As Gayle Letherby and others have suggested, the strong association between miscarriage and menstrual blood goes a long way in accounting for its 'taboo' nature (Letherby 1993; Murphy and Philpin 2010). Moreover, when a womb appears as a 'place of death', this upsets the usual and expected order of things – birth before death, pregnancy versus death – which can be extremely distressing for those whose bodies are thus marked: 'I felt like a "human coffin"'

(Bueno 2019: 89; see also Howes 2019, 21; Moua 2019: 251; Reza 2019: 200). And while in very early miscarriages an embryo may be reabsorbed into the body, people whose miscarriages occur at a later stage of pregnancy may come into direct visual or tactile contact with an intact foetus as it leaves their body (like those who experience stillbirth), and must make decisions about disposal (see e.g. Kamal 2019: 181–2; Zucker 2021: 3–13). This is a bodily encounter with the foetus as 'corpse' or 'waste' that is very far from the shadowy foetal images that appear on ultrasound screens, or the appealing 'cute' foetuses we see in films, magazines and pregnancy manuals (Morgan 1999).

Feelings of failure, shame, exposure and humiliation that so often attend these experiences are routinely managed through concealment or self-imposed silence, which can further entrench the idea that miscarriage is a 'private matter' (Millar 2018: 207). This may be particularly true, as Ceballo and colleagues argue, for those who occupy devalued social positions, as 'silence shields women's sense of shame, difference, and personal failure from public view' (2015: 508). But on the other hand, disclosure of miscarriage can exacerbate feelings of isolation if met with the silence or awkwardness of others – particularly when this serves as a painful contrast to previous investment in the pregnancy when all was proceeding as expected. When the relational work of 'calling the foetus into personhood' is suddenly discontinued, as Cahill contends, what can result is 'an emotional isolation that is itself confusing and damaging to self-trust and bodily integrity' (2015: 45; see also McLeod 2002). While only the pregnant person has the 'privileged relation of *feeling with* the foetus' (Young [1984] 2005: 61), pregnancy is never a purely individual matter, as discussed in Chapter 2. Indeed, given the fundamentally *asymmetrical* nature of the relation between a pregnant person and their foetus, transforming that relation into a meaningful psychosocial bond requires considerable imaginative effort.

As such, a pregnant subject's relations with others in corroborating their sense of that relation with their baby as real and valuable are especially important. So when this relational, imaginative and emotional work is cut off, dismissed or depreciated, it can be experienced as a kind of unravelling or betrayal. Indeed, it could be regarded as a form of 'gaslighting',[13] as the miscarrying/unpregnant person's very sense of reality can be shaken when the status of their pregnancy is demoted to the merely 'private', when previously it had the status of a socially acknowledged and collective reality:

> There's no acknowledgment they existed, like it was just all in my head, my body, my mind, like it didn't really mean anything to anyone else. (Bellhouse et al 2018:6)
>
> With childbearing, my child is also their child; in miscarriage, my loss is my own. (Scuro 2017: 193–4)

Atmospheres of awkwardness, avoidance and embarrassment that so often surround miscarriage are therefore no trivial phenomenon. They can have severe consequences, depriving miscarrying/unpregnant people of the intersubjective contexts required for making sense of their embodied reality and becoming intelligible to others (Cahill 2015). Though in fact we can see this in many ways as a continuation of the gendered epistemics of pregnancy, given that pregnant women are consistently regarded as irrational, overemotional, out-of-control subjects that need to be *told*, particularly those who are not framed as a 'responsible decision maker' (Chinyere Oparah et al 2018: 64). Further, while the deconstitution of their baby is experienced by some as an unravelling or taking-away of what was previously forthcoming, for others, the denial, dismissal and betrayal that occur in the event of miscarriage may well appear as just more of the same. The pregnancies of poor women and women of colour, for instance, are regularly viewed by the dominant white society as more of a 'problem' than a 'baby on the way' that must be treasured; even the lives of their natal babies or children are systemically treated as not fully mattering.

Those whose foetuses are diagnosed with 'abnormalities', too, know all too well how provisional, selective and hypocritical the social attribution of 'baby', 'person' or 'child' status can be. As Katz Rothman has argued so forcefully, against a backdrop of social pressure not to 'bring into the world' an atypically bodied child, routine testing for genetic conditions or impairments means that pregnant people are effectively being asked to be willing to abort their 'damaged' foetuses at the very same time they are encouraged to 'think about the needs of the coming baby, to fantasize about the baby, to begin to become the mother of the baby' (1986: 227). If the test indicates that the 'wrong' kind of child might be born (requiring some kind of social rearrangement or redistribution of resources and energies), 'the baby' returns to being an object for diagnosis: a foetus in all its particularity and hence the 'problem' of the pregnant person, who may or may not feel it to be their baby or child, and must make the decision to abort or continue.[14] We might also consider here assisted conception through IVF, as people trying to become pregnant are supported and encouraged to invest in pregnancy as 'having a baby', but to be prepared at the same time for a 'foetal reduction' in the event of multiple conceptions occurring (Deutscher 2016).

'Baby loss awareness' and 'foetocentric grief'

The 'culture of silence' surrounding miscarriage has become a well-documented phenomenon within feminist scholarship. Since the 1990s, however, there has been a much wider recognition of miscarriage in the public sphere, such that some feminist critics like historian Leslie Reagan have proposed that this 'cultural silence' has actually become overstated (Reagan 2003: 358–9). Articles about miscarriage now regularly appear in mainstream magazines and national newspapers that seek to 'dismantle the stigma' and 'break the silence', including personal revelations by celebrities such as Meghan Markle, Beyoncé and Gwyneth Paltrow.[15] A 'booming' publication industry promoting literature on coping with miscarriage or pregnancy loss has also emerged (Layne 1997: 297–8), as well as dedicated podcasts and campaigns on social media sites – like the #IHadAMiscarriage campaign[16] or the #LGBTBabyLoss blog series[17] – and discussions on Internet forums populated by acronyms such as 'Miscarriage Worries and Concerns' (MWC), 'Recurring Miscarriages' (RM) and 'Gone to Heaven' (GTH).[18] Layne and others identify a full-blown 'pregnancy loss movement' in the US, wherein pregnancy loss support group networks like SHARE[19] and UNITE[20] enable 'subjective reconstitution' through the sharing and validating of experience, and participation in mourning and remembrance rituals (Layne 2003: 16). In the UK, the Miscarriage Association[21], Tommy's[22] and SANDS[23] are the foremost organizations offering support for those who experience miscarriage and stillbirth, as well as campaigning for greater public awareness – for example via 'Baby Loss Awareness Day' begun in 2002[24] – and improved medical research and treatment.

If we can speak in broad terms of a mainstream 'pregnancy loss movement' spanning the US and the UK, one of its key aims is to promote more sensitive practices within medical institutions; and as acknowledged above, considerable success has been achieved here despite unevenness and continued inequalities. Both Layne and Reagan suggest that this shift can be attributed in part to the feminist movement and its demands for respectful medical treatment for women more generally (Reagan 2003: 369; Layne 2003: 55–7). However, they also argue that this is where the overlaps between feminism and mainstream pregnancy loss activism – as a form of what Layne terms 'women's self-help' – reach their limit (2003: 55–6). Reagan, for example, points out that the demand for recognition of women's grief is a challenge to medicine that can actually be met 'without radically changing physician practices, hospital routines or the gendered hierarchy of power in the hospital', because attention to the 'emotional fall-out of pregnancy loss is a task that subordinate, lower-paid (possibly volunteer), and mostly female workers perform' (2003: 269). Feminist scholars have also questioned the kind of support on offer within some pregnancy loss support forums and literatures that represent miscarriage in unequivocal terms as 'baby loss' and imply that the expected response to miscarriage is devastating grief, even 'devastation-that-is-exactly-the-same-as-the-devastation-you-would-feel-if-a-born-child-had-died' (Cahill 2015: 46; Millar 2018: 140). While the term 'angel babies' is commonly adopted ('*I have two children and an angel baby*'), sometimes no distinction is drawn at all between early miscarriages, stillbirths and newborns that have died (Reagan 2003: 366).

The designation of 'pregnancy loss' as synonymous with 'baby loss' is generally intended as a supportive acknowledgement of those who personally experience it that way, and as a way of breaking down what Lovell has termed the 'hierarchy of loss' which presumes the earlier the miscarriage, the lesser the loss (1983). But equating 'pregnancy loss' with 'baby loss' *as a matter of course* means that other ways of feeling and understanding what has happened are rendered marginal, and in some cases, illegitimate or even suspicious. Moreover, when 'baby loss' is framed more as the loss *of* an autonomous 'baby-person' than as loss *to* a particular pregnant person and those close to them, 'baby loss' discourse comes troublingly close to the language of the anti-abortion movement and its promotion of what Erica Millar calls 'foetocentric grief' (2016: 503; 2018).[25] Tommy's, for example, describes its interventions and research into improving pregnancy outcomes as 'saving babies' lives', and within such terms, even ectopic pregnancy can be treated more as 'a life lost' than 'a life saved' (Reagan 2003: 368).

The links between the pregnancy loss movement and the anti-abortion movement are variable and not always clear. For instance, while some founders and leaders of the pregnancy loss support groups that Layne researched in the US are openly supportive of abortion rights and access, 'others clearly feel their work in this area complements their anti-abortion stand' – a stand which may or may not be known by the group members (1997: 297). As feminist writer Dania Rajendra recounts:

> I tried the support group – once. I never went back, though, because of politics – the politics of personhood. After an awkward conversation around a table at a room in the library, I found myself exiting the parking lot, my car behind one of the other ladies. My head-lights illuminated her pro-Personhood sticker. I felt sick.
>
> (2019: 111)

Something else disturbing from a feminist viewpoint is the sharing of symbolism between the anti-abortion and pregnancy loss movements. The symbol of baby/foetal footprints adopted by the US pregnancy loss movement, for instance, is said to have been originally cut and pasted from 'pro-life' materials, with the 'pro-life' membership blanks beneath the image removed (Reagan 2003: 368). Though the footprints image may appear to have been reappropriated as an 'apolitical symbol of grief and memory', argues Reagan, it continues to do ideological work: 'As women wear baby/fetal-footprint pins to signify their losses – without necessarily subscribing to an anti-abortion view or realizing the association – the pro-life movement is strengthened' (2003: 368).

To be clear: these critical feminist interventions are not objecting to the tactful and respectful treatment of a particular person's miscarriage as the loss or death of their baby or child, if this is how they understand what has happened. Networks of solidarity and mutual care are also recognized as essential, as is memorialization for many people as a way of honouring the experience and integrating loss into their lives. Christa Craven and Elizabeth Peel, for example, explore the significance of memorializing queer pregnancy loss in light of the intense heteronormativity of mainstream pregnancy culture which marginalizes and invisibilizes queer pregnancy (2014: 225). The feminist concern, rather, is that mainstream pregnancy loss culture is entrenching anti-abortion logics and imaginaries (both wittingly and unwittingly), and limiting how miscarriage can be expressed and understood. Instead of miscarriage-grief being silenced and 'disenfranchized' (Doka 2002), the impression given by certain pregnancy loss websites, forums and books today is that grief is in fact expected and presumed (Freidenfelds 2020: 2). For example, on the Tommy's website, there are places where it acknowledges variation in experiences, yet at the same time it regularly refers to miscarriage as the death of a baby.[26] The miscarriages of marginalized social groups also get incorporated into this universalizing frame within popular media: 'trans people who miscarry have specific concerns that cisgender women don't, but in the end, the pain of losing a pregnancy is universal regardless of the parents' genders' (Prager 2020).

It could be countered here that the people who seek out support groups and forums are likely to be those most significantly affected by miscarriage, and therefore that centring grief is appropriate in these arenas. But people seeking support during or following miscarriage could be looking for help with an emotional response other than grief, or practical advice on any economic costs or work-related issues that may arise. They may also be trying to find information about the physical stresses and effects of miscarriage, what to expect from an 'expectant miscarriage' or what to do if an identifiable foetal body is passed.[27] But when confronted with universalizing claims about 'baby loss' and the devastating grief miscarriage will cause, this can cause confusion and self-questioning, or concern about being 'cold' and 'heartless': 'I can't help but wonder if I have grieved enough' (Shekmus 2014); 'I felt like a weird mother that doesn't care' (Kilshaw 2017b). As psychologist Jessica Zucker writes, 'shame often occurs when a woman does not feel sad about her miscarriage but instead experiences relief, gratefulness, or simply no profound feelings at all … Women should want to be pregnant. Women should want to *stay* pregnant' (2021: 49).

Such expectations may also contribute to assumptions that care for someone going through miscarriage is conditional upon the expected kind of response. Carolyn Sufrin, for example, considers how staff in the Californian jail she worked in would judge miscarrying inmates worthy of care if they demonstrated 'appropriate maternal sentiment' (2017: 138–40):

> Initially [Nellie] had wanted an abortion. Then as the days passed in jail, she had decided to continue the pregnancy ... The day she excitedly resolved to keep this baby ... in a cruel twist of fate, the embryo had no heartbeat ... Nellie's response to her miscarriage, at least outwardly, was the appropriate and expected one: grief. Unlike the woman whom the deputies disparaged for not lovingly holding her newborn baby, Nellie elicited sympathy. Her conventional affective response to reproductive loss enabled jail staff to deem her a deserving subject, worthy of caring gestures like barbeque chicken and words of solace.
>
> (2017: 139)

What causes particular alarm amongst feminist scholars is the growing *institutionalization* of grief expectations within medical and therapeutic settings. Reagan, for instance, tells of receiving a folder full of material in the early 2000s from the US hospital where her miscarriage was treated, including a pink and white pamphlet describing the ultrasound images taken during the pregnancy as 'pictures of the baby' to be preserved and treasured, and a letter with the foetal footprints symbol printed on each page (2003: 367). UK-based sociologists, anthropologists and researchers in nursing studies have also expressed concern over the past couple of decades. Carol Komaromy, for example, suggests that the practice of showing foetal bodies in late miscarriage and stillbirth to parents has become something of an 'orthodoxy' in the UK hospitals she researched, and that 'prescribed forms of managing grief' may not provide sufficient space for the expression of ambivalence or emotions other than those expected or 'permitted' (2012: 194). Fiona Murphy and Susan Philpin have also argued that early miscarriage is increasingly being reconceptualized in UK hospital settings as 'loss and bereavement': a perspective 'in which the psychological is privileged over the physical and aspects of caring for the physical body tend to be neglected' (2010: 535).

The politics of silence

Those who experience miscarriage in this contemporary conjuncture are thus confronted with yet another set of contradictory social pressures, practices and discourses. On the one hand, the proleptic treatment of pregnancy as 'having a baby' can produce intensely hypocritical forms of social awkwardness and silence when the imagined baby does not materialize. But on the other hand, the culture of proleptic pregnancy has led to an increasingly dominant compensatory representation of miscarriage as 'the loss of a baby', which covers over the messy material realities and multiple meanings of miscarriage, as well as the social and political realities that produce stark inequalities in pregnancy outcomes. Even those who do experience miscarriage as the loss of their baby or child, and find validation in having this legitimized, may feel unease at universalizing, domesticating narratives of miscarriage as 'baby loss', or excluded by normative representations of the 'grieving mother' in mainstream journalistic and online media:

> I read a lot of essays and blog posts about miscarriage after my experience – all of them by white women of privilege. I suppose that they are the ones with platforms and the time to blog. The blog posts especially are so aesthetically pleasing – littered with photographs of the bloggers, beautifully styled, looking into the distance, or rocking in a wicker chair on a porch with the sun setting behind them – that I cannot stomach it … The women writing about miscarriage don't look like me. They don't sound like me. There is nothing that *resonates*.
> (Nakamura Lin 2019: 137–8)

The pressure on feminists to break their own 'studied silence' on miscarriage has built up considerably over the past couple of decades, since Layne first lamented in the 1990s that 'feminists have simply given the field to the antichoice activists while adding to the silence members of pregnancy-loss support groups find so painful' (1997: 304).[28] As Freidenfelds has argued, over twenty years later, 'those devastated by pregnancy losses often turn to the pro-life inspired public discourse that says that six-week embryos are babies', because 'so many of the promoters of investment in early pregnancy – the medical establishment pushing early prenatal care, the marketers of diapers and cord blood banking, the cheerfully scientific developmental timelines charting "your baby's growth" – seem to have nothing useful to say' (2020: 149); and until fairly recently, feminism has not had much useful to say either. Yet while feminism has a 'long history of demanding the unseen and unacknowledged be seen and heard' (Ryan-Flood and Gill 2010: 1), I do want to question the continued and ubiquitous deployment of the 'breaking the silence' metaphor.

This is firstly because, as Reagan suggests, the idea that there is a blanket cultural silence around miscarriage has become somewhat overstated – even if uncomfortable silences remain prevalent at the level of social interactions – and holding on to this idea can end up shielding the prevailing cultural narratives of miscarriage from any kind of critique or contestation, because it frames them as inherently progressive by virtue of 'breaking the silence' or the 'taboo'. That is, simply talking about miscarriage in the public sphere can be framed as a transgressive act if we continue to repeat that miscarriage is never talked about, even if very traditional ideas about femininity, pregnancy and maternity are being recycled. Secondly, the 'breaking the silence' metaphor implies that silence is necessarily a bad thing, when, in fact, silence can have radically different meanings dependent upon context and power (Malhotra and Rowe 2013; Dingli and Cooke 2019). In the case of miscarriage, for instance, the awkward social silences that hover around it are oppressive in part because they occur within a context in which there is such an abundance of noise around 'successful' pregnancy. In other words, it is the contrast that makes these silences so hypocritical and particularly hurtful. But the politics of silence cannot be grasped when silence is presumed to be something *inherently* negative – a void that must simply be filled up.

This presumption, for instance, underpins the predominant *compensatory* approach towards miscarriage which aims for social responses and cultural representations of miscarriage to match up to what is already given or attributed to pregnancy. According to this compensatory logic, if being pregnant means 'having a baby', then miscarriage should be reframed as 'the loss of a baby' in return; if there are Hallmark cards for pregnancy, there should be Hallmark cards for miscarriage. But while these gestures may be an effective way of bringing comfort to many people who feel isolated and excluded from 'pregnancy world', from a broader politically oriented perspective, it must be recognized that they operate in tandem with the rituals of pregnancy 'success' rather than subverting them.

In contrast, a critical and transformative feminist approach will set its sights on eradicating the normative pregnancy scripts and images that amplify or set up loss in the first place: for example, demanding that corporate marketing materials urging people to make shopping lists for the baby as soon as they become pregnant stop being routinely distributed by General Practitioners and midwives in NHS clinics.[29] This may well seem like a classic case of 'feminist killjoy' (Ahmed 2010a), when upbeat magazines and pictures of smiling cartoon foetuses might soften an anxious trip to the antenatal clinic. But do gestures of care and support have to come in such ontologically distorted, condescending and commercialized forms? Though there may be good feminist reasons to decry full-blown 'medicalization' of pregnancy, the propagation of proleptic pregnancy culture in a medical setting gives the impression that in the case of pregnancy, there is no need for ontological reticence or caution – that embryos and foetuses simply *are* babies to the *normal* pregnant person.

The core point I am making, then, is that 'silence-breaking' does not necessarily serve a feminist politics of miscarriage, because a truly transformative approach depends on tackling what makes silence oppressive, as well as being critically alert to what silence is broken *with*. Campaigns for greater recognition or awareness of miscarriage are not enough if they rely on a compensatory logic that leaves normative pregnancy culture unscrutinized and unchallenged, and indeed are counterproductive if they reinforce its core principles and symbols. The liberatory effects of 'replacing silence with storytelling' (Zucker 2021: 210), accordingly, will hinge on the diversity of storytellers and the complexity and range of stories that are told. 'Ritual affirmation of a shared experience', as Sarah Hardy and Quill Kukla argue, need not depend on a unitary and reductive narrative. On the contrary, 'when social space does not provide a full repository of stories about a certain sort of event or experience, it is challenging for anyone involved – whether first- or third-personally – to make sense of what has occurred' (2015: 123).

Feminist campaigns to transform public attitudes towards miscarriage, therefore, would arguably be better framed in terms of deepening, expanding and complicating the conversation rather than 'breaking the silence' – aiming at what Jackie Leach Scully describes as 'narrative enrichment' by facilitating the breakthrough of a more nuanced and expansive representation of lived experiences (2021: 163). This should of course include grief, sadness and loss, but we need to be very careful that the 'overwhelming grief experienced by some' does not get 'projected on to all' (Reagan 2003: 367; 359), instead giving voice to a wider range of overlapping emotions including anger, rage, anxiety, despair, confusion and resentment, as well as relief, pride, courage, trust, empathy and gratitude. The process of narrative enrichment is thus in large part about multiplication, but as Scully insists, it must also keep up the critique – interrogating the forces and institutions that enable the greater circulation and take-up of certain narratives, while others remain repressed or marginal (2021: 163–4). Why, for instance, are celebrity narratives of miscarriage as 'losing my baby' or 'losing my child' so readily promoted and consumed, while those that express relief or conflicted feelings may still feel unspeakable?: 'I'm scared to tell anyone I was ambivalent about motherhood – they'll think that's why I lost the pregnancy' (Zucker 2021: 47).[30] And why is there so much more focus on the psychological aspects of miscarriage than on its physical manifestations and effects, or the deep inequalities that govern and inflect its treatment?

What I also want to emphasize is that while some practices of silence are deeply oppressive,[31] and others can be deeply sad, silence can also be experienced and understood as necessary and generative. As Ahmed argues, silence can signify the limits of knowledge and language which do not just have to be seen as constraints, but rather, 'as productive sites of enquiry' (Ahmed 2010b: xx). Likewise, Sheena Malhotra and Aimee Carrillo Rowe contend that pauses and silences can function as 'space[s] of possibility' that allow for reflection, space clearing and open-minded listening, ultimately providing access to 'deeper nuances of knowing' (2013: 9). Following this thought, instead of seeing silence as something necessarily negative that must always be broken, could we instead regard the silences and discomfort that miscarriage can engender as potentially instructive and transformative?

Encounters with ambiguity

The common phenomenon of 'not knowing what to say' or being 'lost for words' when miscarriage occurs can be approached as a social failing that a set of standardized cultural scripts and social norms could remedy. But these moments of social silence can also be understood as generative 'moments of disorientation' (Ahmed 2006) – a break in the usual narrative that compels us to pause, confront and explore the ambiguities of pregnancy which proleptic pregnancy culture would wish away. Ambiguity, as Erinn Gilson explains, is not simply synonymous with uncertainty or unfixedness;[32] it also refers to the 'holding together' of that which binary systems of thought and language would separate but which 'in experience and existence is inseparable' (2021: 90). So I am suggesting that in disrupting the narrative of proleptic pregnancy, miscarriage can bring us back to ambiguity and help us see what was there all along.

Take, for example, ultrasound scanning, that technology so deeply associated with the ubiquitous 'public foetus'. Ultrasound scans are now widely accepted as a way of 'seeing the baby' – far surpassing their function as a diagnostic tool – and feminist critics have often regarded the widespread embrace of ultrasound images by pregnant people as something of a problem. Barbara Duden, for example, presents this as an embarrassing case of false consciousness as women collude in their own 'skinning' and subordination to the cult of the foetus (1993: 7). But by looking closely at how pregnant people speak and write about having an ultrasound scan as an embodied encounter, other feminist scholars are less certain that pregnant people have uniformly come to identify their foetal images as a 'true representation of the inhabitant of their own bodies' (Kukla 2005: 112). Niamh Stephenson, Kim McLeod and Catherine Mills, for example, conducted interviews with pregnant women about their ultrasound experiences and found their participants to be deeply attuned to ontological ambiguity – speaking of the ultrasound images '"revealing" their foetus', or 'the reality of the baby,' while also demonstrating an acute awareness that these images are 'highly crafted and mediated by technology and expertise' (2016: 18). The women described their scans as a mystifying, 'weird', surreal, awe-inspiring encounter that added even more layers of complexity and indeterminacy to their pregnancies, rather than settling the status of the foetus as a 'baby' separate from themselves (2016: 23).[33]

Stephenson and colleagues do not present these experiences of ambiguity as a problem to be resolved. On the contrary, they argue that such 'encounters with ambiguity' are to be trusted and valued, as they demonstrate 'possibilities for connecting' during pregnancy in ways that maintain 'a kind of openness and ethical responsiveness irrespective of the future of the foetus' (2016: 18–19). They suggest, further, that ontological, aesthetic and epistemic ambiguity are constitutive of pregnancy experiences 'not only where ultrasound affirms "good" and "normal" development, but also in pregnancies pervaded by prospects of pathology and in those that end in miscarriage or termination' (2016: 28). In their study, they found that the women whose ultrasound scans involved 'declaration of foetal demise' or 'the naming of a potential anomaly' often 'eschew[ed] the stabilisation of such events and invoke[d] the ambiguities and uncertainties of continuous experience' (2016: 29). Though it might appear that a clear announcement of miscarriage during a scan would be 'pretty definitive', those who had been informed of a 'missed miscarriage' did not express a sense of clarity. Instead, they described the medical diagnosis in a 'cautious, distancing way', suggesting that the 'definitive news' conveyed via ultrasound in fact 'acts as an entry point into the epistemic ambiguity of foetal development and demise'. In other words, these women may have learned that their foetus had no heartbeat, but what to make of this knowledge and how to respond was taken up as 'a task not of their choosing' (Cahill 2015: 56) that would yield no simple or obvious answers. Moreover, while ultrasound images of miscarried pregnancies may be retained as 'mementoes', such images are not necessarily accepted as a fixed, stable or direct representation of the 'baby' that was lost. To make such an assumption, as Stephenson and colleagues argue, 'fails to recognise the possibility of multiple ontological realities entailed in the encounter', and to appreciate the openness that pregnant people regularly exhibit towards the ultimately ambiguous and unknowable character of their foetuses, alive or otherwise (2016: 21; 29–30).[34]

Insistence upon ambiguity has become fairly routine within academic feminist theory today, though it might seem divorced from the practical worlds and politics of pregnancy. 'Ontological ambiguity now!' is unlikely to take off as a t-shirt slogan. But I want to end this chapter by contesting the idea that ambiguity is only for academia. Though the anti-abortion movement may seem to have pushed feminists into an either/or corner, wherein a foetus is either a baby or it is not, I agree with Brittany Leach that nuanced accounts of pregnant embodiment which embrace variation, ambivalence and ambiguity can 'strengthen normative defences of reproductive freedom', because they 'resonate more expansively' with people's actual experiences of pregnancy (2020: 143; 148).[35] However much the 'public foetus' has come to dominate our political and cultural imaginaries, there is still wide variability and fluidity in how pregnant people themselves conceptualize, imagine and relate to their foetuses, both during and after a pregnancy – a process shaped by personal histories, ideological commitments and social circumstances. Discourses of 'proleptic pregnancy' have indeed 'moved up the time and pace' with which many people in the US and the UK begin the process of 'calling the foetus into personhood'; but this does not have to be understood as a one-dimensional or unilinear process. As outlined above, the ways that pregnant/miscarrying/unpregnant people grapple with ontological ambiguity and multiplicity as a matter of everyday existence must not be underestimated. Personal accounts of pregnancy consistently convey a complex sense of space and time as the narrator describes their foetus/baby as both known and unknown, seen and unseen, already-here and not-here-yet: 'confound[ing] the relationship between past, present and future' (Blewitt 2017: 50); and 'wobbling back and forth' between 'relating to the in utero being as a baby, as if it were a baby, and/or merging their dream, womb and actual babies' (Mullin 2005: 92).

Talk of 'babies' thus does not automatically mean that pregnant people think of their foetuses/babies in fixed and singular terms as autonomous 'baby-persons' who are 'other' to themselves. Likewise, it should not be assumed that those who grieve following a miscarriage have attributed 'fully fledged personhood' to their loss (Layne 2003: 8), or that we must establish 'settled coordinates' for miscarriage 'on the map of grief' (Bueno 2019: 15). Grief is fluid and can be a highly indeterminate experience even in relation to natal people that have died. As Millar argues:

> Grief does not necessarily derive from the death of a loved one, but also from the loss of an ideal or belief. Thus, if experienced, grief following [abortion or miscarriage] could relate, for example, to a woman's fantasies pertaining to her pregnancy. Such fantasies could

involve an imagined future (as a mother or co-parent with a loved one, for example) and could include the possibility, but by no means inevitability, that the woman envisioned the foetus as separate to herself.

(2016: 508)

This is not to say that articulating or embodying ambiguity is easy. But as Diprose insists, 'when there is a sociocultural intolerance of ambiguity, it not only close[s] off possibilities for existence', but also makes ambiguity difficult to live with because it is found wanting in the face of cultural ideals of completeness, singularity and fixed identity (2002: 56). So instead of trying to do away with ambiguity, the aim instead is to get more comfortable with it, devising more nuanced representations and frames of understanding as well as promoting those which already exist. Maggie O'Farrell's memoir *I am I am I am* (2017), for instance, is a masterclass in communicating the complex entanglements of flesh and fantasy, as she reflects on the ambiguity and ambivalence that have characterized her miscarriage experiences, even as she strongly understands these miscarriages as the loss of her children:

> You feel the notion, the idea of the child leaving you with each step. You feel its fingers disentangling themselves from yours. You sense its corporeality disintegrating, becoming mist. (2017: 107)
>
> There is a baby inside you, I say to myself, but it's dead. It's still in there. I imagine it clinging to the sides, those stretchy velvet walls, with its fingertips, refusing to let go. I want it out, more than anything. More than anything, I want it to stay. (2017: 109)

Likewise, Lucy O'Donnell's art exhibition 'Sitting with Uncertainty' captures the coexistence of conflicting emotions, strange temporalities and 'persistent encounters with uncertainty' that she had throughout her four pregnancies that ended in miscarriage. It includes shadowy drawings that evoke the 'pace and sensation of uncertainties' concerning the future as well as what has been lost in the present. Experiences of loss 'filter through into the drawings, sometimes with words, sometimes with ambiguous shapes that appear like blobs or splats, while other times more recognizable forms come forward, such as nappies or bottles: the things that have also been taken away' (O'Donnell 2019).

Candice Carty-Williams' novel *Queenie* gives another powerful account of the disorienting effect miscarriage can have – in this case, when pregnancy has been unsought:

> Why had this happened? … I was twenty-five, I wasn't going to have a baby … my choice would be to not actually carry a child to term and then raise it, but that isn't the point …; I wasn't hurting anymore, but in the place of the pain was something else, something sitting heavy that I couldn't quite identity.
>
> (2019: 12; 19)

Public art and literature thus have a vital role to play in building up our collective capacity to bear with ambiguity and ambivalence, and foster richer languages and images of pregnant embodiment, miscarriage and loss. But as emphasized above, silence does not always need to be filled up. 'Narrative enrichment' is also about building more generative forms of silence: understanding when not much can or needs to be said, and engaging in 'open-minded listening' – giving people who experience miscarriage the time and space they need 'to develop their account experimentally, through multiple tellings and retellings that are likely to change over the months and years', and remaining 'alert to articulations that do not align comfortably with the common motifs' or traditional narrative forms (Scully 2021: 165). Such flexibility and alertness are essential within social, familial and intimate spaces but also within the clinical context. As Komaromy argues, while 'the lack of clear scripts can leave parents floundering in terms of what to do at a very difficult time', it 'might be worse to offer them an inappropriate protocol on how to behave' (2012: 217).[36]

Yet however sensitive, nuanced and open-minded guidelines may become, they cannot be realized without radical material transformation. Just as truly diverse and accessible public art and literature cannot be fostered by an austerity economy,[37] clinical flexibility, patience and curiosity cannot be properly cultivated without appropriate physical spaces, secure working conditions, careful and detailed training, and above all time: to be still and sit down, to allow for shock to settle, information to be fully explained and absorbed, questions to be asked and decisions to be reached, or perhaps revoked and changed (Bueno 2019: 88).[38] Deeply entrenched structures of social, economic and racial inequality are also a major obstacle to 'clinically inflected ontological tact' and therapeutic assistance becoming accessible to all, as well as meeting the costs of disposal and memorialization if required (Deutscher 2016: 172).[39] So while 'the agents in these scenes – both the providers and patients, as well as the technicians and other specialists who are part of the larger interpretive processes – can change its interpretive parameters' (Reynolds 2020: 178), this must be approached as a material social justice project, as much as an interpretative one.

Chapter 4
Suspension

The loss of the fantasy, of the anticipation, the expectations and thoughts and hopes...suddenly it all sort of crashed....[1]

Loss divided time into 'before' and 'after', and I felt suspended between them both.[2]

When a known pregnancy ends in miscarriage, it engenders temporal reorientations that often have an unsettling effect on those involved, however the pregnancy may have been understood or experienced. Anticipations of the imminent future require adjustment (*this time next week* or *this time next month*), as do projections into the longer-term future, as the miscarrying/unpregnant person navigates a present that can feel suddenly 'emptied of expectations' (Gerber 2017: 49). Of course, miscarriage may be experienced as relatively insignificant, or indeed, as a relief or reprieve – an event that reopens possible futures that pregnancy had presumably foreclosed. But miscarriage stories also frequently describe a sense of a 'lost' or 'fragile' future 'ebb[ing] further out of reach' (O'Donnell 2019), which in some cases brings intense anxiety. 'The future that had been so intimately involved in making sense of the present', in Cahill's words, 'blinks, or fades, or painfully erodes out of existence, leaving the present unmoored' (2015: 54).[3] And as the present becomes 'unmoored', questions may also arise about the pregnancy itself: looking back, what sense can be made of this bodily transformation, and this duration of time, that did not amount to what it was 'supposed' to? Productivist values and essentialist notions of 'the ticking clock', for instance, strongly contribute to assumptions that a pregnancy which ends in miscarriage is 'wasted' or 'lost' time; as do cultural narratives of pregnancy which elevate the event-horizon of birth, and the future of the 'mother and child', as the sole guarantors of pregnancy's meaning.

In the previous chapter, the critical focus was on the proleptic model of pregnancy, which collapses a predetermined future in on the present, presenting the foetus as already an individuated child, and the pregnant person as already a mother simply by virtue of being pregnant. In this chapter, I interrogate a more straightforwardly linear model, wherein the pregnant person is imagined to inhabit an in-between time of 'liminal' transition as they move away from the past status of 'not-mother' and towards the future status of 'mother' following birth. This is arguably preferable to the proleptic version, as it affirms the ambiguous nature of pregnancy (as being not quite one thing or another) and signifies the future as still *to come*, rather than as somehow already here. Nevertheless, the future remains the privileged temporal horizon, as pregnancy is inscribed as a one-way passage to motherhood, and above all, a forward-time of *being-towards-birth.* Ambiguity, then, is presented as only a temporary phase to be ultimately overcome, such that the miscarrying person appears as suspended or 'stuck' within an arrested journey that never arrived at its destination, or as ejected from pregnant time altogether. And indeed, miscarriage is frequently experienced this way – as a state of 'limbo', or a directionless duration of time that does not move forward.

My aim in this chapter, however, is to shatter the presumed opposition between pregnant time and miscarriage time by rethinking both through the lens of 'suspended time' – a theoretical move that shifts the accent from the future as the dominating frame of reference to the lived present. Suspended time has emerged as an important theme within feminist/queer theory in recent years: for example, in the work of Kathryn Bond Stockton (2009), Lauren Berlant (2011) and Lisa Baraitser (2017), who each demonstrate that suspended time is not equivalent to a cessation of time, even as it is 'radically outside of the [linear] time of normative development' (Baraitser 2017: 92). In what follows, I argue that this body of work on suspended time is not only pertinent to thinking through experiences and representations of miscarriage, but also to rethinking pregnant time more generally. Through *suspending the future to encounter the present*, I suggest, we can bring to light overlooked temporalities of pregnancy and miscarriage that operate not so much in the mode of futural projection or futural loss, but rather, through present-oriented forms of adjustment and sensing, attachment and intimacy, maintenance and care. Ultimately, I propose, this enables us to resist the oppositional framing of pregnancy and miscarriage, because if pregnant time is not represented in exclusively future-oriented terms as *being-towards-birth*, or a means to an end, then miscarriage need not be understood as pregnancy's *undoing*.

Betwixt and between

The representation of pregnancy as 'liminal' is pervasive within academic literature on pregnancy across a range of disciplines. In continental feminist philosophy, claims about the 'liminality' of pregnancy are often rooted in the work of Julia Kristeva, where the 'liminal' or 'abject' names that which is excluded or inexpressible but persists on the margins and poses a perpetual threat to the stability and unity of the established symbolic order (see e.g. Stacey 1997; Oliver 1998; Ziarek 1999; Longhurst 2001). Though this Kristeva-inspired body of work is rooted in psychoanalytic theory, it is broadly congruent with the phenomenological work I have explored in this book, by Diprose, Cahill and others, in understanding pregnancy as a phenomenon of particularly thoroughgoing intertwinement that disturbs masculinist metaphysics and exposes the fundamentally intercorporeal conditions of subjectivity more generally.[4] Within pregnancy scholarship across a wider range of disciplinary contexts, however, including anthropology, philosophy and psychology, the understanding of 'liminality' is more commonly derived from the classic anthropological notion developed by Arnold van Gennep and subsequently Victor Turner, where the 'liminal' names the 'in-between stage' of a social rite of passage.

In his 1909 text *The Rites of Passage,* van Gennep proposes that social rites of passage manifest a sequential tripartite structure. Individuals undergoing a rite of passage or ritual initiation are symbolically detached from a fixed point in the social structure, before undergoing a liminal period of transition, during which they reside at the margins of society with no clearly defined status or role (van Gennep 1960). Finally, they are re-incorporated into the community with a new social status. Turner further developed this idea, analyzing liminality as a 'betwixt-and-between' period of 'mid-transition' (Turner 1964: 243). His ethnographic work is devoted to demonstrating how symbols and metaphors of the liminal vary: for instance, they may denote pollution and transgression, or revolve more around ideas of growth and maturation. But the 'most characteristic mid-liminal symbolism', Turner argues, 'is that of paradox, or being *both* this *and* that' (1977: 37). 'Liminaries', he writes, 'are betwixt and between established states of politico-juridical structure. They evade ordinary classification, too, for they are neither-this-nor-that, here-nor-there, one-thing-not-the-other'.

The predominant spatial metaphors for the liminal in these classic anthropological accounts are borders, thresholds, margins, limits and boundaries. The 'liminary' or 'liminar' is represented as being both 'inside' and 'outside' their society or community, occupying an 'in-between' space in which 'one is suspended, straddling or wavering between two worlds, neither here nor there, betwixt and between settled states of self' (Carson 2002: 80). Such spatial metaphors are also coupled with temporal metaphors that portray liminality as an intermediate stage in the life course characterized by temporariness and transitoriness. It is said to constitute the middle passage between the 'no-longer' and the 'not-yet', between the point of departure and point of arrival. Both van Gennep and Turner refer to pregnancy as a symbolic and literal illustration of liminality. Turner notes that liminal states of being can be expressed by symbols of 'gestation, parturition, lactation and weaning' and novices treated as 'embryos in a womb' (1977: 37); while van Gennep refers to pregnancy as a transitional liminal state between 'woman-not-mother' and 'woman-mother' – a movement of a woman from her former position towards, but not yet occupying, her new status (1960: 11).[5]

Within more contemporary academic accounts of pregnancy, the notion of pregnancy as an 'in-between' state of being continues to be a common theme.[6] Emma Kowal, for example, writes that the pregnant subject 'inhabits a liminal space of waiting, a space structured both by what is emerging and what is being left behind'. She is 'stranded between her life as an independent woman and a lifetime of service to her baby' (2009: 215; 213). Robbie E. Davis Floyd's account of pregnancy from a 'Turnerian perspective' describes it as 'both a state *and* a becoming'. First comes the 'separation process', during which 'the newly pregnant woman gradually separates herself from her former social identity' (1992: 22), and then comes the 'liminal phase' where she is presented with a 'set of possibilities from which to choose how she will interpret her own unique experience of becoming a mother' (1992: 24). Denise Côté-Arsenault and colleagues also draw on van Gennep's and Turner's work to propose that the pregnant person is in a state of liminality: 'no longer who she was, and not yet who she will be'; 'the woman who once existed becomes hidden for a time and the act of creation is defined by what has not yet happened' (2009: 73, 75).[7]

In the narrative sketched out in these accounts, the rite of passage is finally fulfilled when 'the mother returns home after birth, with the new child in her arms, anticipating the inclusion of the new baby and family unit into the community and family' (Côté-Arsenault et al 2009: 73). Or as Kowal writes, 'after the birth, the mother finally grasps what she meant when fashioning her child through her words and actions. The pregnancy is complete and can begin retroactively to have meaning' (2009: 217). The question arises, however, as to the status of those who do not fulfil such expectations of 'completing' the 'successful role transition' from 'woman to mother' (or indeed, those whose identity as 'mother' or 'woman' is contested or rejected to begin with, or who have no 'home' to 'return' to).[8] Referring to van Gennep's distinction between physical birth and 'social parenthood', Côté-Arsenault and colleagues propose that in cases of adoption or surrogacy, or when a newborn remains in intensive care for a long time, the liminal period is prolonged or left 'unresolved', as the rite of incorporation into parenthood is 'unclear' (2009: 73). In cases of miscarriage or stillbirth when there is 'no baby to take home', such irresolution is presented as essentially intractable, as the passage to parenthood can never be completed:

> The mother entered liminality but is left in this frightening place of being between roles ... She engaged in the rituals and communitas that she needed, but the death of the child prevented reintegration either as a mother or a woman ... she is left being simply a woman ... she is unable to become a mother in a way that society would recognize and unable to return to thinking of herself as being only a woman.
>
> (2009: 84)

This depiction of miscarriage in terms of an incomplete rite of passage also appears in the work of anthropologist Linda Layne (2003) and philosopher Alison Reiheld (2015), both of whom refer to van Gennep and Turner to anchor their arguments. As a state of 'betwixt and between', Reiheld contends, miscarriage falls between the stable identities of 'not-a-parent' and 'parent'; between 'not-having-procreated' and 'having procreated'; between 'old normal' and 'new normal'. Having departed from a social status or position, she claims, return is impossible: the transition is 'halted' more than it is 'reversed' (2015: 11). As such, the 'no-longer' still applies, but the 'not-yet' becomes simply a 'not'. What was supposed to be a transitional, temporary condition has become permanent and the process of becoming a parent through pregnancy can now never be realized, at least in relation to this particular might-have-been-child. The pregnancy that does not lead to parenthood is thus a 'becoming that never becomes', leaving the unpregnant person 'trapped in liminality' (2015: 14), or in more colloquial terms, a state of 'limbo' (Layne 2003: 60). Both Reiheld and Layne propose that the liminality of the embryo/foetus is also in play here too: during gestation, the embryo/foetus is in an ambiguous state of being, and in death it represents another 'border crossing'. It can also be 'liminal in yet a third way' when it is found to have 'severe congenital malformations' (Layne 2003: 65). Layne thus categorizes the dead embryo/foetus as 'superliminal', serving as 'an unwelcome reminder of the fragility of boundary between order and chaos, life and death' (2003: 65).

For these scholars, it is vital that we properly recognize miscarriage as a 'liminal' event, so as to better understand its 'taboo' status and identify the need for more adequate cultural representations and social rituals to support those who go through it. They argue that while there are rituals such as childbirth classes and baby showers designed to guide pregnant people through the 'liminal' passage and 'cushion the transition from woman to mother' (Côté-Arsenault et al 2009: 78), there are no equivalent conventions for those whose pregnancies end unexpectedly without the production of a living child. The idea, then, is that more care and attention must be paid to those instances when the rite of passage *goes awry*, such that miscarrying/unpregnant people can be 'reincorporated' into regular social life, despite not having 'completed' their pregnancy.

But has enough been done to interrogate the conventional notion of pregnancy as a linear passage towards the 'fixed point' of motherhood or parenthood in the first place? The analyses offered up by Layne, Reiheld and others are certainly insightful inasmuch as they make sense of miscarriage through the dominant cultural logics of pregnancy. That is, in contexts within which pregnancy is treated as a teleological passage towards childbirth, it is no wonder if pregnancies that do not arrive at the 'rightful endpoint' are stigmatized as 'incomplete' and 'falling short'. But from the point of view of feminist/queer time studies, it is rather surprising to see the traditional 'rite of passage' model being deployed so persistently as the primary analytical framework within this body of work on pregnancy and miscarriage, given its rootedness in those heteronormative 'conventional logics of development, maturity, adulthood and responsibility' that feminist/queer theorists have so fiercely resisted (Halberstam 2005: 13).

It should be stressed that many of the feminist scholars mentioned above are fiercely critical of hegemonic linear narratives of pregnancy. Floyd Davis, for example, laments that 'the progress of the ritual will feel inevitable and unchanging, with a pre-determined order and progression from which there is no deviation possible' (1992: 19); and Layne strongly castigates the relentless promotion of 'happy endings' and presentation of the 'trimesters' of pregnancy *inevitably* following one another (2003: 71–73). But reinscribing the traditional 'rite of passage' model as the master frame surely keeps us locked within the very same linear logics and imaginaries under critique. Reiheld even provides illustrative diagrams to emphasize her claim that miscarriage needs to be understood as 'liminal': straight lines with 'non-parent' and 'hasn't procreated' at one end, and 'parent' and 'has procreated' at the other, with 'miscarriage' in the middle (2015: 11–13).

My point, then, is that continuing to work within the terms of this analytic model (where 'liminality' is understood in the van Geppian rather than the Kristevan sense) can end up reinforcing presumptions that childbirth is ultimately the whole point of pregnancy and its only guarantor of meaning. It implies that even if we view pregnancy as a creative or generative mode of being not-quite-one-thing-or-another, its ambiguity is ultimately a *temporary phase* (rather than an inescapable aspect of intercorporeal existence) that would ideally be resolved through birth/motherhood as a purportedly 'stable' event or 'clear' end-state of being. But as reproductive justice scholars have argued time and again, 'mother' or 'parent' is not a fixed or settled identity, especially for those whose motherhood/parenthood is consistently challenged, denigrated or denied within racist, xenophobic, homophobic, transphobic and ableist social contexts. Giving birth is not always sufficient grounds for being granted the full social status of 'mother' or 'parent', and although birth does represent a crucial political-legal threshold, it is hardly a fixed point of individuation or psychosocial resolution.[9] Moreover, repeatedly depicting the miscarrying/unpregnant person as 'trapped' or 'stuck' within a 'becoming that never becomes' makes it very difficult to get beyond the assumption that a present disconnected from an expected or prescribed future must be emptied of meaning and substance – a zone of 'arrested development' or 'thwarted' becoming (Winnubst 2006; Lahad 2017). Certainly the experience of ambiguity and irresolution can be difficult to bear, as acknowledged in the previous chapter, but this is only exacerbated by linear models of the 'life course' that perpetuate an impossible identity template whereby ambiguity is deemed inherently problematic and must be eliminated as far as possible.

To reject the 'rite of passage' model as an analytic paradigm does not mean denying the powerful ways pregnancy may be actually experienced as an 'in-between' temporality of transition and anticipation, or miscarriage as an 'arrested journey' or state of 'limbo'. Plenty of sociological and anthropological research, such as Layne's, attests to such personal experiences, as well as first-person narratives of pregnancy and miscarriage across a range of online and print media. But from the point of view of philosophical feminist theory, as well as acknowledging and bringing these experiences to view, it is also imperative to articulate a more thoroughgoing challenge to the cultural predominance of this particular cache of temporal tropes – *passage, arrival, arrest, stuck-ness* – and the normative linear framework to which they are wedded.

The rest of this chapter, then, will explore alternative temporal frameworks and tropes that enable us to think more concretely and deeply about pregnancy as a multi-layered, multi-directional, polytemporal *lived present*, rather than a transitional stage or 'middle passage' on the way towards something else. If pregnancy is not to be understood simply as the retrospective or prospective 'past' of a 'mother-and-child', then what kind of 'present' does it embody or enable? Can we think of pregnancy as a complex and heterogeneous duration of lived time, rather than simply the cumulative amount of time it takes for a foetus to develop (or not) into a baby? (Duden 1993: 97).

Sensing, shaping and growing sideways

Terms like 'presentness' have acquired 'an excess of (mostly negative) ontological and epistemological baggage' within academia over the past few decades (Bayly and Baraitser 2008: 341). From a phenomenological perspective, the very idea of a discrete 'present' that can be separated from past and future as fluid modes of temporal orientation is nothing but an illusion brought about by abstraction and the 'vulgar' notion of time.[10] However, motivation for turning attention back to 'the present' often emerges in contexts where an expected or prescribed future has been extinguished or called into question, especially by those who are positioned outside or against normative futural imaginaries. Within queer theory, for instance, the dominance of 'the future' as a normative horizon has been one of the most intensely debated topics in recent years, in the wake of Edelman's polemical critique of 'reproductive futurism' (Edelman 2004).

Edelman's work, as acknowledged in the Introduction of this book, has certainly sparked controversy, not least amongst feminist critics,[11] and to turn away from futurity may seem tantamount to ceding or abandoning the terrain of struggle. 'To answer death with utopian futurity', as Alexis Pauline Gumbs writes, 'is a queer thing to do … A thing that changes the family and the future forever' (2016: 21). Yet Edelman's polemic has also served as a catalyst for many fruitful interventions that 'defuturize' time, considering what it might mean to suspend the future horizon from its privileged position within political imaginaries. In her discussions of 'crip futurity', for example, Kafer interrogates how disability has been consistently rendered the site of 'no future', as the future for disabled people is presented as either a bleak or diminished future that 'no one wants', or a curative future where disability has been eradicated (2013: 2). But in its very frustration of the normative 'investment in controlling the future', as Rosemarie Garland-Thomson argues, disability constitutes an alternative 'narrative resource' for re-imagining lived time and futurity in ways that do not 'trade the present in on the future' (2012: 352).[12] To pursue this kind of reasoning is not to deny the phenomenological point that futurity in the Husserlian sense of 'protention'[13] 'laces every moment of human existence', such that we simply cannot avoid being aligned with it (Chakrabarty 2000: 250–1), nor to refute that different kinds of political futurity are possible. Rather, to 'suspend the future' is 'to refuse it as the dominating frame of our worlds ... to suspend the desirability of fixed endpoints' (Winnubst 2006: 200).

Edelman's own refusal of 'reproductive futurism' turns him towards the 'pulsive force' of negativity, rather than a renewed conceptualization of the 'present' as such. But for others, suspending linear temporalities and the overbearing 'weight of the discourse of futurity' (Bond Stockton 2009: 101) does explicitly invite a different way of conceptualizing the present. In *Cruel Optimism*, for example, Lauren Berlant identifies an 'urgent need to wrest the present both from the forms we know – the burden of inheritance, of personality, of normativity – and from future-oriented ones to which the claims of the present are so often oppressively deferred' (2011: 157). In this text, the present is endowed with a new vitality and legitimacy as a site of theoretical interest – as much more than just a 'rest stop between the enduring past and the momentous future' (158). *Cruel Optimism* thus develops a sense of the present as an extended, ongoing 'stretch of time that is being sensed and shaped' (199), which Berlant suggests can be captured through the concept of 'impasse'. Though usually this term designates 'a time of dithering from which someone or some situation cannot move forward' (4), in Berlant's formulation, it is a term for 'encountering the duration of the present' as a 'thick moment of ongoingness' – for discovering 'a rhythm that people can enter into while they're dithering, tottering, bargaining, testing ...' (28). Another temporal concept Berlant deploys to articulate the elongated, suspended, stretched-out present is the 'situation':

[A] state of things in which something that will perhaps matter is unfolding amid the usual activity of life. It is a state of animated and animating suspension that forces itself on consciousness, that produces a sense of the emergence of something in the present that may become an event.

(5)

Berlant's concepts of the 'present', the 'impasse' and the 'situation' in *Cruel Optimism* are devoted specifically to theorizing economic and social precarity within post-1980s liberal capitalism, and the 'openings within and beyond the impasse of adjustment that constant crisis creates' (6). Their relevance to a feminist re-imagining of pregnancy and miscarriage may not, therefore, be immediately apparent (though of course contemporary pregnancies are significantly shaped by such conditions of precarity). But as Lisa Baraitser argues, Berlant's work on suspended time and the lived present can be brought to bear upon multiple sites of enquiry, opening up broader questions about 'the nature and quality of this time, and its relation to time as development, progress, departure and arrival' (2017: 52). Along such lines, I suggest it has much to offer as we seek to 'encounter the duration' of pregnancy without being over-determined by the future-horizon of birth; to conceptualize pregnant time aside from the usual tropes of *forwardness*, *being-towards* or *passing through*.

For instance, Berlant's notion of the present as a suspended 'stretch of time that is being sensed and shaped' nicely captures the acute tentativeness expressed within so many first-person accounts of pregnancy: the sense of being in uncertain or unchartered territory, and the everyday practices of adjusting oneself, hesitating, improvizing and feeling out how to 'be' pregnant or 'do' pregnancy:

> I am pregnant. I am pregnant, but nothing is assured. The ground shakes. I vomit, once, twice. I get dressed, I go to work. What to think. What to feel. What to do. (Tyler 2000: 288)
>
> Really I had no idea how I felt and nor did I have any gauge against which I could measure what was normal. (Greengrass 2018: 153)
>
> Freshly pregnant, but also fresh from the sadness of losing a pregnancy, I found myself asking the same question over and over: 'Now what?' … I wasn't able to just go about living my life as usual. I had a hard time simply 'being' pregnant, and I felt compelled to 'do it' properly. (Garbes 2018: 15)

When encompassed within the 'rite of passage' model of pregnancy, such feelings of tentativeness, dislocation, strangeness and not-knowing become quickly subsumed by rituals and platitudes designed to resolve uncertainty, hesitancy and aimlessness, and usher the pregnant person along the 'pregnancy journey' by way of key 'milestones' – the scans, the check-ups, the markers of foetal development. 'All must be directed for the sake of a child produced' (Scuro 2017: 189). But Berlant's exhortation is for us to 'pause for a bit' (2011: 154) and 'hold the present open' (197), examining its qualities and contours without subordinating all experience to the forward pull of future investment and projection. This means *'staying with'* feelings and practices of 'sensing and shaping' that may not be 'hooked on any future' or future-directed temporality (14) and are more about making- and being-present, adjusting and surviving within the shifting and tenuous parameters of one's present situation. Indeed, for those whose pregnancies are deemed 'high risk', the focus may be more on *staying* pregnant than anything else (Alcade 2011; Nakamura Lin 2019).

This kind of present-oriented approach does not entail ignoring the many different ways in which pregnancy is experienced as a fluctuating time of change, growth or possibility; rather, it untethers the concepts of change and growth from the future-dominated frameworks within which they are usually thought. We are generally primed to think of change as a transitional process of turning from A into B – a gradual passage forward (as in the traditional 'rite of passage' framework), or an abrupt break with what has gone before. But Berlant proposes a different definition of change as 'catching up to what is already happening' (2011: 54), as an 'an impact lived in the body before anything is understood' (39). This reconceptualization offers a different way of thinking about pregnancy as a time of change: a lived time oriented as much around *what is already happening* as it is towards the *to-come,* and structured through rhythms of negotiating and renegotiating a changing bodily situation. In cases of unplanned pregnancy, this notion of change as 'catching up to what is already happening' might seem particularly applicable; but however planned, intended or desired a pregnancy may be, it entails a continual re-assessment of bodily sensations and re-evaluation of the pregnant body in relation to the pre-pregnant body, as well as to stringent regulative ideals of the 'conscientious' pregnancy, as discussed in

Chapter 2, which dictate what the pregnant body should be and how it should be managed and maintained (Neiterman 2012).[14]

By way of illustration, we can turn back to Young's phenomenological essay 'Pregnant Embodiment', also considered in that earlier chapter, in which she proposes that pregnancy has a 'unique temporality of growth and change', as the pregnant person 'experiences herself as a source and participant in a creative process' ([1984]2005: 54). One way to interpret this would be to envisage a temporality that is developmental and future-oriented – propelling the pregnant subject onwards towards a future of birth and parenthood as that which prospectively, or pre-emptively, gives meaning to the pregnancy. And as I have argued elsewhere, exclusive emphasis upon active transformation and developmental change during pregnancy has the effect of erasing or marginalizing those pregnant bodies that do not 'grow and change' as they are expected to (Browne 2017). Yet, in the personal account of her own pregnancy that she weaves through the text and uses to substantiate her philosophical claims,[15] Young describes a discontinuous lived temporality that is arguably better parsed by Berlant's conception of change as 'catching up to what is already happening':

> In pregnancy my prepregnant body image does not entirely leave my movements and expectations, yet it is with the pregnant body that I must move ... I move as if I could squeeze around chairs and through crowds as I could seven months before, only to find my way blocked by my own body sticking out in front of me ... my habits retain the old sense of my boundaries.
>
> ([1984] 2005: 50)

What Young is describing here is less a 'forward time' of developmental change from A to B, and more a kind of *time-lag* whereby the habitual body image is somewhat out of sync with the dynamic body schema that moves and engages with the world, 'catching up' to it as the pregnant person conducts their daily life. And in turn, this notion of change as a process of 'catching up to what is already happening' can prompt us to revisit the common depiction of pregnancy as a time of 'growth'. To 'grow' is usually understood to refer to a process of maturation and development into something else: as such, when Young speaks of pregnancy having a 'unique temporality of growth and change', we might again presume she is invoking a developmental temporality pertaining to the gestation of the foetus as an unfinished baby, or the pregnant person's 'growth' towards the endpoint of childbirth and parenthood. But does growth always have to be understood in forward, developmental, teleological terms? Kathryn Bond Stockton, for example, in *The Queer Child*, proposes the concept of 'growing sideways' as a means of 'deflat[ing] the vertical, forward-motion metaphor of growing up' towards full stature and maturity (2009: 11). The 'growing sideways' concept is specifically aimed at capturing the experience of the 'queer child' out of sync with their peers and 'repelled by the future mapped out for her', who feels there is 'nowhere to grow' and hence a sense of 'growing toward a question mark. Or in a haze. Or hanging in suspense – even wishing time would stop, or just twist sideways, so that one wouldn't have to advance to new or further scenes of trouble' (13).[16] However, Bond Stockton is clear that 'growing sideways' should also be taken as a more capacious concept, suggesting that 'the width of a person's experience or ideas, their motives and motions, may pertain at any age', and that we all need 'new words for growth' which reach beyond a 'simple thrust toward height and forward time' (14). From this perspective, 'growing toward' appears as a 'short-sighted, limited rendering of human growth, one that would oddly imply an end to growth when full stature (or reproduction) is achieved' (11).

Bond Stockton's concept of 'sideways growth' thus offers a promising way of breaking with the idea of pregnant time as a narrowly or exclusively forward time directed towards birth and parenthood. On the one hand, 'growing sideways' can be taken quite literally in the sense of a pregnant person that physically spreads out and takes up more space.[17] But it can also serve as a temporal metaphor for aspects of pregnancy that do not conform or slot neatly into developmental, forward-moving time: the attachments, affinities and affective activities that organize and 'bind people to the present' (12). Bond Stockton describes such intercorporeal practices of connection, kinship and solidarity as 'moving suspensions' and 'unruly contours of growing that don't bespeak continuance', locating 'energy, pleasure, vitality and (e)motion in the back-and-forth of connections and extensions that are not reproductive' and exceed normative teleologies of the future (13). To consider this in relation to pregnancy, we can turn to

an affecting portrait of such 'sideways' relations in *The Argonauts,* as
Maggie Nelson recalls a pregnant summer spent alongside her partner
as he undergoes and recovers from top surgery:

> 2011, the summer of our changing bodies. Me, four months
> pregnant, you six months on T. We pitched out, in our inscrutable
> hormonal soup, for Fort Lauderdale, to stay for a week at the
> beachside Sheraton in monsoon season, so that you could have
> top surgery by a good surgeon and recover ... The air was hot and
> lavender with a night storm coming in. There was always a night
> storm coming in ... The crowds were loud and repulsive and a little
> scary but we were protected by our force field ....

(2015: 80)

In Nelson's depiction, the two protagonists are by no means turned
away from the future – 'I had started showing ... Maybe there would
be a baby' – and they are filled with a sense of change: 'we were
two human animals undergoing transformations beside each other,
bearing each other loose witness. In other words, we were aging'
(83). But the account here is focused more on their mutual lived time
over that summer – on the possibilities of connection enabled by
their changing pregnant and post-op bodies – than a projected final
endpoint when the pregnancy or surgery will have led to an ultimate
result or conclusion.

The extracts quoted above, by Nelson, Young and others, offer
only snapshots of specific pregnant lives, and as emphasized
throughout this book, there are 'a thousand ways of living a
pregnancy' (Guenther 2006: 55). But they give an indication of
what it might mean to understand pregnancy as a lived present
and an open-ended 'process of emergence' rather than the linear
unfolding of a predetermined path (Berlant 2011: 6), or a generic
passage that can be simply marked off as one goes along (*fourteen
weeks to go!*). They illustrate how pregnancy can be meaningful and
significant in itself, regardless of whether it culminates in a live birth
that retrospectively gives pregnancy meaning as the prehistory of a
postnatal future. As emphasized previously, 'suspending the future'
and foregrounding the 'presentness' of pregnancy does not equate
to a denial of the future-oriented features of pregnancy structured by

anticipation, expectation, preparation, hope and longing, as well as anxiety, fear or dread. In *addicted.pregnant.poor*, for example, Kelly Ray Knight documents how pregnancy is experienced by many of the subjects of her study as a 'ticking time bomb' (2017: 8). Nor does it discount the ways that pregnancy 'milestones', timelines, schedules and rituals can serve as experientially significant temporal anchor points. The intention, rather, is to attend more carefully to those aspects of pregnant time that are so often overlooked or skipped past within the usual representations of pregnancy: temporalities of adjustment, sensing and improvisation; of connecting and witnessing; of impededness, slowness or directionlessness; indeed, of nothing very much happening at all.

A more complex polytemporal understanding of pregnant time thus begins to appear: as multi-layered, multi-rhythmic and multi-directional, and far removed from normative future-dominated depictions which subordinate pregnant time to the teleology of the future 'mother-and-child', or reductively align it with the developmental time of the foetus. In the following and final section, I will consider how this temporal strategy of *suspending the future* can simultaneously open up a different way of thinking about miscarriage.

Staying with suspension

When pregnant time is imagined as a linear progression towards birth, the time of miscarriage can only appear as an arrest of, or ejection from, pregnant time. But through *suspending the future* in order to 'encounter the duration' or lived present of pregnancy, we eliminate the presumption that the future horizon of birth provides the sole measure and structuring principle of pregnancy, and that pregnancy is only to be valued for its 'product'. In turn, then, we also eliminate the presumption that a pregnancy which has not culminated in birth and a baby is necessarily a 'waste of time' that amounted to nothing. Reframing pregnancy in non-teleological terms as a 'situation' entailing multiple complex temporalities can thus help to address the *problem of meaning* that arises in the event of miscarriage. My point here is not that negation, lack and loss ought to be banished from determining the meaning of a 'miscarried pregnancy'. The idea, instead, is that when pregnancy is re-framed as a complex lived present rather than a singular one-way journey, it can be fully grasped as significant in itself, and not only because of where it is presumably headed.

Accordingly, if there is a sense of disorientation or loss in the event of miscarriage, this can be understood not only as the loss of a developing foetus or baby with whom one was in relation, or an imagined future of parenting an expected child, but moreover, as the loss of a particular form of embodiment and way of being in the world. So even when there is no baby or child at the end of it all, this does not mean the pregnancy has amounted to nothing. There are 'contours of growing', in Bond Stockton's words, that are not procreative in the conventional sense, and are not just *cancelled out* in the event that a projected future does not materialize. Pregnancy is a transformative situation that can enable changes and connections that spread or spiral outwards in the world, and do not only acquire meaning in a prospective or retrospective sense. Hence if the meaning of pregnancy does not depend entirely on its future outcome, then miscarriage need not be understood as pregnancy's *undoing*, as if pregnant time simply halts or is erased with the onset of miscarriage time.

Theoretical accounts of suspended time within feminist/queer theory also help to push back against the idea that the miscarrying/ unpregnant person is 'trapped' in a kind of *non-time* that is the absolute negation of pregnant time. Though miscarriage is often presumed to be a singular event that happens 'in a moment' and brings the 'pregnancy journey' to a sudden halt, it incorporates a dis-synchronicity or time-lag between demise of the embryo/foetus and expulsion or removal from the pregnant body (Hardy and Kukla 2015). In the case of 'missed miscarriage' it can take days or even weeks for a body's hormonal signals to register that the embryo/foetus is no longer developing (Freidenfelds 2020: 5). This gives rise to an array of temporal experiences that may well include a sense of going backwards: 'you will watch your body backtrack, go into reverse, unpicking its work; the sickness recedes, your breasts shrink back, your abdomen flattens, your appetite disappears' (O'Farrell 2017: 103). But the temporalities of miscarriage also share common traits with the pregnant time with which the time of miscarriage overlaps, such as the temporality of 'catching-up' to a changing bodily situation that is largely out of one's control. Just as being pregnant entails adjustment and 'catching up to what is already happening', so does becoming unpregnant: 'It felt like my body had only just realized I wasn't pregnant anymore' (Hintz-Zimbrano 2015).

Another recurring temporal theme within personal accounts of miscarriage and its aftermaths is that of waiting: 'waiting for the fetus to expel itself, waiting for an appointment for a surgical extraction, waiting for grief to lessen' (Hardy and Kukla 2015: 107). Waiting often conjures assumptions of an entirely passive and blank time, especially if it is not an intentional 'waiting for the baby' but rather for a miscarriage and its after-effects to be over. Within feminist philosophy and theory, for example, the temporality of waiting is often understood as a 'passive present' which operates as a formative structure of women's lived existence and subordination (Burke 2019: 112; see also Beauvoir [1949]1997; Rich [1976]1992). And indeed, waiting is often described in miscarriage stories as a kind of 'limbo' – a suspended, futureless time that 'stretches out endlessly' (Miscarriage Association 2014). 'Limbo' is a particularly common trope within narratives of recurrent miscarriage, which often describe a sense of life going 'on hold' while 'the repeated cycle of pregnancy and loss takes over' (Bueno 2019: 130). But as Baraitser argues in *Enduring Time* (2017), while it may be experienced as obdurate, arduous, even unbearable, suspended time should not be understood as stilled or as 'outside of time'. It is a form of lived time that has duration, even if it is not experienced as flowing or progressing towards a tangible, anticipated or longed-for future. Moreover, though it might be imagined that suspended time is empty or dead, that 'suspension of the flow of time would mean a failure to live and feel' (Baraitser and Riley 2016), suspended time is commonly felt to be 'thick' and 'viscous', or 'oddly lively' (Baraitser 2017: 89). Indefinite periods of waiting in miscarriage, for instance, are often emotionally complex and highly intense, 'saturated with complicated bodily and social meanings' (Hardy and Kukla 2015: 107–8).

If our temporal imaginaries remain tethered to the conventional 'rite of passage' framework, accounts of being 'on hold' or 'in limbo' during, or following, miscarriage can only appear as the very antithesis of what the time of pregnancy is supposed to be: a hopeful movement forward towards a future birth and new identity as a 'mother' or 'parent'. But like Berlant and Bond Stockton, what Baraitser incites us to do is to pause and 'stay with' suspended time 'rather than passing through it' (2017: 5), to stop measuring all life experiences and events against an idealized model of developmental or progressive time as 'proper time' itself. This opens up a way of thinking about miscarriage that is less about trying to *rescue* the 'liminar' from temporal suspension through re-incorporation into normative social time, and more about attending to and reflecting on 'the *qualities* of time that has nevertheless been suspended':

> The thought of carrying a dead embryo inside me drove me crazy … that time … was an eternity, it simply didn't pass. (Gerber-Epstein et al 2009)
>
> The next few months were a blur. I put one foot in front of the other, but I'm still not sure how I managed to make my way in the world. (Hintz-Zimbrano 2015)
>
> I feel gelatinous, a bit like putty, neither solid nor liquid. Like I no longer have edges to contain me. (Gibney 2019: 101)

Living through suspended forms of time during or following miscarriage can be distressing, unsettling, disorienting, depressing, exhausting, desperate, even tortuous. Yet just as 'no baby' need not equal 'no future', it generally does not equate to a complete cessation or breakdown of the lived present either. Indeed, personal accounts of miscarriage consistently describe a wealth of emotional and material practices of endurance, survival, care and solidarity – the forging of 'sideways relations' through the sustaining of people and things, connections and ties, that do not depend upon a certain or projected future as a guarantee of meaning or purpose. This is not so much 'the time of generation or production', as Baraitser describes it, but the time of 'trying to keep something going – keeping things functioning' through pain, loss, sadness and uncertainty (2017: 52), of saying to each other 'we are *here*' (Gibney and Yang 2019: 8). Feminist writers Dania Rajendra and Angela Garbes, for example, each depict the process of reckoning with their miscarriages as a re-immersion into everydayness and the political realities of the present conjuncture, rather than a journey of 'moving-on' or refocusing all attention on a future goal of parenthood:

> We paid $10 each at the door of a juke joint where the price of admission included a red Solo cup, allowing us to help ourselves to

unlimited refills from a keg that sat on the floor, late into the night. We were sad, but we were drunk, and we talked loudly about the importance and beauty of our freedom ... In Jackson I saw a family burning wood and trash in a drum on their front lawn. The windows of their house were broken; the fire was for heat.... (Garbes 2018: 77–8)

I walk around in a warm and living body that carries a brittle length of something hollow, full of dark, cold, missing person-potential ... Everydayness is a blessing – a binding sign of the fullness of this life – my life. (Rajendra 2019: 112–4)

Experiences of miscarriage can of course be 'wildly divergent, even within one life' (Garbes 2018: 83), and as argued in the previous chapter, it is highly problematic to assume that there is always an experience of grief, sadness or loss, or an onset of something like suspended time that is necessarily lived in a particular way. The aim, rather, is to try and consider these kinds of temporal experiences in terms other than *lack, antithesis* or *falling short*, and to call for greater social patience and openness in relation to miscarriage. This means expelling all assumptions that a miscarrying/unpregnant person must 'move on' as soon as possible – a response of *shutting down* that is particularly directed towards those deemed too young or too poor, to be pregnant anyway and thus not permitted to feel sadness or grief, those expected to be 'strong' (in line with the 'Strong Black Woman' stereotype), or those with living children already (Kamal 2019: 182). It means resisting the impulse for 'fixing and ... manic repair' (Baraitser and Brook 2021: 244) through immediately reinserting the miscarrying/unpregnant person back into linear reproductive time – 'pointing [them] toward happiness' (Ahmed 2010a: 576) with talk of '*trying again*' and '*better luck next time*'. This impulse finds consistent expression within various pregnancy loss support communities, where books, blogs, newsletters, and articles talk of hope and the future – the chances of being able to become pregnant again, of future pregnancies culminating in live birth and a 'rainbow baby', of reaching the end-goal of parenthood.

Certainly, the thought of future pregnancy, birth or parenthood, can function in many cases as an important source of hope, energy and optimism. It is also important to recognize that for those whose reproductivity has been cast as a threat to social futures, or for whom the future has been effectively foreclosed, insisting upon generation and futurity can be a vital form of both persistence and resistance (Vergès 2020: 124; Gumbs 2016). But as Garbes argues, the incessant focus within some pregnancy loss communities and wider society upon fixing problems and 'reinforcing that you can and will get pregnant again as the goal' leaves 'no room for the possibility of not trying over and over to get pregnant again' (2018: 87) – a process that can be an economic and emotional drain. Moreover, it obscures the often difficult and slow work of reckoning with complex feelings and corporeal repercussions in the present, sidestepping grief as something to be *'grappled with'* by presenting it as a time-limited problem with a clear resolution (Scuro 2017: xiii).

In Berlant's words, then, we must eschew the temptation to approach the present as 'more or less a problem to be solved by hope's temporal projection' (2011: 12), being wary of the 'cost of future projection' (Deutscher 2016: 4) when it functions as a diversion from the work of caring and world-making in the present. Maria Puig de la Bellacasa, for instance, describes 'care time' as a time which 'suspends the future and distends the present' (2017: 207), in order to make time for the 'hovering and adjusting' that constitutes caring attention. Or as Baraitser and Brook explain, 'care time' demands a commitment to 'fostering forms of connection that consist of waiting *with*' rather than waiting *for*, 'enduring with, staying with, staying alongside' (2021: 244). Social attitudes towards pregnancy and miscarriage would then be oriented less around *When are you due?* or *You can try again*, and more around *What makes you feel cared for?*[18] *What enables you to care? What structures of support are needed now?*

Chapter 5
Solidarity

I experience such a flash of hatred for her that I have to turn away, ashamed.[1]

The commonness of the experience became real to me ... what had first appeared as an interruption in my story I later came to see as an opening ... .[2]

Expressions of anger, envy and resentment towards those who are 'successfully pregnant' can often be found within miscarriage stories. This is a completely understandable response, particularly within a competitive social environment that pits women against one another, while also rendering negative emotions a shameful threat to the atmosphere of 'pregnancy world' as a scene of happiness. At the same time, miscarriage stories repeatedly attest to a strong sense of connection amongst those who go through it: 'I received immeasurable support from women who were already a part of this club that nobody wants to be a member of' (Smalkoski 2019: 91). It is also possible, though rarer, to find expressions of empathy and solidarity that extend across 'miscarriage', 'pregnancy' and 'abortion' as sites of experience. For instance, the lived experience of an accepted or wanted pregnancy can reinforce a pro-choice/pro-access position by enabling new insight into the need for abortion: 'to unwillingly bear a pregnancy like this in the center of one's being would be one of the worst forms of torture' (Bigwood 1991: 59; see also Manninen 2010). And various feminist writers strongly reassert their pro-choice/pro-access politics as they mourn their miscarriages, emphatic that there is no contradiction in so doing (see e.g. Rajendra 2019; Valvidiamo 2019).

In this final chapter, I want to seize on such moments to consider how solidarity could be further strengthened and extended to encompass the full spectrum of pregnancy 'independent of the outcomes or expectations of childbearing' (Scuro 2021). To call for full-spectrum solidarity is not to demand that those who experience miscarriage must feel or understand it a certain way, or to claim that anger, envy and resentment are 'unfeminist'. As Sara Ahmed affirms, 'we cannot always close the gap between how we feel and how we think we should feel' (2010a: 581); and it can simply be unbearable to witness or engage with the pregnancies of others when one's own has ended unexpectedly. I am talking here about forms of political solidarity and alliance-building that dismantle the false barriers separating 'pregnancy' from 'miscarriage' and 'abortion', such that they cease to be treated as mutually exclusive 'clubs' and become fully integrated into feminist struggles for social justice instead of 'single issue' politics.

To demonstrate the urgency of this political project, the chapter will begin by highlighting the increasingly punitive treatment of miscarriage and stillbirth in the US, as hundreds of women – overwhelmingly poor and disproportionately of colour – have been arrested, prosecuted and incarcerated for allegedly causing their miscarriages/stillbirths through drug-use, or for disguising illegal 'self-abortion' as miscarriage/stillbirth. Though it may seem that this rising criminalization of miscarriage necessitates a protective response that insists on its 'innocence' and separateness, I will argue instead for a feminist refusal of 'divide and rule' politics that would have us defend 'innocent' miscarriage at the expense of 'guilty' abortion or 'irresponsible' pregnancy. The chapter will turn then to the rising 'full-spectrum doula' movement in the US – which offers support and care to all pregnant people whether their pregnancy ends in birth, abortion, miscarriage, stillbirth or adoption – as an inspiring practical example of feminist solidarity that paves the way for coordinated struggle at a wider level.

Criminalized miscarriage

As miscarriage gets taken up as a feminist issue, critical reflection often centres on the question of how it is possible to acknowledge the sadness and grief that miscarriage may cause without compromising the principles of pro-choice/pro-access politics. But there is another political predicament that pertains not so much to how different people feel about their miscarriages, but rather to the ways in which some individuals are held accountable for them. This returns us to the discussion in Chapter 2 about the consequences of the individualist model of pregnancy as a controllable 'project', which makes 'successful' pregnancies appear as a matter of individual achievement and responsibility. At the upper ends of the privilege scale, this means that many people report feelings of guilt and self-blame for somehow causing their miscarriages or not doing enough to prevent them, even as they are reassured by sympathetic medical professionals and others that there was 'nothing they could have done'. But at the lower ends of the scale, sympathy is far more likely to be displaced by scrutiny and suspicion (Bommaraju et al 2016). In the present era, neoliberal ideologies of self-control and individual responsibility combine with patriarchal ideologies of 'foetal motherhood' and 'foetal personhood' to produce increasingly draconian forms of social censure, state intervention and criminal punishment targeted particularly at low-income women and women of colour.

Since 1973, there has been a 'skyrocketing' number of arrests, detentions and equivalent deprivations of physical liberty of women in the US, 'in which being pregnant was a necessary element of the crime or a "but for" reason for the coercive or punitive action taken' (Paltrow and Sangoi 2016; NAPW 2021a). As Lynn Paltrow and Lisa Sangoi explain, 'otherwise non-criminal acts such as attempting suicide, falling down a flight of stairs, drinking alcohol, failing to get bed rest, not consenting to surgery, and using drugs (as opposed to possessing drugs) become criminal acts because the woman is pregnant' (Paltrow and Sangoi 2016). There were 413 recorded arrests and forced interventions in the US between 1973 and 2005 – 71 per cent of those affected were living in poverty and 59 per cent were women of colour (Paltrow and Flavin 2013) – and approximately 1,254 more arrests, detentions and equivalent deprivations of physical liberty have been documented between 2006 and 2020 (NAPW 2021a).

Many of these cases have involved the arrest and prosecution of women for exposing their 'unborn child' to drugs under a variety of laws such as 'child endangerment' or 'child neglect'.[3] Though the minimal welfare state may provide 'opportunities for rehabilitation and redemption' for drug-addicted or drug-using pregnant people, as Kelly Ray Knight demonstrates, it also ensures that 'adjudication and punishment will follow, should these fail' (2015: 11).[4] In 2004, in Oklahoma, Theresa Lee Hernandez was sentenced to fifteen years in prison for 'second-degree murder' after her baby was stillborn and tested positive for methamphetamine (NAPW 2007). In 2019, Lindsay R. was placed on Arizona's Central registry for twenty-five years for committing 'civil child neglect' for using medical marijuana while pregnant (NAPW 2021c). In October 2021, Brittney Poolaw was convicted of 'first-degree manslaughter' in Oklahoma for having a miscarriage at seventeen weeks – the prosecutor blamed her alleged use of controlled substances while pregnant – and sentenced to four years in state prison. Prior to the conviction, she had already been incarcerated for eighteen months having been unable to afford the $20,000 bond set by the court (NAPW 2021e).[5]

A significant number of cases also involve the accusation that illegal 'self-abortion' has been disguised as miscarriage or stillbirth. One of the most high-profile of these cases occurred in 2015 when Purvi Patel became the first person in the US to be charged, convicted and sentenced for 'feticide' in relation to her own pregnancy. In 2013, she had been admitted to an emergency room in Indiana, claiming to have suffered a miscarriage and disposed of the foetal body on the way to the hospital. The prosecution, however, argued she had deliberately sought to terminate the pregnancy through taking abortion-inducing drugs ordered online (though the toxicology report found no evidence of the drugs in her body).[6] Patel was also charged with neglect of a dependent, as the prosecution proposed that the foetus had in fact been born alive, and could have survived if medical attention had been sought. Though the charges appear contradictory (and the evidence for both was fiercely contested), the prosecution contended that a person can be guilty of 'feticide' for deliberately trying to end a pregnancy by illegal means, even if the foetus survives; and that in such cases, a person can also be guilty of letting them die after birth. Patel was indeed found guilty of both crimes – class A felony 'neglect of a dependent' and class B felony 'feticide' – and sentenced to twenty years in prison (Bazelon 2015).

Indiana's 'feticide' statute, introduced in 1979, refers to 'a person who knowingly or intentionally terminates a human pregnancy with an intention other than to produce a live birth or to remove a dead fetus', or to perform a legal abortion.[7] It was designed with violent third parties in mind whose actions cause a pregnancy to end in miscarriage or stillbirth (through intimate partner violence or assault for example), rather than those who attempt an illegal 'self-abortion' or endanger their own pregnancy. Indeed, the Indiana Court of Appeals ultimately vacated the 'feticide' charge against Patel, conceding that 'the legislature did not intend for the feticide statute to apply to illegal abortions or to be used to prosecute women for their own abortions'.[8] This clarification of the Indiana law came too late for Kelli Leever-Driskel, however, who was arrested in February 2018 after a stillbirth, and charged with 'feticide' and involuntary manslaughter based on her alleged drug use while pregnant. She spent several months in jail before the charges were dismissed (NAPW 2018).

With cases like Patel's or Leever-Driskel's, the onus on the legal defence is to show that existing laws are being improperly applied, or otherwise to 'prove it's a miscarriage' or stillbirth[9] and moreover an 'innocent' one, thereby summoning a series of binary distinctions – chosen versus unchosen, intentional versus spontaneous, voluntary versus involuntary, reckless versus responsible – that could hold the key to an individual's freedom from incarceration and other forms of punishment. But from a broader theoretical viewpoint, what kind of response might these criminalized cases generate? What have feminists had to say about miscarriage and its place within the politics of pregnancy, and how might this inform the challenge to its criminalization in the US and beyond?

Alison Reiheld is one feminist philosopher who has turned their attention to such questions, attributing the criminalization of miscarriage to its 'liminality'. Unlike 'pregnancy' and 'abortion' which have 'clear event status', she argues, miscarriage falls between these 'well-defined social categories' and is thus susceptible to being 'enrolled' in discussions and legal battles over their control (2015: 16). 'A thing poorly understood', Reiheld writes, 'but too-like states or events which we believe we understand is quite likely to be drawn into debates over those other states or events' (23). Accordingly, if miscarriage were better theorized and understood as a 'liminal' event 'in its own right', and separated from the opposing 'poles' of 'pregnancy' and 'abortion', it might not be so easily subjected to sets of laws and policies (proposed or enacted) seeking to control pregnancy and abortion, namely: those which require pregnant people to prove their pregnancy has ended involuntarily rather than voluntarily; those which allow healthcare providers to opt out of treating miscarriage because it can require similar techniques as abortion (most notably D&C); and those which hold individuals criminally responsible for their own miscarriages or stillbirths where their actions or behaviours are deemed to have played a causal role (23). Reiheld acknowledges that in light of the persistent obsession with 'foetal personhood' in the US, it is unlikely that we can 'avoid entirely' the treatment of miscarriage as suspicious or shameful. Nonetheless, without a notion of miscarriage that is 'clearly distinct' from the 'binaries' it falls in between, including 'pregnancy' and 'abortion',

> I fear we will repeat again and again the negative ethical fallout of failure to understand miscarriage's liminality. The result? Women who miscarry will again and again be isolated, their troubles sequestered, their experiences and fates enrolled in debates which hardly bear on miscarriage at all.
>
> (23)

The call to treat miscarriage as a case apart does make practical sense in certain situations. For example, people undergoing miscarriages or stillbirths often find it distressing to be treated in the same spaces within medical institutions as those having check-ups for ongoing pregnancies or those in labour. But at the level of political principle and strategy, the argument to separate out miscarriage from pregnancy and abortion needs to be further questioned. What makes miscarriage 'clearly distinct' from pregnancy and abortion, as Reiheld contends? Is a pregnancy that ends in miscarriage or abortion not still a pregnancy? Can 'women who miscarry' (19) not also be 'women who abort' and 'women who give birth'? Do 'debates' over abortion 'hardly bear' on miscarriage? And if miscarriage is 'too like' abortion, does this imply we should be devoting our theoretical energy to trying to separate them out?

Stigma, choice and responsibilization

Assumptions that pregnancy, miscarriage and abortion should be treated as discrete phenomena usually revolve around two key concepts: stigma and choice. In short, pregnancy and abortion tend to be framed as a matter of choice in contrast to miscarriage; while abortion and miscarriage are understood to be stigmatized in contrast to pregnancy because neither produces 'the all-miraculous, all-coveted BABY' (Nelson 2015: 109). But when examined in light of feminist work on the politics of 'stratified reproduction', such assumptions soon begin to falter or collapse altogether.

First, as I have argued throughout the book, it is not straightforwardly the case that 'miscarriage' and 'abortion' are stigmatized while 'pregnancy' is not. The argument put forward by Reiheld, for example, is that 'pregnancy' is celebrated and surrounded by a host of well-established, 'clear cultural scripts', whereas miscarriage in contrast is 'sequestered' and seldom discussed, therefore occupying a liminal position as 'taboo' (2015: 13). But this kind of claim obscures the fact that social support for pregnancy is highly conditional and variable, depending upon who is pregnant. Demonized pregnancies – of so-called 'benefits scroungers', for example – are just as socially stigmatized as miscarriage, arguably even more so if we are talking about the miscarriages of the wealthy and privileged compared to the pregnancies of the scapegoated poor. Further, while scenes of criminalized pregnancy depicted in the news – like the disturbing images of Purvi Patel in handcuffs – may seem a far cry from the frothy magazine articles and casual social interactions Reiheld presumably has in mind when she speaks of 'clear cultural scripts' for pregnancy, such banal discourses are a primary vehicle of 'childbearing teleology': the scripts and rituals that differentiate the 'right' kind of pregnancy from the 'wrong' kind, and validate only its productive aspects (Scuro 2017). Defining miscarriage as a stigmatized phenomenon *in contrast* to pregnancy therefore seems to somewhat miss the point, as if the ubiquitous scripts and symbols of normative pregnancy were not themselves the source of the problem. Indeed, the more banal and seemingly benign this symbolism is, the more ordinary and commonplace it becomes.

Second, the framing of miscarriage as 'unchosen' in contrast to pregnancy and abortion as 'chosen' must also be examined more closely. The ideal pregnancy today is presented within normative public discourse as a deliberately chosen and carefully controlled individual 'project', as previously outlined in Chapter 2. An effect of this is that pregnancies which are unplanned, unintended or forced disappear from view, as does the ineluctable contingency of even the most desired and planned-for pregnancies. Another effect is that unchosenness appears to belong more properly to miscarriage than 'successful' pregnancy.[10] This impression is also strengthened by the centrality of choice to the construction of abortion as a political issue. Though both miscarriage and abortion are stigmatized by virtue of the fact that neither delivers up the baby, they are often treated as oppositional phenomena because when abortion is framed as, above all, the chosen act of an autonomous individual, miscarriage again seems distinct in its lack of chosenness.[11]

From a patriarchal perspective, then, while both abortion and miscarriage are to be feared, it is for different reasons: abortion for its apparent exercise of sovereign power over life and death (Cavarero 1995: 64), miscarriage for its unruly eruption of uncontrollable feminine matter. The miscarrying body may be marked by an essentialist logic as 'unnatural' in its failure to fulfil its 'most natural function', as discussed in Chapter 1, but the feminized subject who miscarries can – if she conforms to the archetype of the 'good foetal mother' – nevertheless be deemed *innocent*. She may have been 'helpless' but at least she was 'willing if not able' (Ahmed 2014: 111).[12] In contrast, a feminized subject who opts to deliberately terminate her pregnancy appears as the very 'antithesis of womanhood' in wilfully refusing the reproductive imperative of 'the female body'. One appears as a 'failed' or 'incomplete' woman, the other as *no kind of woman at all*.

Abortion stigma has thus conventionally been premised as much upon intention and choice as upon outcome. And outside of patriarchal discourses too, there is a widespread assumption that 'whether a pregnancy is terminated voluntarily or not constitutes an enormous distinction' between experiences of abortion and miscarriage (Cahill 2015: 57). This, presumably, is behind Reiheld's claim that 'the line between completing or accelerating a miscarriage and performing an induced abortion seems clear to me' (2015: 23). Yet for as long as the rhetoric of individual choice and voluntarism has been attached to abortion, it has also been subject to feminist interrogation, which should make feminist theorists and activists wary of these kinds of claims. This is not to say that chosenness and unchosenness are not significant or relevant to the discussion. In plenty of cases, abortion is experienced as an empowering exercise of choice, while many personal accounts of miscarriage describe it as an event that brings a depleted sense of control and agency in its unchosenness. Jennifer Doyle, for example, writes of her sense that 'the abortion I had as a student at Rutgers in the 1980s was one of the most singularly empowering experiences I've had as a sexual subject' (2009: 26), while Angela Garbes describes feeling 'powerless' as her miscarriage occurred (2017: 76). But the line between miscarriage and abortion can also feel much finer. Many people who have 'terminations for medical reasons' – or 'TMR' as it is often referred to in pregnancy loss forums online – do not categorize the experience as 'abortion'; and as Barbara Katz Rothman argued in *The Tentative Pregnancy* over thirty years ago: 'The decision to abort a foetus with spina bifida when you live in a fourth-floor walkup in a city designed without access for wheelchairs is not really an exercise in free choice' (1986: 9; see also Reza 2019, or Squires 2019).

There is clearly a danger in highlighting these kinds of 'fine lines'. In the first instance, the example given above by Katz Rothman can easily be made to fit the normative narrative of the 'right' kind of abortion: the regretful one involving a moral dilemma, or a difficult and painful choice in response to extraneous circumstances. This narrative belongs to what Erica Millar calls the 'mushy middle' that is 'at once pro-choice and anti-abortion', professing support for women to choose and have abortions, 'so long as they feel "really, really bad" about them' (Pollitt in Millar 2018: 2).[13] Narratives of abortion as a 'choiceless choice' (Ross and Solinger 2017: 102) can also be summoned in support of the 'pro-life' claim that women are 'victims' of abortion as much as the 'unborn', as no woman in their right mind or in the right circumstances would ever choose abortion. As Millar demonstrates, since the early 1980s, the transnational anti-abortion movement has 'increasingly shifted rhetorical focus away from protecting foetal life to feigning equal concern with the impact of abortion on women' (2016: 501). This turns on reframing abortion as 'loss' rather than 'murder', and transposing the foetus into 'a constant, absent presence in the woman's life, constantly judging her for making the wrong decision and retrospectively organising her pregnancy as involving an eternal relationship between a mother and her child' (2016: 508). The 'wrongness' of the abortion choice is recast as a wrong against women themselves and their 'maternal nature', such that women need to be protected from the bad choices they might make under the spell of feminist doctrine. As Mary Mahoney and Lauren Mitchell put it, the strategy to make abortion an 'unthinkable option' has been 'to say that it was something women might regret, and to save women from the pain of regret, they should not have the choice' (2016: 19). Choice is thereby voided through claims that abortion could never be a valid choice, and, further, that it is a 'loss even when it is chosen' (Millar 2016: 507).

So if the distinction between miscarriage and abortion hinges upon individual choice, voluntarism and intention, then in practice it is being eroded quite effectively by anti-abortion campaigners, through the language of loss and mobilization of 'foetocentric grief' (Millar 2016). Indeed, as discussed in Chapter 3, this form of anti-abortion activism can be both wittingly and unwittingly strengthened by certain strands of the pregnancy loss movement: for example, when terminating a pregnancy for medical reasons ('TMR') is presented in universalizing terms as always 'a heartbreaking decision'.[14] This kind of statement, as emphasized in that chapter, is generally intended as a legitimating gesture that provides social recognition or 'uptake' to a set of feelings and experiences that so often generate social awkwardness, avoidance and discomfort. But the effect of this kind of compensatory discourse is that variation, ambiguity and ambivalence tend to disappear from view, such that 'foetocentric grief', as Millar argues, becomes 'the only intelligible emotion that women experience upon the cessation of pregnancy through either miscarriage or abortion' (2016: 503).

At the same time, the presumption of miscarriage as a passive event that is *undergone* rather than chosen is being steadily eroded through regulatory discourses of 'foetal motherhood' and 'conscientious pregnancy', which not only maternalize abortion but responsibilize pregnant individuals for the outcomes of their pregnancies. As considered in Chapter 2, the neoliberal construction of the 'conscientious' and 'active' pregnancy as an individual 'body project' places intense pressures upon pregnant people of all social positions and incomes to 'do' pregnancy correctly and conform to the demanding public standards of the 'good pregnant mother'. 'Every choice that a woman makes', argues Pam Lowe, 'from eating to prenatal testing, is taken as evidence of her willingness to perform idealised motherhood … whilst nominally "choices" can be made, there is often only one "right" choice for responsible women to make' (2016: 109). Hence, though it might well be recognized that miscarriage itself is not actively chosen or intended, the pregnant person can nevertheless be held responsible for their choices or 'substandard care' of their foetus up to that point (Bommaraju et al. 2016: 63). This logic reaches its dreadful realization through the US criminal justice system when predominantly poor women of colour are arrested, prosecuted and charged for 'culpable miscarriage', the message being that it does not matter whether the ending of a pregnancy was chosen, intended or undertaken deliberately, because a pregnant individual can still be held responsible for failing to 'act like a mother'.

All this might well suggest that the feminist response to the 'merging' of miscarriage and abortion should be to do just the opposite and reinforce the distinction between the two. But if such a distinction depends upon a reinforcement of chosen vs. unchosen as the decisive criterion, or presumptions about which pregnancies are 'willed' and 'wanted' and 'nurtured' and which are not, this only brings us back to all the problems that ensue when individual choice and intention are placed front and centre of reproductive politics. The marshalling of individual autonomy – 'My body, My choice' – certainly carries a powerful charge as an act of reclaiming what patriarchal ideologies and laws seek to obliterate; and meaningful choice is of course a necessary condition of reproductive freedom. But as reproductive justice theorists and activists have tirelessly argued, in isolation from campaigns for full access and 'enabling conditions', the mantra of individual choice only serves to eclipse the gross structural inequalities that materialize through differential access to reproductive services including abortion care, as well as modes of reproductive coercion, censure and sanction (Ross and Solinger 2017: 122; see also Matthieson 2021). In reality, the apparatus of 'choice' works for some but against others, when the moralized and gendered responsibility to make the 'right' choices, want the 'right' things, and apply the 'right' kind of control, functions as a form of disciplinary power exercised particularly over the 'wrong' sort of women. Further, as Millar points out, the tables are easily turned when 'choice' is appropriated and marshalled by anti-abortion activists. While, on the one hand, they claim that women's choices to abort are against their 'maternal nature' and hence can never be genuine, they themselves deploy the discourse of choice when they assert that knowledge of 'post-abortion syndrome', as well as incremental restrictions on abortion, including mandatory counselling and 'cooling-off' periods, 'provide women with informed and "real" choices' (Millar 2016: 506).

What we are dealing with, then, is a terrain in which 'chosen' and 'unchosen' may continue to hold subjective meaning (in terms of how an individual might understand and frame their own abortion or miscarriage), but their political meaning has become subsumed by powerful discourses of proper and responsible behaviour, and a new kind of consequentialist logic whereby outcome, above all, is deemed sufficient grounds for culpability. In response, what is required at the level of political strategy is not so much a renewed feminist defence of individual 'choice', but joined-up resistance to the mechanisms of responsibilization that put people who experience both abortion *and* miscarriage at risk of censure and criminal punishment. This means suspending questions about choice and intent, and reckoning instead with the gendered, raced and classed norms that position certain individuals on the right side of social approval and the law while rendering others reckless or suspicious. *Whose* miscarriage looks 'too like' abortion? If there is a 'right' and a 'wrong' kind of abortion, how does this relate to the 'right' and 'wrong' kind of miscarriage, and the 'right' and 'wrong' kind of pregnancy? How well is someone able to narrate their miscarriage or abortion to meet the requirements for 'responsible decision-making', 'conscientious pregnancy' or 'innocent loss'? (Deutscher 2016).

It also means reckoning with the impacts, implications and costs of abortion and miscarriage – quite literally for those without adequate medical insurance or who are gestating for money[15] – in light of how they map on to wider social inequalities. When we widen the focus like this, what appears most politically significant with regard to cases of criminalized miscarriage like Purvi Patel's is not what the individual in question may have chosen or intended – was it deliberate? – but the conditions that make adverse pregnancy outcomes, interventions and arrests far more likely for some than for others; in which pregnant people may refrain from seeking help for drug or alcohol addiction for fear of being reported to the police; and in which the options for some pregnant people are so severely constrained that a risky 'DIY abortion' in unsafe conditions may emerge as the only option.[16]

This redirection of attention away from individual choice and intention might cause feminist concern, if it seems that the agency of pregnant/ unpregnant people is once again disappearing from view. But to recall the argument of Chapter 2, de-individualizing pregnancy is in fact a prerequisite to understanding the nature of agency as an affective relational capacity that is actualized through intercorporeal interactions which can never be fully controlled. From the intercorporeal perspective, agency is not an innate property of the 'self-made, self-contained and self-moving' individual who acts to bring about their self-determined ends (Cahill 2015: 51). Rather, it is only through embodied encounters in specific contexts that possibilities for making decisions and having an impact in the world are opened (or closed) in any substantial way (Diprose 2002: 72). Consequently, examining how intersecting structural factors and power relations shape the possibilities of a pregnancy, and enable or constrain socially conditioned processes of choice, is a much better way of grasping the complex operations of agency than simply hailing 'choice' as a proxy for agency. As Keren Epstein-Gilboa argues, for instance, 'choice' can serve in clinical settings as 'a means of appeasing, silencing, controlling and isolating' rather than advocating for patients, because once a choice has been made, it is presumed that agency has been exercised and hence that no further questions are necessary (2017: 113). Or as Penelope Deutscher demonstrates, the language of choice discounts and diminishes people 'whose agency might not be legible as choice' (2016: 187), which includes those who experience miscarriage.

Full-spectrum solidarity

What the above discussion has demonstrated is that miscarriage and abortion cannot be distinguished from 'pregnancy' on the presumption that miscarriage and abortion are stigmatized while 'pregnancy' is socially supported; or on the grounds that pregnancy and abortion are chosen while miscarriage is not. Not only do such distinctions frequently falter on further examination; they are also integral to oppressive social discourses of 'successful' pregnancy and 'foetal motherhood' which, to quote Berlant, 'retraumatize a set of already vulnerable bodies: the body of the woman unsettled by pregnancy and already exposed to misogyny and the state; the impoverished, the young, the often African American or Native American women who have had little access to reproductive health support apart from a scandalous history of state chicanery ...' (1994: 149). From this critical perspective, it is not that miscarriage is wrongly 'enrolled' in laws and debates over the control of pregnancy and abortion due to conceptual error. It is rather that struggles over the criminalization of miscarriage are *inextricable* from struggles over the control of pregnancy and abortion. When pregnant people are treated as dangerous subjects, it is inevitable that those who have experienced miscarriage or stillbirth will be 'swept up' into the criminal justice system, at least those whose reproductivity and existence have already been marked as suspicious or threatening.

The impulse to *rescue* or shield those who go through miscarriage from the 'fallout' of abortion politics through insisting upon its difference may be strong; but in 'turn[ing] away less from those who have experienced miscarriage' (Reiheld 2015: 22), it is vital not to turn away more from those who have experienced abortion. In particular, there is a need for vigilance concerning the assumptions and implications that lie behind the idea that it is *especially* bad for someone to be punished for inducing an abortion when in fact the cessation of pregnancy was involuntary. Of course there is a particular cruelty to being punished for something one did not do. This adds the injustice of wrongful accusation into the mix, and if the pregnant person did not want the pregnancy to end, a wretched kind of irony. But who is to say it is necessarily less painful to be punished for something that one has actually done, especially within a cultural climate that is so anti-abortion that even some pro-choice activists refer to it as a 'necessary evil'? And if we entertain, even for a second, the idea that abortion is something to distance ourselves from, or that punishing miscarriage is necessarily 'worse' than punishing abortion, we risk fuelling anti-abortion sentiment and support for restrictions and bans even further.

Accordingly, instead of trying to refine categorical distinctions and treating miscarriage as a case apart, there is much more to gain from pursuing a relational politics of solidarity, considering different pregnant realities and outcomes in relation to one another, and to the wider socio-economic structures and ideological contexts within which they are embedded. A powerful example of this approach can be found in the 'full-spectrum' doula movement in the US that aims to provide accessible doula care to any pregnant person, however their pregnancy proceeds or ends.[17] Usually a doula – a nonmedical caregiver – attends to, and advocates for, a pregnant person as they prepare for and give birth. But the full-spectrum doulas have expanded the definition and provide support for pregnant people whatever kind of pregnancy or pregnancy-ending they are experiencing, including abortion, miscarriage, stillbirth, live birth and adoption.

In their book *The Doulas: Radical Care for Pregnant People* (2016), Mary Mahoney and Lauren Mitchell describe how the full-spectrum 'Doula Project' they co-founded in New York in 2007 emerged as a 'direct descendent' of the reproductive justice framework developed in the 1990s by women of colour who put 'choice' into context by analyzing and exposing 'the intersections – including gender, race, sexual orientation, and access to resources – that affect how a person makes decisions and whether that person has meaningful choices around reproductive health'. Understanding systemic oppression, they write, is thereby 'crucial to the way we approach doula care' (Mahoney and Mitchell 2016: xxiii-iv). The reproductive justice framework, moreover, promotes the idea that 'abortion should not stand alone', and instead be approached as 'one part of a person's entire reproductive life. The same individual may have an abortion, give birth, and then have a miscarriage', and support and care should be equally available in every case (5–7).

The Jane Collective has also been a major source of inspiration – the underground abortion network that operated in Chicago between 1969 and 1973, putting together pop-up abortion clinics in apartments and providing counselling and phone support[18] – and the Doula Project seeks to recapture the ethos of this collective by providing free non-judgemental support and 'mixing abundant idealism and social responsibility' (6). While private doula care is expensive and hence has become something of a 'boutique service' for the privileged (Parker 2016: 283), the full-spectrum Doula Project is run by a network of volunteers to ensure their services are free and accessible to low-income people and people without existing support structures. As of 2019, the Project is run by around fifty volunteer doulas and partners with New York City-based healthcare providers.[19]

The Doula Project is primarily a direct caregiving local service that works with individuals to provide emotional, physical and informational support, and since 2007, it has supported 'hundreds of birth clients and over ten thousand people through abortion and fetal loss'.[20] Yet in breaking down boundaries between birth, abortion, miscarriage and stillbirth, full-spectrum doula care goes far beyond the individual. In the words of Loretta Ross, the intention is to 'weave diverse pregnancy experiences into a holistic service and advocacy model that challenges stigmatized, artificial divisions among pregnancy outcomes' (2016: x), building alliances between direct caregiving and advocacy work, as well as between abortion activists and birth activists who usually work separately and may indeed see their respective agendas as incompatible. 'Many in the birth community', recount Mitchell and Mahoney, 'were affronted not only by the abortion work we were doing but by the very idea that we would expand the doula name in this way' (2016: 23). But as the director of the National Advocates for Pregnant Women, Lynn Paltrow, argues, though the 'abortion issue' operates as a pernicious mechanism of division and diversion, we need to recognize the damaging effects of 'pro-life' policies and logics of 'foetal rights' upon *all* pregnant people and not only those who seek to terminate. 'The justification for locking women up and forcing them to have court-ordered C-sections', she writes, 'stems from the same legal justifications developed for restricting abortions' (Paltrow in Mitchell and Mahoney 2016: 10).

As well as resistance from some birth doulas, Mahoney and Mitchell discuss the concern expressed by some pro-choice activists that the Project gives an impression of women being 'so fragile they need ... a complete stranger to hold their hand at the doctor's' (2016: 17). There is also a prevalent fear that acknowledging abortion can be an emotional and complicated experience might 'feed' the anti-abortion movement (19). But as argued in Chapter 3, it is essential to refuse the anti-abortion traps that would force us into a totalizing commitment to an either/or position. To challenge universalizing redefinitions of miscarriage as 'baby loss' is not to deny that many people do understand their own miscarriages in this way, just as insisting on abortion on demand without apology does not equate to a claim that abortion never has ethical or existential significance. Indeed, as Brittany Leach contends, downplaying experiences of attachment or loss is counterproductive, because 'if some women feel excluded or affronted by narratives which preclude viewing fetuses as persons or future children, this creates an opening for pro-life discourses to persuade these women by offering narratives that better represent experiences minimized by pro-choice discourses about pregnancy and abortion' (2020: 159). Andrea Smith makes a similar argument, positing that by dividing the field into a rigid 'pro-choice' versus 'pro-life' framework, we 'often lose opportunities to work with people with whom we may have sharp disagreements but who may, with different political framings and organizing strategies, shift their positions' (2005: 132).

The ultimate aim of full-spectrum activists and advocates, then, is to find 'common threats and threads' that can serve as a uniting force across a divided and divisive political landscape (Paltrow 2005).[21] This is not what Verónica Gago describes as a 'simple' or easy mode of political solidarity that appeals only to similarity; nor one which takes the distanced paternalistic approach of being in solidarity with 'something that is not "ours"'. On the contrary, full-spectrum solidarity seeks to produce, in Gago's words, 'a common plane without homogenizing differences': a logic and practice of intersectional coalitional connection which sees complexity and variation as a strength rather than a weakness (2020: 197-8). This is where the distinct political contribution of the 'direct care' model becomes clear, because it offers an opportunity to listen to those who speak from 'within' abortion or 'within' miscarriage, and experience, support and bear witness to 'the kind of pregnancy that people don't want to talk about, the kind that is considered painful, shameful and complicated' (Mahoney and Mitchell 2016: xxiii). In so doing, the full-spectrum doulas exemplify the liberatory feminist process of forging solidarity via complex narrative constellations and practices of care:

> Being a doula speaks directly to the part of myself that is complex and contradictory, and it doesn't let me hide it … It opens up a space for things to be messy, unpackaged, raw ….
>
> (Mahoney and Mitchell 2016: 40)

[Full-spectrum] doulas aren't just talking about the good abortion story or the uncomplicated one but multiple stories that run the gamut … it complicates things in ways that are important. Hopefully, it allows us to open up the doors around abortion but also around pregnancy. (2016: 258)

Afterword

In December 2021, at the time of this writing, the US Supreme Court heard arguments in *Dobbs v. Jackson Women's Health Organization* challenging a newly introduced Mississippi law that bans abortions at fifteen weeks: nine weeks earlier than the designated point of 'viability' established by *Roe v. Wade,* and at present, the point at which a person's pregnancy is no longer deemed legally their 'own' (Carmon 2021).[1] The involvement of the court indicated that at least four of the justices, the minimum required to take a case, were seeking to eradicate the 'viability' threshold and move back the limit to fifteen, even twelve weeks, such that 'the right to abortion would survive, battered but extant' (Stern 2021). In fact, it appears that the court may be gearing up to overrule *Roe v. Wade* entirely, which would mean that total or near-total abortion bans would likely be implemented in roughly half the states.[2] Conservative justice Amy Coney Barrett, for example, seemed to suggest that adoption and 'safe haven' laws – which allow people who have just given birth to surrender their parental rights, and leave the baby at a designated place such as a hospital or fire station without being prosecuted – could 'take care of the problem' of 'forced motherhood' (Matthews 2021). That just leaves us with forced pregnancy and forced birth, then, classified by a United Nations report in 2016 as a form of torture.[3]

Of course, the constitutional right to abortion in the US has long been unrealizable for many people within disadvantaged social classes, as the Hyde Amendment prevents funds for government programmes such as Medicaid being used for abortions, and 'TRAP laws' have forced many clinics to close, making accessing abortion even more difficult for those without the ability to travel, take time off work, find childcare or the money to pay.[4] As of 2017, 99 per cent of Mississippi counties had no clinics that provided abortions, and around 91 per cent of women in Mississippi lived in those counties.[5] But as the National Advocates for Pregnant Women point out, it is not only abortion that is at stake here. Taking a full-spectrum approach, they examine the impact of *Roe*'s likely over-ruling upon all women and people with the capacity for pregnancy. In their legal brief supporting the challenge to the Mississippi law, NAPW point to all those cases in which police, prosecutors and judges have used their power to criminalize pregnancy and all its possible outcomes including abortion, miscarriage, stillbirth and live birth, and argue that if the court overturns *Roe*, the state power exercised in the name of 'foetal protection' or 'the unborn' will be greatly increased, to the disproportionate detriment to low-income women and women of colour (NAPW 2021d). At the same time, they highlight the new alliances, networks and forms of activism that are emerging as *Roe* looks set to fall, highlighting the efforts of organizers and healthcare workers across the country to find access for people seeking abortion care, and to fight for reproductive justice and freedom across the pregnancy spectrum with renewed energy, solidarity and creativity (Paltrow 2021).[6]

The ultimate aim of this book has been to make a philosophical contribution to the full-spectrum model of pregnancy. The primary focus has been on miscarriage, exploring how miscarriage puts normative reproductive imaginaries 'out of joint', thereby opening up alternative logics, temporalities, relations and ways of being (Kafer 2013: 36). But this has implications for how all kinds of pregnancies and pregnancy-endings are understood, including abortion and birth itself. Throughout the book, I have sought to highlight points for solidarity in the face of 'common threats' (Paltrow 2005) that include ideologies of 'foetal personhood' and 'foetal motherhood', ideals of 'normal' and 'natural' pregnancy, and individualist doctrines of pregnancy as a 'project', which set us up for failure and entrench egregious pregnancy hierarchies. At the same time, the book has sought to identify 'common threads' (Paltrow 2005), and to articulate an intercorporeal philosophy of pregnancy which embraces variation, invites us to sit with ambiguity, contingency and suspension, and enables us to see subjective agency in all pregnancies, even as they are shaped by biological, political and social forces beyond our personal control. It has promoted a relational politics of full-spectrum access and care, rather than individualized choice and responsibility; and a present-oriented attitude to pregnancies of all kinds based upon patience, openness and responsiveness, rather than normative projections and investments that subordinate the lived present of the pregnant person to the teleological or proleptic future.

In the final chapter, I turned to the full-spectrum Doula Project in New York for a practical illustration of what full-spectrum care can look like in action; and it is also important to highlight the proliferation of community-based doula networks led by women of colour in recent years, such as the Black Doula Project in the District of Columbia and Maryland,[7] Sista Midwife Productions in New Orleans[8] or Chicago Volunteer Doulas.[9] Doulas without Borders in the UK is another notable organization working with marginalized and disadvantaged pregnant people including refugees, asylum seekers and migrants who have been targeted by the UK's 'hostile environment'.[10] But care should not have to depend upon volunteer networks to fill the void created by neoliberal individualism and organized state abandonment. Initiatives like these rely on volunteers to ensure their services are free, which, as the founders of the Doula Project highlight, does bring benefits. The lack of wage structures, for instance, enables them to cultivate non-hierarchical ways of organizing care and support away from paternalistic and bureaucratic state procedures. But they also acknowledge the limitations of 'volunteerism' given that taking time away from paid work is simply not an option in most cases. And as Loretta Ross points out, the full-spectrum doulas take considerable risks given their exposure to the physical and emotional dangers posed by violent anti-abortion vigilantes (2016: xi).[11] Jennifer Nash, like Ross, emphasizes the 'tremendous physical, affective, and spiritual labor' of volunteer and precariously employed doulas, who work without job security or adequate wages, and argues that an overemphasis on volunteer or low-paid doulas as 'the answer to the problem of Black maternal mortality' detracts from the true causes of the 'Black maternal health crisis'. For instance, she writes, 'the hospital all too often feels like a carceral space, subjecting birthing Black people to myriad forms of violent surveillance. Yet the current political attention to doulas suggests that Black birthing people simply need to hire doulas as bodyguards to protect them from the violence that masquerades as medical care' (Nash 2021a).

The Covid-19 pandemic has worsened health and reproductive inequalities and exposed the structural injustices that create and exacerbate them. For example, in October 2021, the UK Care Quality Commission found that while NHS targets had been set for ensuring that pregnant people from Black and 'minority ethnic' groups received continuity of care in order to tackle racial disparities in pregnancy outcomes, only small numbers of women were actually receiving this support, and in some areas the 'active continuity of carer' teams had been 'put on hold or disbanded' due to Covid-19-related staff shortages.[12] In this fragile context, many on the Left in both the UK and US have sensed an opening – a public appetite for an alternative to neoliberal capitalism that goes way beyond simply 'resilience and repair' (Berlant 2016: 393). As Berlant suggests, in certain 'crisis times', politics is defined by 'a collectively held sense that a glitch has appeared in the reproduction of life ... the revelation of an infrastructural failure' (2016: 393). Yet while 'crisis framing' has its strategic uses, we must remain aware of how 'crisis talk' and its inference of a sudden rupture can misrepresent the 'duration and scale of the situation'; or can come to 'stand in for political work designed to ameliorate the very conditions that produce the "crisis"' (Nash 2021b: 12; see also Wood and Skeggs 2020).[13] Moreover, while 'social reproduction' is at the heart of recent texts like *The Caring Manifesto* (Chatzidakis et al 2020) or *The Care Crisis* (Dowling 2021), it is vital that pregnancies which do not 'reproduce' in the usual sense of the word are not sidelined once again, and that the insights and methodologies of full-spectrum reproductive justice theorists and activists are fully integrated into the conversation: 'connect[ing] the dots' between social issues that seem unrelated to traditional views of reproductive politics, from decarceration and prison abolition to environmental justice (Ross and Solinger 2017: 69).[14]

In the 1970s and early 1980s, for example, activists across the US – from Love Canal in New York to San Jose in California – engaged in an effective campaign to politicize pregnancy and miscarriage by raising public awareness of higher-than-average rates of miscarriage in areas affected by chemical contamination, and demanding intervention. The struggles were highly localized, but as Leslie Reagan argues, these grassroots movements 'infused miscarriage with new political meaning as a marker of American industrial negligence' (2003: 365). Media coverage of the effects of environmental conditions and corporate power on pregnancy was short lived, and soon refocused on the lifestyle and behaviour of the 'individual woman' (2003: 363–4). But a moment like this from the recent historical past does attest to the possibility of a shift back in the opposition direction: from individualized responsibility towards social responsibility, and a politics of care that does not tolerate the gross inequality of access to necessary pregnancy services including abortion, or the existing links between poverty, long working hours, exposure to pollution, structural racism and increased rates of miscarriage.

To enact such a shift does not mean treating pregnant/unpregnant people as passive victims of circumstance. Indeed, most of the Love Canal and San Jose residents calling for corporate, social and political accountability became political activists precisely because of personal experiences of pregnancy and miscarriage. It is also not to revert to controlling futurist fantasies which imagine that uncertainties and 'unhappy endings' would simply be eliminated under the right kind of technological conditions. But social support and material conditions do make a significant difference to pregnancy experiences and outcomes, and this, as a society, we *can* do something about. Not in the deferred future, but here, now, in the ongoing present.

Notes

Preface

1 Thank you to my sister for permission to share this.
2 Heidegger, for example, barely mentions birth in *Being and Time*. Towards the end, he does acknowledge that 'Death is only the "end" of Dasein; and, taken formally, it is just *one* of the ends by which Dasein's totality is closed round. The other "end", however, is the "beginning", the "birth"' ([1927] 2009: 425). But it is the 'bornness' of the existing individual that has ontological significance for Heidegger, rather than birth itself as a relational event. And it is up to the individual to grasp the possibilities granted by birth as if they had taken them for themselves, rather than receiving them through birth – 'converting the unchosen passivity of birth into a possibility that is *mine*, and that still comes toward me' (Guenther 2008: 104).
3 The term is taken from *The Phenomenal Woman* by Christine Battersby (1998).
4 For example, I received an anonymous peer review of an article, included here as Chapter 4, which suggested that a theoretical discussion of miscarriage would only be relevant to people who had experienced miscarriage themselves. Fortunately, the other reviewer and editors did not agree, and the article was published in *Hypatia* in 2022.

Introduction

1 This book focuses on the collective imaginaries, social discourses and structural conditions of pregnancy/miscarriage within the contemporary UK and the US. For academic discussions of miscarriage in different regional contexts, see e.g. Van der Sijpt (2018) or Kilshaw (2020).
2 The 'Baby on board!' badges were introduced by Transport for London in 2005. At present, TfL supplies free badges in partnership with the

company BABYZEN and actively encourages readers of the TfL website to 'visit BABYZEN to find out more about their innovative YOYO+ stroller'. See here: https://tfl.gov.uk/transport-accessibility/baby-on-board. Critics of the badges argue that they encourage women to refrain from directly asking for things they need or want, and favour pregnant people over others who have bodily conditions that might make standing difficult. Spoof versions of the badge have appeared as a response – from the serious ('Cancer on board') to the playful ('Hangover on board!'). In 2017, TfL introduced a generic 'Please offer me a seat' option (Transport for London 2017).

3   Thank you to Transport for London for permission to include this image here.
4   I am drawing here on Alison Kafer's analysis of the depolicitization of disability in *Feminist, Queer, Crip* (2013), where she demonstrates how disability is treated as a 'natural' affliction and a private problem that has nothing to do with existing social arrangements and distribution of resources.
5   In this book, I am working with the existential concept of 'situation' as developed by Simone de Beauvoir in *The Second Sex*. In this text, she explains that one's 'situation' is not simply the brute facts of one's bodily existence: 'if the body is not a thing, it is a situation … it is the instrument of our grasp on the world, a limiting factor for our projects' ([1949]1997: 66). Moreover, she affirms that 'individual "possibilities" depend upon the economic and social situation' within which the individual exists ([1949]1997: 670). Our situation thus 'encompasses both the objective and subjective aspects of experience' (Moi 1999: 68); or as Charlotte Knowles explains, 'we are both *in* a situation and (our bodies) *are* a situation' (2019: 245).
6   'Neoliberal' is a ubiquitous and contentious term that I use in the book to refer to a set of economic and political practices aimed at reducing public spending and deregulation and privatization of public services, which is both produced by, and productive of, an ultra-individualist ideology of personal responsibility and entrepreneurialism. Though it is often framed as 'laissez faire', neoliberalism must be understood, as David Harvey emphasizes, as a highly orchestrated and managed capitalist project of state abandonment (Harvey 2005). And as Imogen Tyler insists, against a 'thin' notion of neoliberalism as market rule, it is important to develop 'thick' accounts of neoliberalism as a form of governance 'through which public consent is procured for policies and practices that effect inequalities and fundamentally corrode democracy' (Tyler 2013: 5). For more feminist analysis of neoliberalism see e.g. Fraser 2009; Funk 2013; Brown 2015; Cooper 2017.
7   The US National Centre for Health Statistics' report on pregnancy rates in 2010 claims that around 6.2 million people became pregnant that year: around 4 million (65 per cent) ended in live birth, around 1.1 million (17.9

per cent) in abortion and around 1 million (17.1 per cent) in 'foetal loss' (including stillbirths) (Curtis et al. 2010). The provisional data for 2020 shows there were around 3.6 million reported births, but does not include data on reported abortions, miscarriages and stillbirths (Hamilton et al. 2021). The Centre for Disease Control and Prevention (CDC)'s 'Abortion Surveillance System' states that in 2019, the 'abortion ratio' was 195 abortions per 1,000 live births (Kortsmit et al. 2021). The UK Office for National Statistics states that in 2019, in England and Wales, there were around 821,089 reported conceptions, 25.2 per cent of which ended in abortion (2021). The stillbirth rate in England was 3.8 stillbirths per 1,000 total births, and in Wales, 4.6 stillbirths per 1,000 total births (Office for National Statistics 2020). There are no official statistics in the UK reporting miscarriage.

8   This statistic is cited by the National Advocates for Pregnant Women. See here: https://www.nationaladvocatesforpregnantwomen.org/issues/ pregnancy-loss/. The UK National Health Service website says that 'among women who know they're pregnant, it's estimated about 1 in 8 pregnancies will end in miscarriage'. See here: https://www.nhs.uk/ conditions/miscarriage/.

9   Data on miscarriage is particularly unreliable because not all miscarriages will be reported (for instance, if the pregnancy has been diagnosed at home with a shop-bought pregnancy test rather than at a clinic), and some pregnancies and miscarriages are never known about. Estimates are as high as 31–50 per cent when including individuals who miscarry before knowing they are pregnant. See, for example, the National Advocates for Pregnant Women webpage: https://www. nationaladvocatesforpregnantwomen.org/issues/pregnancy-loss/. It should also be noted that in the US, states are not required to report abortion data to the CDC's 'Abortion Surveillance System'. See here: https://www.cdc. gov/reproductivehealth/data_stats/abortion.htm.

10 In this essay, 'America, "Fat", the Fetus', Berlant argues that this inversion of maternal value can be demonstrated through another 'prior negation of it: the slave mother's absolute power to determine the meaning and status of her child. To "follow the condition of the mother" was the slave child's legal and experiential condition in antebellum America. By focusing solely on the maternal context, the often violently biracial genealogy of slave children was occluded, made non-knowledge, and circumvented the law's gaze. This maternal line of entailment without entitlement set up the horizon of the slave child's relation to embodiment – that is, to futurity, identity, and political self-sovereignty. To name fetal motherhood following this juridical and cultural logic marks a similar delegitimation of agency, history, and identity for the reproducing woman' (1994: 147).

11 In the words of Claudia Dey: 'Pregnancy is bathed in sunlight, moonlight, God light. What could be more beautiful than the pregnant woman, deliverer of pure promise?' (2018).

12 Roberts also discusses Black women being given the 'choice' of an extended prison sentence or Norplant – a long-acting contraceptive injection that was taken off the market in the UK in 1999 and the US in 2000 due to its serious side effects. The use of another controversial long-acting contraceptive injection, Depo-Provera, continues to be disproportionately targeted at young, impoverished, disabled and/or racially minoritized women and girls (Roberts 1997: 176; see also Watkins 2010; Volscho 2011).

13 As another example, in 2008, State Representative John LaBruzzo proposed to pay poor women in Louisiana $1,000 to undergo surgery to have their fallopian tubes tied in order to 'reduce the number of people going from generational welfare to generational welfare' (Knight 2015: 153). In the UK, the 'two-child' benefit limit is a piece of legislation that both feeds and feeds off popular beliefs about 'scroungers' and 'benefit broods' (McRobbie 2013; Jensen and Tyler 2015).

14 Briggs points out that private health insurers in more than ten states in the US are required to provide infertility treatment to their employees, but none of those states provide it as a Medicare benefit. Although the US Supreme Court has concluded that private employers need not cover employees' birth control, Medicare mandates it, without a co-pay, and also covers sterilization. Consequently, 'those who have private insurance can get ARTs but not necessarily birth control, and those on Medicaid can get birth control or sterilization but not ARTs' (2017: 108).

15 For instance, 'between 1973 and 2005 African Americans in Florida made up approximately 15 percent of the state's population and whites composed 81 percent. Yet approximately three-fourths of Florida's cases were brought against African American women, while only 22 percent were brought against white women' (Paltrow and Flavin 2013: 311).

16 In another high-profile case in the UK in 2015, a judge authorized health authorities and social services to force entry into the home of an intellectually disabled woman and use 'necessary restraint' in order to sterilize her (Sabin 2015). Elizabeth Tilley, Sarah Earle and colleagues suggest that sterilization of intellectually disabled people may go under the radar because it commonly results from private negotiations between medical practitioners and families, bypassing consent and formal legal procedures (2012).

17 Relatedly, Amia Srinivasan points out that anti-abortionists are essentially engaged in a 'symbolic politics', because a 'real movement' to abolish abortion would have to be premised upon a programme for serious structural change, including state-guaranteed parental leave, universal childcare, social care and pregnancy healthcare, as well as safe, free and accessible contraception and massive investment in sex education (2021: 155).

18 As Khiara Bridges demonstrates, however, many low-income pregnant people do strongly welcome and seek out increased monitoring through

Medicaid prenatal programmes, even as it can be regarded by feminist critics as intrusive, excessive and pathologizing (2011: 15).

19 Briggs also notes that infant mortality rates are elevated for Native Americans, Asian Americans and Latinx communities, particularly Puerto Ricans, but she argues that this data set has greater variation because of the different health experiences of the different groups, which have not been made into coherent groups the way African Americans have (2017: 133–4).

20 A 2020 study indicates that disabled women in the US, including those with 'cognitive, physical, and independent living disability', have higher odds of experiencing miscarriage than non-disabled women, but the authors contend that further research is required to understand why this is the case (Dissanayake et al. 2020).

21 The *Observer* also reports that jailed women in the UK are five times more likely to experience stillbirth (Murray and Summers 2021).

22 For more on trans pregnancy, see More 1998; Currah 2008; Rosenblum et al. 2010; Wallace 2010; Riggs 2013; Hoffkling et al. 2017; Hines et al. 2021.

23 To be clear, condemning the injustices and inequalities that permeate commercial and noncommercial surrogacy at present is not to oppose surrogacy *per se*. Sophie Lewis, for example, pits a 'critical-utopian gaze against the reality of commercial gestation', reclaiming 'the productive web of queer care (real surrogacy)', which currently existing forms of commercial surrogacy are 'privately channelling, monetizing, and, basically, stealing from us' (2019: 29).

24 See, for example, the research project based at the University of Leeds funded by the UK Economic and Social Research Council, from 2017 to 20: 'Trans Pregnancy: An International Exploration of Transmasculine Practices of Reproduction': https://transpregnancy.leeds.ac.uk. The project conference led to the publication of a special issue of the *International Journal of Transgender Health* in 2021: 'Trans pregnancy: Fertility, Reproduction and Body Autonomy' (Hines et al. 2021).

25 'Originary' is an existential concept which does not refer to a point of origin as a discrete moment in time. As Joanna Hodge summarizes, an originary event does not take place at the beginning of a sequence of events, from which the sequence then proceeds. Rather, 'the originary from which a particular discursive formation emerges has to be repeatedly enacted and reinscribed if the formation is to stay in place …(it) articulates itself as an omnipresent and recurrently affirmed set of parameters that open up certain lines of possibility while closing off others' (1994: 192).

26 As Alison Stone explains it from a psychoanalytic perspective, 'psychoanalysis has also spearheaded the recognition, increasingly widespread in the twentieth century, that our early relations with our mothers are central in forming our selves. Often, though, it has been

thought that our mothers lay the foundations of our selves or of capacities for subjectivity which nonetheless require a break from the mother for their complete realization or exercise' (2011: 12).

27 Ewa Ziarek follows Kristeva in arguing for 'the impossibility of thinking the otherness of the child (and consequently the mother's "sameness") in terms of relations; the alterity is neither inaccessible to me nor similar to me, but radically interrupts "my relation" to myself, to "my" body' (1999: 337).

28 Luce Irigaray envisages the placenta as a mediating figure that enables the dual existence of the pregnant person and foetus as both distinct and merged at the same time (1993). As Lisa Guenther summarizes: 'even in the womb, there is no fusion between woman and fetus, nor is there an empty interval between them, but rather a semipermeable membrane of connection and distinction' (2008: 100).

29 For more on the intersection of logics of gender, race, property and kinship, see Spillers 1987.

30 I want to acknowledge here that in some of the work I have published prior to this book I have myself unthinkingly treated the 'pregnant body' and the 'maternal body' as synonymous, designated the pregnant person as 'the mother', and used the generic term 'pregnant women' without considering how this reinforces gender essentialism and excludes trans and nonbinary pregnant people from the conversation – a salutary experience regarding the pressure and rush to publish and a reminder that developing nuanced and informed perspectives is a slow process that requires, above all, time (see e.g. Browne 2016a).

31 Further, renaturalizing maternity precludes recognition of the ways that motherhood is in fact withheld or applied differently to different groups of women. The motherhood of women of colour, poor and queer women, for example, is consistently discounted and discredited, and so for many people, being pregnant does not necessarily confer social status as 'mother' (Ross 2016: xvi–ii; see also Collins 2005).

32 Within feminist philosophies of 'natality', the significance of pregnancy usually appears through retrospection. Adriana Cavarero, for example, writes of the 'intrauterine duration' primarily from the perspective of the born child reflecting on their gestation, and 'look[ing] in the direction from which s/he came, as a presence that was revealed from a given starting point' (1995: 82–3).

33 The other core component of Guenther's argument is that for the child, gestation signifies an 'anarchic' past time that made possible her existence but cannot be recollected (2006: 4).

34 Sophie Lewis points out that this is also true within Marxist feminist theories of pregnancy as 'gestational labour'. Mary O'Brien, for example, in *The Politics of Reproduction* (1981), does not take up the question of abortion or miscarriage at all, because taking account of 'withdrawals,

mutations, and failures of gestational labor' would only undermine her central thesis that 'gestating advances history and creates synthetic value' (Lewis 2019: 9). Amy Mullin similarly contends that O'Brien's use of Marx's theory of productive labour means her analysis remains focused on the 'product' of pregnancy (2005: 17).

35 This continuity is captured by the concept of the 'fourth trimester', which has gone some way to deflating the overwhelming focus on birth as the 'climax' of pregnancy.

36 In phenomenological philosophy, what is 'bracketed' is the 'natural attitude', which is a state of uncritical or unquestioning absorption in the assumptions and routines of the everyday world. The idea is that once these have been bracketed, the philosopher can describe exactly how an object of perception is experienced, which, in turn, reveals the structures that make any meaningful experience possible. Within 'critical phenomenology' this includes not only transcendental structures such as intersubjectivity or the transcendental ego, but moreover, historical and social structures such as racism and sexism that shape our experience in 'quasi-transcendental' ways. 'Bracketing', then, is understood as a way of shining a light on 'ways of seeing' and 'ways of making the world' that otherwise go unnoticed and are simply taken for granted as 'natural' and unchangeable (Guenther 2019: 11–12). As Jennifer Scuro writes, a phenomenological account of pregnancy must therefore bracket off 'both the everyday sense and significance of pregnancy from the entailments of childbearing as well as the medicalization of pregnant experience' (2017: 191).

37 As Emily Lind writes, 'There are moments where I regret my abortions. In those moments of regret, I am forced to confront the fact that such regret assumes that I would have had a normative pregnancy and a normative child. My regret is a form of disavowal, as it denies the possibilities my pregnancies could have ended in miscarriage or stillbirth' (2017: 148).

38 For examples of research studies in psychology and nursing since the 1960s see e.g. Bruce 1962; McLenahan 1962; Bourne 1968; Wolff et al. 1970; Lewis 1976; Borg 1982; Leroy 1988; Hey 1989; Oakley et al. 1990; Farquharson 2002.

39 Best known amongst sociologists and anthropologists who have written on the subject of miscarriage and 'reproductive loss' are Gayle Letherby and Linda Layne. See e.g. Letherby 1993, 2009; or Layne 2003. See also *Understanding Reproductive Loss: Perspectives on Life, Death and Fertility* edited by Sarah Earle, Carol Komaromy and Linda Layne (2012).

40 Indeed as Stella Sandford argues, 'philosophy' in its traditional disciplinary form resists feminist theory because it cannot incorporate the necessarily transdisciplinary content of its concepts, which derive from its relationship to feminism as a political practice. In a strict disciplinary sense, 'feminist philosophy' thus appears as a 'contradiction in terms' (Sandford 2015).

41 For a feminist analysis of 'experience', see Joan Scott's famous essay 'The Evidence of Experience', in which she critiques appeals to first-person experience as an unquestioned 'foundation' or 'origin for knowledge' that buttress referential notions of evidence – 'what could be truer, after all, than a subject's own account of what he or she has lived through?' – and preclude questions about the constructed nature of experience and how subjects are differently constituted within specific sociohistorical contexts (1991: 776–7). Over a decade later, Johanna Oksala acknowledges the important shift that Scott's essay helped to inaugurate from 'a narrow focus on the issues of identity and victimization to a broader study of their constitutive conditions' (2014: 388); but argues that 'a critical study of the evidence of experience – when experience is understood in its traditional philosophical meaning as a subjective apprehension of reality – does not have to imply metaphysical or epistemological foundationalism'. Indeed, she argues that it is 'indispensable for challenging them', and hence that we must 'hold onto the evidence of experience as an important resource for contesting sexist discourses and oppressive conceptual schemas' (2014: 389). It does not follow, then, that if experience is discursively produced it should be dismissed as evidence. On the contrary, when we recognize that personal experiences are 'culturally contingent and politically constituted, and not a manifestation of an essential and naturalized identity, they can function as an important source of critical reflection and societal transformation' (2014: 397).

42 In *Battling Birth: Black Women's Birthing Justice*, for example, several of the respondents discuss the role their religious/spiritual beliefs played as they processed their miscarriage experiences: 'My strong belief is I will see my son again. I believe in an after life and I believe that he's waiting for me there so I do have a lot of hope' (Chinyere Oparah et al. 2018: 42) 'In the dream there were these two little kids … And the little boy was pulling back and saying "No, No, I don't want to go"… you know in African spirituality we believe that some children are just spirit children they're never meant to be here' (2018: 43).

43 For a brief history of the transformation of the NHS into a market-based healthcare system since the 1980s, see El-Gingihy 2015. A decisive moment was the Health and Social Care Act 2012 which abolished Primary Care Trusts and transferred healthcare funds to clinical commissioning groups, designed to increase marketization of the NHS and the use of private providers (Department of Health and Social Care 2012).

44 The *British Medical Journal* reports that as part of the government's 'hostile environment' anti-immigration policy, legislation passed in 2014 increased restrictions on the entitlement to NHS care. In 2017, further legislation in England introduced 'mandatory upfront charging before treatment for those unable to prove their eligibility, and denial of non-urgent care for those unable to pay'. Maternity services can be provided at the point of need but charged for at a later date (Russell et al. 2019).

The organization Maternity Action documents many instances of women in the UK being charged, retrospectively and also up front, for maternity care, and increasing withdrawal from prenatal and postnatal care for fear of incurring debts or being reported to the Home Office. The charging regime impacts especially upon: 'women whose asylum claim has been refused and who are therefore not entitled to asylum support; destitute women whose relationship has broken down and who are not entitled to work or to access mainstream housing or benefits; women wholly dependent on the very limited financial support and housing provided by their local authority; women whose visa has expired and who do not have the funds to apply for renewal' (Maternity Action 2018). See also Patients not Passports: https://www.patientsnotpassports.co.uk/; and Docs not Cops: http://www.docsnotcops.co.uk/.

45 We should note here the situation in Northern Ireland, where abortion was decriminalized in 2019, but the Northern Ireland Department of Health has still not commissioned abortion services (Nelson 2021).

46 It should also be noted here that legal regulation of surrogacy is another area of difference: in the US, commercial surrogacy is legally permitted whereas in the UK, a surrogate can be paid for 'expenses' but cannot be paid a fee.

47 For the first-person quotations I use to open the chapters, their sources are indicated in endnotes rather than in-text citations – a technique of what Clare Hemmings has termed 'de-authorization', intended to emphasize that these quotations are taken to be exemplary of recurring themes and tropes that I analyse as socio-cultural phenomena (Hemmings 2011: 22). This was a source of frustration to my anthropologist friend who kindly read a couple of draft chapters, as they wanted to hear more of the personal stories behind the extracts. But while I recognize what gets lost in this method, I wanted to move from personal testimony and anecdote towards a more integrated philosophical–political analysis in this book, and so have made the trade-off.

48 Against those who see phenomenology and discursive analysis as opposed projects, this group of feminist philosophers regard them as intertwined and complementary. For example, as Gail Weiss puts it, while 'we understand our bodies (and are shaped as subjects) through a series of disciplinary practices that socially categorize bodies and submit them to hierarchical differentiations', exclusive emphasis on disciplinary discourses runs the danger of disembodying our body images 'by presenting them as merely the discursive effects of historical power relations' (1999: 2). See also Oksala 2014, mentioned above.

49 In biomedical terms, 'foetus' only comes into effect after the eighth week of gestation. However, the term is often used for earlier gestational ages (Kilshaw 2020: 6–7).

50 See here for the NHS definitions of miscarriage and stillbirth: https://www.nhs.uk/conditions/miscarriage/; https://www.nhs.uk/conditions/stillbirth.

The British Parliament supported a change to the stillbirth definition from 'after 28 weeks' to 'after 24 completed weeks' in 1992, following consensus from the medical profession about the age of viability, meaning that the foetus's/baby's death at twenty-four weeks or after must be registered and a stillbirth certificate issued. In 2014, Conservative MP Tim Loughton introduced a bill to enable parents to register a pre- 24 weeks' gestation death. The bill did not succeed, but there have been other calls for the law to be changed, including a recent campaign led by Labour MP Sharon Hodgson proposing optional birth certificates or registration for miscarried pre-24 weeks' gestation foetuses/babies (Kilshaw 2020).

51 Another term used in academia is 'reproductive loss' which is even more expansive as it includes the sense of loss that can be felt when pregnancy never even occurs (see e.g. Earle, Komaromy and Layne 2012).

52 According to the NHS, stillbirth happens in around 1 in every 200 births in England: https://www.nhs.uk/conditions/stillbirth; while around 1 in 8 known pregnancies end in miscarriage: https://www.nhs.uk/conditions/miscarriage/.

53 Please note that for simplicity I refer throughout to 'singleton' pregnancies rather than pregnancies that involve multiple foetuses.

54 For example, when the Scottish government tweeted that 'Over 55,000 pregnant people in England & Scotland have had the #coronavirus vaccine', several social media users, including some politicians, were sharply critical of the use of gender-neutral language. Former SNP MP and subsequently Alba Party candidate Tasmina Ahmed-Sheikh replied: 'You spelled "women" incorrectly. Women get pregnant. Women matter. Stop trying to erase us. We won't let you' (Herald Scotland 2021).

Chapter 1

1 This quotation is taken from 'Néna's Story', published on the Miscarriage Association website (Miscarriage Association 2016): https://www.miscarriageassociation.org.uk/story/nenas-story/. Thanks to Néna and the Miscarriage Association for permission to use it here.

2 This quotation is taken from *How to be a Failure and Still Live Well: A Philosophy*, by Beverly Clack (2020: 9). Thanks to Beverly and Bloomsbury for permission to use it here.

3 The UK miscarriage charity Tommy's conducted a poll in 2015 as part of its #MisCourage campaign and reports that 79 per cent of the 6,000 participants said they felt like a failure: https://www.tommys.org/get-involved/campaigns/miscourage. We should note, though, that the survey was conducted via Tommy's Facebook group, so it must not be taken as representative of the UK population overall.

4 As Susan Bordo remarks, though Michel Foucault is consistently credited with this insight, it has actually been present within feminist thought for

decades, even centuries (1993). Mary Wollstonecraft, for example, argued that while the 'physical superiority' of men'is a 'law of nature' that 'cannot be denied' ([1792] 2017: 4), it is cultural norms and social practices that produce the 'weakening' of women's bodies as well as the 'cramping' of their minds ([1792] 2017: 44). The very physicality of women, then, in Wollstonecraft's account, is determined in part through activities such as sewing in warm stuffy rooms, or the wearing of restrictive clothes.

5   For touchstone feminist accounts of the mutually constitutive nature-culture relation, see e.g. Bordo 1993; Butler 1993; Gatens 1996; Roberts 1997; Spivak 1999; Price and Shildrick 1999; Weiss 1999. In a recent lecture, Dorothy Roberts argues that the presumed boundary between 'biology' and 'society' is now 'exploding'. 'Dramatic new knowledge', she said, 'acquired over the last several decades about the way genes function renders untenable the view of heredity as immune from social influences. More than that, discoveries about epigenetics, brain function, and the microbiome demonstrate that the social environment profoundly affects biological processes, so that society becomes *embodied*. In other words, the biological and the social are inseparable' (2018: 101).

6   Thank you to Jen Scuro for permission to include this image here.

7   For example, Aristotle says that while the existence and formation of the eye is 'for the sake of something', i.e. seeing, its being blue is not, and in such cases the causes of the eye's blueness 'must be referred back to the matter and to the source which initiated their movement', i.e. the material and the efficient or moving causes rather than the 'final' cause (Aristotle 1953: 487).

8   It is A. L. Peck who translates 'Nature' with a capital N: for example, in his 1953 version of Aristotle's *Generation of Animals.*

9   In *Parts of Animals*, Aristotle similarly asserts that: 'In every animal there is something natural and good; that which is for the sake of something is present most of all in the works of Nature; and the end for the sake of which each animal has been constituted takes the place of the good' (Aristotle 2006: 645a21–5).

10 Ahmed references Mary Poovey's *Making a Social Body*, where she explores the compatibility between eighteenth-century medical descriptions of the relationship between body parts as 'sympathetic' and ideas about social sympathy in the work of philosophers such as Adam Smith and David Hume (Poovey 1995: 79–81).

11 In Janet Zandy's discussion of the workers' hands, for example, 'human beings [are] reduced to working parts, just so many hands' (Zandy 2004: 1–2).

12 As Kafer explains it, 'these procedures, known as "the Ashley Treatment", were seen as necessary by her parents and doctors to protect Ashley from future harms. According to this logic, Ashley's body required intervention because her body was growing apart from her mind … As a result, she was embodied asynchrony' (2013: 21).

13 In this book, Vergés focuses on the colonized island of Reunion and the contradiction between pronatalism in France and population control in the colonies, as well as the ways in which the women's liberation movement of the 1970s in France defended the reproductive rights of white French women at the expense of women of colour. Many of the insights into the racialized and violent legacies of slavery and colonialism, however, are applicable to the racialized politics of reproduction in the UK and the former British colonies including the US (Vergés 2020).

14 For more on the ways in which concepts of disability shaped American slavery alongside concepts of race and gender, as well as the effects of disability on the valuation of enslaved people as property, see e.g. Boster 2015; Barclay 2014.

15 Within social reproduction theory, there is a debate around whether the reproductive labour of women should be understood as fully commodified in the sense of being generative of human capital, or whether it has been viewed as a 'natural resource' laying outside the sphere of market relations. Federici, for example, argues that in the early history of capitalist production, women became 'the commons' as their reproductive labour became defined as a 'natural resource' (Federici 2004). For more on social reproduction theory, see e.g. Bhattacharya 2017; Mezzadri 2019.

16 This eugenic strand also runs through certain forms of 'planned parenthood' advocacy. Marie Stopes, for example, was a member of the Eugenics Society; and in 2020, Marie Stopes International changed its name to 'MRI Reproductive Choices' to break the association with her legacy (BBC 2020a). The organization was established in the 1970s in the former Marie Stopes Mothers' Clinic in London, and was named after her, but the website claims that 'today, the legacy of Marie Stopes, the woman, is deeply entangled with her views on eugenics: opinions which are in stark contrast to our values and principles. Although our organisation was not founded by Marie Stopes, there were understandable misapprehensions that MSI had a meaningful connection to her and her views': https://www.msichoices.org/who-we-are/our-history/.

17 It must be emphasized here that it is not only Black anti-abortion activists who deploy this rhetoric of 'Black abortion as Black genocide'. As Lisa Guenther points out, 'The leaders and spokespersons of the state-based personhood movements are almost invariably white and male. But this does not prevent them from connecting their cause to the liberation of black people. In a video posted on the Personhood USA website, called "A Day to Advance," a white-sounding male speaker declares that "Personhood is the new civil rights movement for the twenty-first century," while a video image of Dr. Martin Luther King, Jr. flashes onto the screen …' (Guenther 2013b). The irony here, Loretta Ross contends, is that 'Martin Luther King and Coretta Scott King were strong supporters of family planning in general' (Ross 2008).

18 Accordingly, biological motherhood tends to be more highly valued than social motherhood in that biological motherhood enables a woman to 'fulfill' her expected biological and social roles. Adriana Cavarero, for instance, refers to the 'totalizing coincidence of feminine identity with its maternal role', such that if a woman does not become a mother 'something essential is denied: her value, function, role ...' (1995: 89).

19 Seline Szkupinski-Quiroga also found that the women of colour she interviewed experienced infertility as a challenge to their racial/ethnic identity, because they saw having children as key to being fully-fledged members of their communities (2002).

20 In *Pregnant Butch*, AK Summers writes of her pregnant body suddenly becoming feminized: 'There is no use denying it. I am eternal woman. I am tears and I am snot. I am anaemic and I am purple veins. I am boobies' (Summers 2014).

21 Amongst those who defend some kind of teleological language in biology, there is a wide variety of views about its scope, nature and relation to natural selection theory. One important question, for example, is whether teleological explanations should be understood *backwards* or *forwards*. According to the *backwards*, or a etiological, account, 'the function of X is Z' means that a) 'X is there because it does Z', and b) 'Z is a consequence (or result) of X's being there' (Allen et al. 1998: 6). Teleological explanations, on this view, are thus explanations of existing states of affairs, and frequently make reference to a history of natural selection that has produced the traits or capacities in question. *Forwards* or *dispositional* accounts, on the other hand, understand teleological explanation to pertain to the disposition of such traits or capacities to contribute to the future survival and reproduction of organisms (Allen et al. 1998: 2). In this regard, they may be essentially a historical in that they aim to '[work] forward through time without the aid of hindsight' (Allen et al. 1998: 7).

22 The term 'teleonomy' is sometimes preferred as a way of referring to end-directed systems with self-regulating mechanisms (Allen et al. 2002: 3).

23 From the perspective of contemporary biology, of course, the taking for granted of binary 'sex' as a given reference class is clearly problematic, as the question of how to biologically define sex has become an increasingly debated area. For a classic feminist text drawing on biological science to question the sex binary, see Fausto-Sterling 1993.

24 Unlike philosophers of biology who emphasize biological variation, Boorse says 'it is only at massive evolutionary timescales that there is constant variation, otherwise at a more short-term level there is a massive constancy – our species and others are highly uniform in structure and function. This uniformity of functional organization I call the species design. To deny its existence on Darwinian grounds would be to miss the forest for the trees' (1977: 557).

25 In contrast, Boorse says 'pregnancy is a painful, disabling, and unusual condition' but not a disease (1977: 547).

26 Boorse writes that 'Sterility, in a world without contraception, might be a heavenly blessing to parents of large families' (1977: 545).

27 'Impaired fecundity' is term that designates an ' impaired ability to have children, including carrying a pregnancy to term' (Crawford et al. 2018).

28 For the NHS 'three in a row' rule, see here: https://www.nhs.uk/conditions/miscarriage/diagnosis/. In the UK, the NICE guidelines are that a person should be offered a referral for medical 'investigation and management' after having three or more consecutive miscarriages before ten weeks gestation, defined as 'recurrent miscarriage', or 'one or more morphologically normal fetal losses occurring after 10 weeks of gestation'. See here: https://cks.nice.org.uk/topics/miscarriage/background-information/definition/. According to Julia Bueno, guidelines published by the European Society of Human Reproduction and Embryology (ESHRE) in 2017 state that 'recurrrent miscarriage' should refer to two or more miscarriages which do not need to be consecutive (as does the American Society of Reproductive Medicine) (Bueno 2019). In the UK, MP Olivia Blake is campaigning for a change to the 'three in a row' rule (Pidd 2021).

29 As Shelly Tremain explains, 'information supplied from a wide number of biological disciplines suggests that we should expect a wide range of functional variation, not a narrow match between functional typicality and functional success' (2010: 41).

30 Ian Hacking charts the historical rise of the concept of 'normal' in relation to the rise of statistics in the nineteenth century (1990). Lennard Davis also tracks the historical emergence of the modern concepts of 'normal', 'normalcy' and 'normality', in the sense of 'constituting, conforming to, not deviating or different from, the common type or standard, regular, usual'. For instance, he draws our attention to the work of the French statistician Adolphe Quetelet (1796–1847), who contributed significantly to a 'generalized notion of the normal as an imperative' through his concept of *'l'homme moyen'* or the average man which he intended to represent 'at once all the greatness, beauty and goodness of that being' (Davis 1995: 1–3). In Quetelet's formulation of the average man, Davis argues, the average paradoxically became 'a kind of ideal, a position devoutly to be wished'. Previous classical ideals never expected that real individuals would conform to the ideal, he argues, and hence contained no social pressure or imperative to strive to approximate that ideal. The concept of the 'normal' that emerges in the nineteenth century, in contrast, as the 'hegemony of the middle' implies that the majority of the population must or should somehow approximate the idealized norm (Davis 1995).

31 Mary Poovey shows how, in the Scottish medical community of the 1820s, the epistemology by which medical scientists claimed to know the body was a complex mix of empiricism and theory. On the one hand, anatomists like Whytt emphasized that scientists should represent exactly what is before them, yet anatomists of the period also tended to use artificial means to highlight parts of the body that were indistinct and to supplement empirical observations with normative judgements: 'because nature presented an infinite variety of bodies to those who sought to standardize knowledge, anatomists produced images of a normative body rather than exact copies of any particular bodies' (1995: 79). So the anatomical figures from this period represent the outcome of numerous observations that have been supplemented with theoretical norms, in keeping with the preference in the eighteenth century for normative over mimetic representation, such that generalization or theory displaces actual bodies (1995: 80).

32 For the NHS advice on seeking investigative treatment for miscarriage, see here: https://www.nhs.uk/conditions/miscarriage/diagnosis/.

33 As the above quotation from the NHS webpage demonstrates, 'weakened cervix' may be used instead of 'incompetent cervix', but the usage of the latter has not been phased out entirely if anecdotal evidence is anything to go by.

34 '11 hours' labour and all natural!' proclaimed the Daily Mail Online after the 'serene' Duchess of Cambridge gave birth to her son 'without recourse to any powerful painkillers' (Chamberlain and Elliott 2013).

35 The term 'natural childbirth' was purportedly coined by physician Grantly Dick Read who was the first president of the UK Natural Childbirth Association founded by Prunella Briance in 1956. He claimed that 'civilized' British women experienced pain during labour because of the cultural production of fear, while 'primitive' women feel no pain during labour because they are in a more 'natural' state. For more on the history of the 'natural childbirth' movement and the ways it has coincided with both neoliberalism and neoconservatism, see Coslett 1994; Mosucci 2003; or Phipps 2014.

36 Chinyere Oparah and colleagues argue, for example, that non-medicalized birth has not been promoted or framed as a genuine option for Black women. They argue that the 'culture of fear' around birth is amplified by knowledge of racial disparities in pregnancy/birth outcomes, which can leave Black women feeling that they have few choices; and that lack of financial resources or insurance coverage may also rule out a birth-centre experience (2018: 109–15).

37 Stanworth's claim is that 'the thrust of feminist analysis has been to rescue pregnancy from the status of the natural' (1987: 34).

38 As Beauvoir caustically puts it: 'The pregnant woman's *raison d'etre* is there, in her womb, and gives her a perfect sense of rich abundance … She is the incarnation of the species, she represents the promise of life, of eternity' ([1949]1997: 518).

39 For more on the #IHadAMiscarriage campaign, see Zucker 2021, or see here: http://shop.drjessicazucker.com/about.

40 For more on the #misCOURAGE campaign run by the organization Tommy's, see here: https://www.tommys.org/get-involved/campaigns/miscourage.

41 According to the World Health Organization (WHO), infertility is 'a disease of the reproductive system defined by the failure to achieve a clinical pregnancy after 12 months or more of regular unprotected sexual intercourse' (2020).

42 See, for example, this report in the *Lancet*, titled 'Miscarriage: worldwide reform of care is needed', which proposes a 'graded model of care, where after one miscarriage women should have their health needs evaluated and be provided with information and guidance to support future pregnancies. If a second miscarriage occurs, women should be offered an appointment at a miscarriage clinic for a full blood count and thyroid function tests and have extra support and early scans for reassurance in any subsequent pregnancies. After three miscarriages additional tests, including genetic testing and a pelvic ultrasound, should be offered. This model represents a substantial move away from the current fragmented system of care, with barriers to access, and better reflects the significant mental and physical event that miscarriage is to many people' (The Lancet 2021).

43 Age-old essentialist presumptions about the 'true calling' of women find contemporary expression in talk of 'biological clocks', 'baby hunger' and so on, and gendered metaphors of 'intrepid', 'victorious', 'purposeful' sperm fertilizing the 'waiting' inactive egg (see e.g. Beauvoir [1949] 1997: 45; Bordo 1993: 12–3; 90; Martin 2001).

44 For the British Medical Association's recommendations on gender-inclusive language, see BMA 2016. In 2021, the NHS trusts of Brighton and Sussex made the headlines for their 'gender-additive' language policy (see e.g. BBC 2021). For the Midwives Alliance of North America, see MANA 2015.

45 Indeed, this can involve rereading those very texts that have established teleological models and infused the 'natural' with the 'good'. For instance, Aristotle himself admits that 'Nature' as teleological system does not always succeed in 'gaining the mastery' over the unruly physical and biological processes involved in coming-to-be and passing away (1953: 413). In a striking passage at the very end of Book IV of *Generation of Animals*, for example, he acknowledges that while 'Nature's aim' is to 'measure the generations and endings of things by the measures of [the heavenly] bodies … she cannot bring this about exactly on account of the indeterminateness of matter and the existence of a plurality of principles which impede the natural processes of generation and dissolution' (1953: 483; see also Bianchi 2014).

Chapter 2

1 This quotation is taken from 'Communicating Miscarriage: Coping with Loss, Uncertainty and Self-imposed Stigma', by Masha Sukovic and Margie Serrato, in Angie Deveau and Emily Lind (eds), *Interrogating*

Pregnancy Loss: Feminist Writings on Abortion, Miscarriage and Stillbirth (2017: 24). Thanks to Demeter Press for permission to use it here.

2   This quotation is taken from *Battling over Birth: Black Women and the Maternal Healthcare Crisis*, by Julia Chinyere Oparah, Linda Jones, Dantia Hudson, Talita Oseguera and Helen Arega (2018: 44). Thanks to Praeclarus Press for permission to use it here.

3   The Tommy's #MisCourage campaign reports that 70 per cent of their 6,000 participants said they felt guilty: https://www.tommys.org/get-involved/campaigns/miscourage. But as said previously, these results should not be assumed to be representative of the wider population.

4   Agency is of course a vast topic in philosophy, and it would not be possible or desirable to attempt anything like an overview of different conceptions and arguments here. For comprehensive analyses of feminist philosophies of agency, see e.g. McNay 2000 or Mahmood 2005. For discussions of degrees and distributions of agency beyond the human estate, see e.g. Bennett 2010, or Connolly 2011.

5   In Sartre's formulation, the existential subject has to 'give birth to himself' – even my own birth is a kind of retrospective choice, in that I alone will decide the significance that birth will hold for me: 'The opacity of my birth calls not for a recognition of its strangeness but for a "projective reconstruction" in which I decide the meaning …' ([1943] 2003: 22). Heidegger makes a similar claim in *Being and Time*, where he writes that the heritage of the past is authentically grasped by 'handing down to oneself … the possibilities that have come down to one, but not necessarily *as* having thus come down' ([1927] 2009: 435); as if the self had not merely received these possibilities, but taken them for itself (see e.g. Guenther 2008: 99–109).

6   The uterus, in Aristotle's account, functions as the 'container' for the foetus providing 'protection, shelter, and concoction' (1953: 35), while the menstrual blood provides the 'matter' for what he calls the 'fetation'. This matter is nutritive but alone is passive and non-generative. It is the semen produced by the male which provides the principle of motion, form and Soul. The feminine 'matter' or 'residue' is shaped or 'set' by the semen, which acts in virtue of the generative power it contains (1953: 117–19). However, as Emmanuela Bianchi argues, on closer examination, a more complex picture emerges in Aristotle's account of matter and form, female and male, which for her is disclosed through what she calls the 'symptomatic' problem of the female offspring (2014: 4). Essentially the problem for Aristotle is this: if the form is always provided by the male, or the masculine principle, then how does the female offspring result? His answer is that the female offspring is formed due to a kind of malfunction or error in the process: due to a deficiency of heat, the male principle 'fails to gain the mastery' and 'does not succeed in reducing the material into its own proper form, but instead is worsted in the attempt, then of

necessity the material must change over into its opposite condition' (cited in Bianchi 2014: 391). This deficiency can be a deficiency in natural heat, for example, when the father is too young or old, or too fluid or 'feminine' in body; or it can be caused by external factors, such as winds in the South, or the couple in question facing South during copulation. Hence the female offspring is essentially a product of deviation or failure, though it is only 'the beginning of deviation', as Aristotle puts it (1953: 401). A greater deviation or 'failure of mastery', he claims, leads to what he terms 'deformities' and 'monstrosities', as well as 'abortions [miscarriages] of which there are many' (1953: 443). But in Bianchi's argument, the female offspring can also be seen as 'symptomatic' in the sense that it draws our attention to the multiple kinds of cause and necessity that exist in the Aristotelian universe, and to those points in the text where Aristotle admits that Nature as teleological system does not always 'gain the mastery' (2014: 413).

7   Feminist thinkers themselves such as Shulamith Firestone have described pregnancy and childbirth as a 'tyranny' from which women must be liberated through progressive socio-technological arrangements ([1970]1999: 213). Pregnancy, then, would be 'be indulged in, if at all, only as a tongue-in-cheek archaism, just as already women today wear virginal white to their weddings' ([1970]1999: 216). For critical essays on Firestone, see Merck and Sandford 2010.

8   In existential philosophy, 'immanence' refers to the 'facticity' of a situation; while 'transcendence' refers to the overcoming of the restrictions of the present situation through the capacity of the conscious self to take up this situation as its own, and to orient themselves 'towards an open future in which I am nothing other than what I choose to become' (Diprose 2002: 79).

9   In this respect, Beauvoir has similar concerns to Hannah Arendt, who is also concerned to differentiate the repetitive securing of survival from the productive, creative and generative sphere of 'work' (Arendt [1958] 1998). For both, reproductive labour is necessary, but alone cannot provide meaning. As Arendt writes: 'It is indeed the mark of all laboring that it leaves nothing behind, that the result of its effort is almost as quickly consumed as the effort is spent' ([1958] 1998: 87).

10 A sample of women's life-writing in Victorian England, for instance, frequently depicts miscarriage as a matter of good fortune, 'providing spacing' between pregnancies as well as averting a 'damaged child or mother' (Littlewood 1999).

11 Adrienne Rich makes the same point: the problem is male domination and control over biology and reproduction; in the right conditions, pregnancy and childbirth could become creative and empowering (Rich [1976] 1992).

12 Young targets Edwin Strauss and Maurice Merleau-Ponty as exemplars of purportedly anti-dualist phenomenological philosophers who continue to preserve a distinction between subject and object because they 'assume

the subject as a unity'. Young does acknowledge, however, that Merleau-Ponty's later work suggests that 'this transcendental faith in a unified subject as a condition of experience may be little more than ideology' ([1984] 2005: 48).

13 Since the time of Young's essay's publication in 1984, the pregnant body has become much more sexualized within mainstream popular culture, such that it is difficult today to see pregnancy as a temporary escape or refuge from sexual objectification to the extent that Young does here (see e.g. Oliver 2012).

14 Helen Hester and Sophie Lewis make the case that alienation can be understood as a necessary part of the feminist strategy to de-normalize and de-naturalize – that we need to become alienated or dehabituated from the hypernormative and naturalized belief-sets and value systems that shape our understanding of who we are and who we might become (Hester 2018; Lewis 2019: 12).

15 As Diprose explains it, though it may rarely appear explicitly in adult life, this preflective 'indivision' between bodies remains as a basic state of being, implying that any operative distinction between the inside and outside of self – that is, between my phenomenal or introceptive body as I live it, my body as it is perceived by others, and the other's body as I perceive it – can never be absolute or final (2002: 54). A key source here is Merleau-Ponty's later work in which he explores the 'indistinction' between self and other, 'my' body and 'your' body, proposing a kind of primordial 'empathy', 'telepathy' or 'compresence' between bodies – a transitive field where 'to feel one's body is also to feel its aspect for the other' (Merleau-Ponty 1968: 244–5; see also Merleau-Ponty 1964). As Diprose writes, 'Just as through the look and touch [to which we might add smell, taste and sound] of the other's body I feel my difference, it is from the same body that I borrow my habits and hence my identity without either body being reducible to the other or to itself' (2002: 54).

16 In support of this idea, Alison Stone refers to the psychoanalytic view that the individual psyche forms through successive identifications with the different figures to whom the individual relates in infancy, childhood and beyond. These internalized figures, she explains, collectively compose the individual's psyche: for instance, 'paradigmatically, the internalized authoritarian father becomes the nucleus of the super-ego and the ego-ideal'. Thus, 'each psyche takes shape as a complex system of agencies, stratified in relations to one another that reflect the relations the individual has had with real others. The web of relations of which each person consists is thus constantly shifting in relation to unique external others, while equally it shapes the character of those present relations' (2010: 365).

17 To clarify, Cahill problematizes relational accounts that propose the pregnant person can attach moral and emotional significance to the foetus and their interrelation 'as though she were somehow outside of

the relationship'. The relation that the pregnancy constitutes 'is constructed here as an object of the pregnant person's attention, choice, emotions; what is missing is a recognition of how pregnancy is transformative of a pregnant person's subjectivity, and how the transformative nature of pregnancy is central to the lived experience of miscarriage' (2015: 48).

18 The phenomenological language of 'otherness' can also be viewed as problematic. To be clear, within Levinasian-inspired phenomenology, the 'Other' does not necessarily refer to another *person*, but rather a 'mode of occurrence' which is beyond our control or comprehension, even though we are bound in relation to it. Yet, as Jane Lymer points out, the language of foetal alterity does seem to entail that the foetus is accepted from conception as an existent alterity that a pregnant person understands to be different to themselves (2016: 53–4), which seems inconsistent with the claim that pregnant intercorporeality is prereflective and preconscious. As Cahill writes, the pregnant body is 'simultaneously receiving and giving corporeality' even 'before the knowledge of the pregnancy is made manifest' (2015: 52); and a major advantage of the intercorporeal model is precisely its emphasis on the profound ambiguity of this situation and the multiple subjective possibilities to which it gives rise. This includes conceiving of a foetus *in utero* as 'other' to the person who is pregnant, but this is one possibility among many.

19 Quill Kukla demonstrates that the socio-medical vision of pregnancy as an 'active project' is traceable at least to seventeenth-century Europe, and therefore cautions against treating it as an entirely new phenomenon (2005: 134). But taking a historical perspective does show how expectations concerning pregnancy have ramped up over the past century or so due to social, medical and technological transformations. Lara Freidenfelds, for example, illustrates that while in previous eras pregnancy in America was regarded as a 'precarious and unpredictable process' and miscarriage as routine and unremarkable, advances in medical care and the rise of 'pregnancy planning' have now created 'unrealistic and potentially damaging expectations about the ability to control reproduction and achieve perfect experiences' (Freidenfelds 2020).

20 The National Maternity Review was launched following an inquiry in 2015 that investigated preventable perinatal deaths at the University Hospitals of Morecambe Bay NHS Trust. The final report of the Review can be found in full here: www.england.nhs.uk/wp-content/uploads/2016/02/national-maternity-review-report.pdf. The report made newspaper headlines with its claim that the introduction of an NHS Personal Maternity Care Budget would give 'impetus to choice'. Personal healthcare budgets have been in place for some time for people with long-term conditions and health needs, who can use their budget to procure a range of items and services, including therapies, personal care and equipment. But given the unpredictable nature of pregnancy and birth, there is no clear practical reason to introduce personal budgeting into pregnancy services, which reveals all the more clearly the underlying economic function of such budgets, which is to further conscript users of health services into the marketization of public health, in line with the Health and Social Care Act of 2012 designed to accelerate 'patient choice and competition'. Moreover, the Review makes a virtue of the fact that the proposed move away from obstetrical settings towards midwife-led care will be much cheaper (see Browne 2016b). In 2019, the Royal College of Midwives produced a document summarizing the NHS Long Term Plan, published by NHS England on 7th January 2019, which states that 'the roll out of Personal Health Budgets will be accelerated', although there is no mention of personal maternity care budgets (2019); and there is no mention of these budgets on the NHS webpages since the initial pilot scheme was announced, so the current situation is not clear.

21 The US chain of stores Buy Buy Baby, for example, offer 'in-store consultations' that help you draw up a long list of all the baby merchandise you must buy, because 'who knew such a tiny bundle of love could need so much stuff?': https://www.buybuybaby.com/store/page/BabyRegistry. Linda Layne's work demonstrates in depth the role of consumer culture in setting standards for pregnancy and parenting experiences (see e.g. Layne 2003; see also Friedenfelds 2020).

22 Margrit Shildrick contends that 'maternal imagination' was a widespread explanatory model for 'birth defects' in Western Europe between the late sixteenth and first half of the eighteenth century (2001: 32–3). The concept of 'maternal imagination', or 'maternal impressions', she argues, held that the 'disordered thoughts and sensations' experienced by a pregnant woman were somehow transmitted to the foetus, such that at birth, the child's body or mind were marked by the corresponding signs (see also Freidenfelds 2020: 22–3).

23 This neoliberal formulation, however, does not exhaust the meaning of 'project'. As Simon Bayly demonstrates, different formulations and enactments of a 'project' can entail a variety of logics and temporalities, from the messianic to the catastrophic (Bayly 2013). Elly Teman's analysis of surrogacy as a 'dyadic body project' also demonstrates that individualist formulations do not exhaust the meaning of 'project' (Teman 2009).

Chapter 3

1 This quote is taken from 'The Loss of Possibility: The Scientisation of Death and the Special Case of Early Miscarriage', by Julia Frost, Harriet Bradley, Ruth Levitas, Lindsay Smith and Jo Garcia (2007: 1012). Thanks to the *Sociology of Health and Illness* journal for permission to use it here.

2   This quote is taken from 'Grief, Shame, and Miscarriage', by Nancy Gerber, in Angie Deveau and Emily Lind (eds), *Interrogating Pregnancy Loss: Feminist Writings on Abortion, Miscarriage, and Stillbirth* (2017: 49). Thanks to Demeter Press for permission to use it here.

3   The overarching theoretical framework I am using here is intercorporeal phenomenology, but another way of theorizing this is via Annemarie Mol's performative notion of ontology which argues that 'there are not just many ways of knowing "an object", but rather many ways of practicing it. Each way of practising stages – performs, does, enacts – a different version of "the" object. Hence, it is not "an object", but more than one. An object multiple' (Mol 2014). Reality, then, is never simply 'there' for us to observe, but is constantly being enacted through practice (see also Mol 2003; Kilshaw 2017a).

4   Legal and medical definitions too are constantly shifting and often inconsistent and imprecise, indicating how much of a challenge that foetuses (living or dead) present to conventional existential boundaries around life and death and the thresholds of 'personhood' (Middlemiss 2021). Aimee Middlemiss, for example, argues that 'governance of the dead, born, foetal body in England is incoherent' which has an effect on 'parental choices about the range of actions available after pregnancy loss in relation to the material body of the foetal being or baby' (2021).

5   'Disavowal', as Jacob Breslow explains, is a psychic mechanism of avoiding, wishing away or refusing to recognize the reality of something one finds disturbing (2021: 29). And as Sally Weintrobe outlines, disavowal 'can arise in individuals, or in groups of people, and it can also characterize a culture' (2012: 8).

6   For landmark feminist discussions of the 'public foetus', see e.g. Petchesky 1987; Franklin 1991; Berlant 1994; Harraway 1997; Morgan and Michaels 1999; Dubow 2011; Mills 2014; Millar 2018.

7   The 'Mommy. Can't wait to meet you' mug is advertised on Etsy here: https://www.etsy.com/uk/listing/913781068/ultrasoundmothers-day-personalized-gift?click_key=0833365f7ebaeb44b6c4f89d0220bcb8a19c6a84%3A913781068&click_sum=2300f1f5&ga_order=most_relevant&ga_search_type=all&ga_view_type=gallery&ga_search_query=ultrasound+mug&ref=sr_gallery-2-1&sts=1. Thank you to Sharon Dippenaar from 'UbuntuDesigns4U' for permission to use it here.

8   The analysis by Layne and Freidenfelds is based on the US, but in many ways is applicable to the UK.

9   Interestingly, Freidenfelds claims that in colonial America, babies were 'not regarded as fully realized humans at birth', but needed guidance to become fully human – hence they were discouraged from crawling out of fear they would permanently move on all fours like other animals (2020: 14).

10 As Layne points out, framed images of miscarried foetuses or stillborn babies do not tend to be socially accepted as a cute and welcome addition to a shared office space or refrigerator door (Layne 2012).

11 Jennifer Scuro makes the case that all postpartum experience is trivialized even when a baby has been produced: the emotional labour and grief work is not recognized and becomes alienating and isolating as the postpartum subject is expected to 'snap back, especially in order to "take care of her baby"' (Scuro 2018).

12 Rayna Rapp refers to it as 'code-switching' (1999: 82–3).

13 For more on how 'gaslighting' causes people to doubt their understanding of reality, see e.g. Catapang Podosky 2021.

14 For more on the diminished personhood typically assigned to foetuses diagnosed with 'anomalies', and to babies and infants who are born disabled, see e.g. Landsman 1998 or Frederick 2017.

15 See e.g. 'Meghan: Duchess of Sussex tells of miscarriage "pain and grief"' (BBC 2020c); or 'Beyonce: Miscarriage and child birth caused star to "search for deeper meaning"' (Sky News 2019).

16 Jessica Zucker created the #IHadAMiscarriage Instagram account in 2014, which was named 'the bravest use of social media' by Women's Health Magazine UK. See here: http://shop.drjessicazucker.com/about.

17 The #LGBTBabyLoss blog series was begun in 2016 to share 'experiences of early miscarriage, recurrent loss, stillbirth, neonatal death, prematurity, preeclampsia and twin loss'. See here: https://thelegacyofleo.com/lgbt-baby-loss/.

18 Maggie O'Farrell dubs these acronyms 'the Morse code of the miserable' (2017: 110).

19 For SHARE in the US, see here: https://nationalshare.org.

20 For UNITE in the US, see here: http://unitegriefsupport.org.

21 For the Miscarriage Association in the UK, see here: https://www.miscarriageassociation.org.uk.

22 For Tommy's in the UK, see here: https://www.tommys.org.

23 For SANDS in the UK, see here: https://www.sands.org.uk.

24 'Pregnancy and Infant Loss Remembrance Day' was first held in the US, and authorized by Ronald Reagan, in 1988 on October 15th, and was first held on the same day in the UK in 2002. Since 2003, it has been expanded to 'Baby Loss Awareness Week' in the UK, coordinated by various organizations including the Miscarriage Association and SANDS. See here: https://babyloss-awareness.org.

25 For example, as Tommy's gives advice on commemoration and creating a 'lasting legacy for your baby', it acknowledges that seeing and holding the foetal body 'may be hard and upsetting', but also claims it is 'very special' and that declining the experience will most likely lead to regret. See here: https://www.tommys.org/pregnancy-information/pregnancy-complications/baby-loss/stillbirth/spending-time-your-stillborn-baby.

26 See the 'What we Believe' section of the Tommy's website: https://www.tommys.org/about-us/what-we-believe.

27 For frank accounts of the physical impacts of miscarriage and advice on dealing with the process, see e.g. Herman 2020, or the 'Your Stories' section on the Miscarriage Association website: https://www.miscarriageassociation.org.uk/your-feelings/your-stories/.

28 Cahill and colleagues similarly warn that 'We ought to be concerned about the risks of furthering the social and academic silence surrounding phenomena that so many have experienced' (2015: 1).

29 For instance, in the UK, at the first 'booking appointment' pregnant people are encouraged to make at their GP surgery before ten weeks of pregnancy, they will be presented with commercially sponsored materials. 'Emma's Diary', a 'pregnancy booklet' endorsed by the Royal College of Midwives presents a highly normative 'pregnancy journey' replete with advertising and free samples and vouchers for nappies and so on. Readers are encouraged to sign up to mailing lists and baby clubs that will share their data with a wide range of companies, which in turn will target them with marketing materials. See here: https://www.emmasdiary.co.uk.

30 For instance, feminist writer Sarah Shemkus frames her relatively rapid recovery from miscarriage as a 'confession': 'I confess it didn't take me long to begin healing', and when she speaks of her feelings of relief says that 'I know I'm not supposed to admit such a thing' (Shekmus 2014a).

31 Kristie Dotson, for example, discusses practices of silencing as a form of 'epistemic violence' (Dotson 2011).

32 Beauvoir, for example, writes that 'the notion of ambiguity must not be confused with that of absurdity. To declare that existence is absurd is to deny that it can ever be given a meaning; to say that it is ambiguous is to assert that its meaning is never fixed, that it must be constantly won' ([1948] 1976: 129).

33 As another example, while the 'public' or 'official foetus' may be presented as appealing and human on posters or in pregnancy manuals, there is a recurring theme within online pregnancy forum chats of ultrasound images looking like aliens. Sometimes this is experienced as disconcerting, disappointing or surprising, with the ritual of 'seeing the baby' not quite going as expected; but frequently a strange or alien-like image is accepted and greeted with shrewdness and humour: '*So we had an ultrasound at 17 weeks, and it literally looks like I'm carrying an alien, I can't help but to laugh at how incredibly creepy she looks!*' Though we may also find the language of 'my baby' and the personifying attribution of gender – '*Alien baby girl*' – at the same time, there is often a clear acknowledgement that the technological image does not straightforwardly prefigure the imagined future baby that the pregnant person is intending to birth and parent.

34 For a fascinating account of the ways that 'angel babies' are constructed through social and material practices including displaying images and buying material products see Layne 2012.

35 For more on the production and potentials of 'maternal ambivalence' see Parker 1995.

36 Pre-made memory boxes may be welcomed by some but experienced as reductive by others. For example, Julia Bueno writes of one of her clients that 'she was bothered by the materiality of something "to keep or not to keep"... she would never have chosen the colour pink' (2019: 219). Current NICE guidelines in the UK state in relation to late miscarriages and stillbirths, 'women should be given the choice of seeing and holding their baby, but ... they should not be routinely encouraged to take up this choice if they do not want to' (in Bueno 2019: 111).

37 As Gary Hall explains, the withdrawal of material support from the creative arts and culture by successive Conservative governments in the UK, alongside exclusion of the arts from the core school curriculum, and the decline in arts and humanities education at universities, has not only left many arts organizations struggling to survive, but has also ensured that cultural production remains largely an occupation of the elite. At the same time as many state schools and universities have had to shrink or scrap their arts and humanities courses, 'many well-funded private schools have invested in substantial arts centres to make certain their alumni continue to lead the field'; and 'arts and humanities education – including media studies, philosophy, history of art, music, dance and performing arts – can continue (in some form at least) at the kind of wealthy "global-brand" institution that admits a lot of private school pupils in a manner it cannot so easily at others'. Hence, it is unsurprising that a 2017 study found that 'half of the country's poets and novelists attended private school and 44 per cent were educated at Oxbridge. Yet just 7 per cent of the UK population go to private school and approximately 1 per cent graduate from Oxford or Cambridge' (Hall 2022).

38 As Bueno writes, 'Time might also have allowed their doctor to tune into their relationship to their pregnancy more closely – to hear their use of the word "baby" and to find out what the miscarriage meant for them both' (2019: 88).

39 See, for example, this interview quoted in *Battling Over Birth: Black Women's Birthing Justice*: 'We wanted to have the remains and we wanted to at least bury it, or cremate it. We had to pay thousands of dollars for that. And it's money we didn't have. It's on my credit card just rolling over year after year' (Chinyere Oparah et al. 2018: 45).

Chapter 4

1 This quote is taken from *The Experience of Miscarriage in First Pregnancy: The Women's Voices*, by Paula Gerber-Epstein, Ronit D. Leichtentritt and Yael Benyamini (2008: 15). Thanks to the *Death Studies* journal, and Taylor & Francis Ltd., for permission to use it here.

2 This quote is taken from *I Had a Miscarriage: A Memoir, a Movement*, by Jessica Zucker (2021: 30). Thanks to the Feminist Press for permission to use it here.

3 Another temporal experience often described within miscarriage stories is the sense of living alongside the imagined or fantasy child that never was: e.g. 'I notice myself attracted to same age children; I think "oh they'd be this age now" ... It's like, it's like [pause] they *have* grown up with me' (Tonkin 2012).

4 Gloria Anzaldúa should also be highlighted here as an important feminist thinker of the 'liminal' in the sense that the 'Borderlands' (1987) or '*Nepantla*' (2015) can be understood as spaces of perpetual liminality that hold the potential for subversion and transformation. Homi Bhabha too considers the liminal as a kind of 'third space' of interstitial cultural enunciation (1994), which subverts established entities and becomes productive of new meanings, relations and identities.

5 It should be noted that in his later work, Turner moved away from focusing on liminality in ritual settings as a transitional phase, speaking more of 'liminoid' phenomena and cultural forms that develop outside the central symbolic sphere but represent an ongoing reminder of the fragility and ambiguity that underpin social life and relations. This would bring him rather closer to Kristeva and others, but it is his earlier work that generally receives most attention, at least in the literature I have examined in my research for this book.

6 The 'liminality' concept is also widely deployed within social scientific research on experiences of illness and disability. See, for example, the literature review by Blows et al., 2012.

7 For further examples of the 'liminality' framework deployed in relation to pregnancy, see also Brubaker and Wright 2006, or McMahon 1995.

8 It would be interesting to consider these analyses of pregnancy as a transition 'from woman to mother' further in relation to gender transition and the pregnancies of trans men, or those who identify and exist otherwise than as a 'woman'. Existing research, for example, documents how pregnant men are repeatedly subjected to being effectively 'de-transitioned' by others, as the essentialist link between pregnancy and womanhood is so deep and enduring (see e.g. Riggs 2013 or Toze 2018).

9 As Baraitser asks, 'Once the baby is out, are there "two" who are so clear for us all to see?' (2009: 124).

10 For more on the phenomenology of time, see Browne 2014.

11 To explore some of the critical pushback against Edelman, see e.g. Muñoz 2009, or Doyle 2009.

12 As Rachel Robertson puts it, 'Breaking the notion of a mapped linear development from dependent child to independent autonomous adult, of a future controlled by past and present, we may find ourselves able both to live in the present without the shadow of the future and imagine a future inclusive of disability and all other forms of human variation' (2015: 10). See also Rice et al 2017.

13 In his lectures on *The Phenomenology of Internal Time-Consciousness*. Husserl proposes that the structures of time consciousness are essentially 'retentional' and 'protentional.' Conscious temporal experience is constituted through retentions of the 'just passed' – the 'comet's tail' of what has been perceived – and protentions, or immediate anticipations of what will be perceived (Husserl [1928]1964: 44–57). Unlike secondary 'recollections' and 'expectations' that come and go, and require an active awareness, retention and protention are passive, immediate phenomena that belong to all experience (68–71).

14 I note that this analysis does not pertain to cases of unknown or denied pregnancy (Lundquist 2009).

15 To consider the philosophical issues that this eclectic approach encounters, see Sandford (2016).

16 The 'growing sideways' concept is also inspired by 'the matter of children's delay' – children grow 'sideways' as well as 'up' because 'they cannot, according to our concepts, advance to adulthood until we say its time' (Bond Stockton 2009: 6).

17 This is experienced by some as a particularly problematic aspect of pregnancy (Bordo 1993: 91). Yet despite the pressures to maintain a 'tightly managed body' and control weight gain during pregnancy, many pregnant women document a sense of release from the 'slender imperative', of being granted permission to spread outwards and take up more space via what is coded as socially acceptable 'heterosexual fat' (Berlant 1994).

18 This question is taken from a research project designed by Kristen Swanson of the College of Nursing at Seattle University, and quoted in Garbes (2018: 82).

Chapter 5

1 This quotation is taken from *I am, I am, I am: Seventeen Brushes with Death*, by Maggie O'Farrell (2017: 109). Thanks to the Headline Publishing Group for permission to use it here.

2 This quotation is taken from 'Communicating Miscarriage: Coping with Loss, Uncertainty and Self-Imposed Stigma', by Masha Sukovic and Margie Serrato, in Angie Deveau and Emily Lind (eds), *Interrogating Pregnancy Loss: Feminist Writings on Abortion, Miscarriage and Stillbirth* (2017: 34). Thanks to Demeter Press for permission to use it here.

3 The National Advocates for Pregnant Women contend that media reporting on the impact of drug ingestion upon foetal development is consistently misrepresentative (2021b). The Guttmacher Institute reports that '24 states and the District of Columbia consider substance use during pregnancy to be child abuse under civil child-welfare statutes, and 3 consider it grounds for civil commitment'. Further, '25 states and the District of Columbia require health care professionals to report suspected prenatal drug use, and 8 states require them to test for prenatal drug exposure if they suspect drug use' (2022b).

4 The term 'addicted', as Kelly Ray Knight explains, is frequently applied to people experiencing 'physical and/or emotional dependence on a controlled substance who continue to use the substance despite negative consequences for themselves and others'; and the term 'drug-user' is often preferred as a way of acknowledging the person's agency. Yet Knight uses the term 'addicted' in her ethnography of drug-addicted pregnant women in the US, partly because the women describe themselves this way, and also because the term can help to 'de-sanitize certain discourses about drugs and drug use that circulate in public health literature' (Knight 2015).

5 NAPW points out: 'Oklahoma's murder and manslaughter laws do not apply to miscarriages, which are pregnancy losses that occur before 20 weeks, a point in pregnancy before a fetus is viable (able to survive outside of the womb). And, even when applied to later losses, Oklahoma law prohibits prosecution of the "mother of the unborn child" unless she committed a crime that caused the death of the unborn child' (NAPW 2021d).

6 The pathologist who testified for the defence told the court the foetus was at twenty-three or twenty-four weeks gestation and that its lungs were not developed enough to breathe. But the pathologist for the prosecution claimed that the foetus was further along than that – at twenty-five to thirty weeks gestation, which is treated as past the point of 'viability' – and was born alive. He also used the discredited 'lung float test' in making his determination. The idea behind the test (which dates from the seventeenth century) is that if the lungs float in water, the baby took at least one breath, but if they sink, then the foetus died before leaving the uterus. For more details, see Bazelon (2015).

7 For more clarification of Indiana's 'feticide' statute, see here: http://www. in.gov/legislative/bills/2009/SE/SE0236.1.html.

8 As for the neglect conviction, it was decided that 'the State presented sufficient evidence for a jury to find that Patel was subjectively aware that the baby was born alive and that she knowingly endangered the baby by failing to provide medical care, but that the State failed to prove beyond a reasonable doubt that the baby would not have died but for Patel's failure to provide medical care. Therefore, we vacate Patel's class A felony conviction and remand to the trial court with instructions to enter judgment of conviction for class D felony neglect of a dependent and resentence her accordingly'. See the Court of Appeals of Indiana case summary,

Purvi Patel v. State of Indiana, 22 July 2016: https://www.in.gov/judiciary/opinions/pdf/07221601tac.pdf.

9   These are the words of lawyer Dennis Muñoz, who represents two imprisoned women in El Salvador where there is a total ban on abortion. Between 2000 and 2011, more than 200 women were reported to the police for suspected abortions, forty-nine of whom were convicted with seven more convicted since 2012 (Watts 2015).

10 This notion of pregnancy as something chosen is actively promoted by normative pregnancy discourses in the popular sphere, but it has also been boosted by feminist phenomenology which has focused on positively accepted, wanted or 'chosen' pregnancies to a much greater extent than pregnancies that are unintended or forced by rape, and unwanted, rejected or denied (Lundquist 2008).

11 Moreover, as Freidenfelds points out, the majority of abortions happen in the first eight weeks when those pregnancies might have miscarried anyway, which means that a greater proportion of miscarriages are happening to 'wanted' pregnancies: 'This contributes to the modern understanding of what differentiates abortion and miscarriage: abortion happens to unwanted pregnancies and miscarriage happens to wanted pregnancies. Miscarriage, then, becomes an unambiguously bad thing, a derailing of an intended process rather than an expected and sometimes welcome part of reproductive life' (2020: 144).

12 Indeed, this kind of logic is key to the de-politicization of miscarriage because it is framed as women's bodies 'acting on their own' and thereby a biological and personal matter.

13 For another illustration, we might contrast two British MPs, Heidi Allen and Jess Phillips, speaking out against Northern Ireland's abortion laws in 2018 through reference to their own abortions. Conservative MP Heidi Allen's account can be heard as the 'right' kind of narrative when she reports that her abortion was an 'incredibly hard decision' and explains she had been very ill with daily seizures and so reluctantly put her health first (Buchan 2018). This is of course not to question her account of her experience, but rather to point out that Labour MP Jess Philips takes a bigger political risk in recounting her own experience of abortion as 'nothing special. I cannot remember the date it happened. I never wonder' (Phillips 2018).

14 See, for example, the Tommy's website section on 'terminating a pregnancy for medical reasons'. It does acknowledge that there is a range of responses to this situation, but the headline is less equivocal, stating that 'When a baby is diagnosed with a life-limiting medical condition in the womb, the parents are faced with the heartbreaking decision of whether to end the pregnancy.' See here: https://www.tommys.org/baby-loss-support/tfmr-terminating-pregnancy-medical-reasons.

15 As stated in the Introduction, one estimate from 2015 is that uninsured women in the US are paying between $4,000 and $9,000 for medical

treatment of miscarriage, while insured women are paying out-of-pocket expenses of between $250 and $1,200, depending upon their co-payments and deductibles (Grose 2015).

16 To be clear: the 'DIY abortion' is not necessarily risky in itself, as argued by feminist campaigns to de-medicalize abortion or to legalize taking abortion pills in a safe home or non-medical setting (see e.g. Bakic Hayden 2011; Presser 2018; Craig 2018). As legal abortion becomes less and less accessible in the US, this will become a more common practice.

17 In the UK, the 'full-spectrum' redefinition of doula care is taking off with some individual doulas offering full-spectrum services, but there is no fully established organization that is equivalent to The Doula Project as yet, as far as I am aware.

18 For more on the Jane Collective, see Kaplan 2019, or O'Donnell 2017.

19 These partner organizations include Planned Parenthood Brooklyn, Planned Parenthood Bronx and several public hospitals. See here: https://www.doulaproject.net.

20 See the Doula Project website here: https://www.doulaproject.net.

21 This kind of approach has also been pursued by various feminist and crip/critical disability theorists seeking to challenge the presumed split between reproductive justice activism and disability activism – critically examining how anti-abortion ideologies get blurred with disability critiques of prenatal testing and working against the assumption that disability activism is necessarily anti-abortion (see e.g. Fine and Asch 1988; Kafer 2013; Jarman 2015). In future work, it will be interesting to consider this body of work in relation to miscarriage and stillbirth as well as abortion.

Afterword

1 The ruling is due to take place by the end of June 2022.

2 For more on which states are certain or likely to ban abortion if Roe is overturned, see Guttmacher Institute 2021.

3 The report is focused on 'circumstances where the suffering inflicted by the denial of abortion services may rise to the level of torture or cruel, inhuman and degrading treatment'. See here: https://www.ohchr.org/Documents/Issues/Women/WG/AmicusBrazil.pdf.

4 TRAP laws (Targeted Regulation of Abortion Providers) requiring excessively high standards of abortion providers have been passed by the health departments of Republican-controlled states since the 1990s.

5 In Mississippi, these are the same groups who lose their Medicaid health insurance sixty days after giving birth, a state in which Medicaid covers more than two-thirds of births. It should also be noted that more people in Mississippi die of pregnancy-related causes in the postpartum period than nearly all other states, with Black women at highest risk (Hensley

and Judin 2021). For more on the Mississippi context, see Guttmacher Institute 2022a.

6   See, for example, the Afiya Centre activists in Texas: https://www.theafiyacenter.org. Or the Plan C national network: https://www.plancpills.org/about.

7   See here: https://www.blackdoulaproject.com.

8   See here: https://www.sistamidwife.com.

9   See here: https://www.chicagovolunteerdoulas.org.

10 See here: https://www.doulaswithoutborders.com.

11 Chinyere Oparah and colleagues also note that because many of the opportunities for doulas of colour to serve people in their communities are voluntary, this undermines their ability to support themselves 'unless they tailor their services to middle-to-upper class white women' who can pay (Chinyere Oparah et al. 2018: 137).

12 For more on the UK Care Quality Commission report, see the *Guardian* 2021.

13 Indeed, Nash suggests that an 'outpouring of attention alongside political stasis' may actually be 'constitutive of the crisis frame' (Nash 2021b: 12).

14 For example, in the UK, the Feminist New Green Deal links reproductive justice with regenerative sustainable economics: http://feministgreennewdeal.com/principles/.

Bibliography

Ahmed, Sara (2004), *The Cultural Politics of Emotion*, Edinburgh: Edinburgh University Press.

Ahmed, Sara (2006), *Queer Phenomenology*, Durham, NC: Duke University Press.

Ahmed, Sara (2010a), 'Killing Joy: Feminism and the History of Happiness', *Signs: Journal of Women in Culture and Society*, 35 (3): 571–94.

Ahmed, Sara (2010b), 'Foreword: Secrets and Silence in Feminist Research', in Róisín Ryan-Flood and Rosalind Gill (eds), *Secrecy and Silence in the Research Process: Feminist Reflections*, London and New York: Routledge, xvi–xxi.

Ahmed, Sara (2014), *Willful Subjects*, Durham, NC: Duke University Press.

Alcade, M. Cristina (2011), '"To Make It through Each Day still Pregnant": Pregnancy Bed Rest and the Disciplining of the Maternal Body', *Journal of Gender Studies*, 20 (3): 209–21.

Allen, Colin, Marc Bekoff and George Lauder (eds) (1998), *Nature's Purposes: Analyses of Function and Design in Biology*, Cambridge, MA: MIT Press.

Amundson, Ron (2000), 'Against Normal Function', *Studies in History and Philosophy of Biological and Biomedical Sciences*, 31 (1): 33–53.

Andrzejewski, Alicia (2018), 'The Then and There of Transmasculine Pregnancy', *Synapsis*, 10 June. Available at: https://medicalhealthhumanities.com/2018/06/10/the-then-and-there-of-transmasculine-pregnancy/ (accessed 23 January 2022).

Anzaldúa, Gloria (1987), *Borderlands/La Frontera: The New Mestiza*, San Francisco, CA: Aunt Lute Books.

Anzaldúa, Gloria (2015), *Light in the Dark/Luz en lo oscuro: Rewriting Identity, Spirituality, Reality*, Durham, NC: Duke University Press.

Arendt, Hannah ([1958] 1998), *The Human Condition*, 2nd edn, Chicago: University of Chicago Press.

Ariès, Philippe (1974), *Western Attitudes toward Death: From the Middle Ages to the Present*, Baltimore: Johns Hopkins University Press.

Ariew, Andre (2002), 'Platonic and Aristotelian Roots of Teleological Arguments', in Andre Ariew, Robert Cummins and Mark Perlman (eds),

Functions: New Essays in the Philosophy of Psychology and Biology, Oxford: Oxford University Press.

Aristotle (1953), *Generation of Animals*, trans. A. L. Peck, Cambridge, MA: Harvard University Press.

Aristotle (2006), *Parts of Animals*, in *Parts of Animals. Movement of Animals. Progression of Animals*, trans. A. L. Peck, Cambridge, MA: Harvard University Press.

Asch, Adrienne and Anna Stubblefield (2010), 'Growth Attenuation: Good Intentions, Bad Decision', *American Journal of Bioethics*, 10 (1): 46–8.

Ayala, Franciso J. (1999), 'Adaptation and Novelty: Teleological Explanations in Evolutionary Biology', *History and Philosophy of the Life Sciences*, 21 (1): 3–33.

Baird, Barbara (2008), 'Child Politics, Feminist Analyses,' *Australian Feminist Studies*, 23 (57): 291–305.

Baker, Jennifer N. (2019), 'The Pursuit of Happiness', in Shannon Gibney and Kao Kalia Yang (eds), *What God Is Honoured Here? Writings on Miscarriage and Infant Loss by and for Native Women and Women of Color*, Minneapolis: University of Minnesota Press.

Bakic Hayden, Tiana (2011), 'Private Bleeding: Self-Induced Abortion in the Twenty-First Century United States', *Gender Issues*, 28 (4): 209–25.

Baraitser, Lisa (2009), *Maternal Encounters: The Ethics of Interruption*, London: Routledge.

Baraitser, Lisa (2017), *Enduring Time*, London: Bloomsbury.

Baraitser, Lisa and Denise Riley (2016), 'Lisa Baraitser in Conversation with Denise Riley', *Studies in the Maternal* 8 (1): 5.

Baraitser, Lisa and Will Brook (2021), 'Watchful Waiting: Temporalities of Crisis and Care in the UK National Health Service', in Victoria Browne, Jason Danely and Doerthe Rosenow (eds), *Vulnerability and the Politics of Care: Transdisciplinary Dialogues*, Oxford: Oxford University Press.

Barclay, Jennifer L. (2014), 'Mothering the "Useless": Black Motherhood, Disability, and Slavery', *Signs*, 2 (2): 115–40.

Barkham, Patrick (2008), "Being a Pregnant Man? It's Incredible", *Guardian*, 28 March. Available at: https://www.theguardian.com/lifeandstyle/2008/mar/28/familyandrelationships.healthandwellbeing (accessed 23 January 2022).

Barnes, Medora W. (2015), 'Anticipatory Socialization of Pregnant Women: Learning Fetal Sex and Gendered Interactions', *Sociological Perspectives*, 58 (2): 187–203.

Battersby, Christine (1998), *The Phenomenal Woman: Feminist Metaphysics and the Patterns of Identity*, Cambridge: Polity.

Bayly, Simon (2013), 'The End of the Project: Futurity in the Culture of Catastrophe', *Angelekai*, 18 (1): 161–77.

Bayly, Simon and Lisa Baraitser (2008), 'On Waiting for Something to Happen', *Subjectivity*, 24 (1): 340–55.

Bazelon, Emily (2015), 'Purvi Patel Could Be Just the Beginning', *New York Times*, 1 April. Available at: https://www.nytimes.com/2015/04/01/magazine/purvi-patel-could-be-just-the-beginning.html (accessed 23 Jan 2022).

BBC (2020a) 'Abortion Provider Changes Name Over Marie Stopes Eugenics Link', 17 November. Available at: https://www.bbc.co.uk/news/uk-54970977 (accessed 23 January 2022).

BBC (2020b), 'Katherine Ryan Says Miscarriage Made Her Feel "Shameful"', 15 May. Available at: https://www.bbc.co.uk/news/entertainment-arts-52674418 (accessed 23 January 2022).

BBC (2020c), 'Meghan: Duchess of Sussex Tells of Miscarriage 'Pain and Grief', 25 November. Available at: https://www.bbc.co.uk/news/uk-55068783 (accessed 23 January 2022).

BBC (2021) 'Brighton NHS Trust Introduces New Trans-Friendly Terms', 10 February. Available at: https://www.bbc.co.uk/news/uk-england-sussex-56007728 (accessed 23 January 2022).

Beauvoir, Simone de ([1948] 1976), *The Ethics of Ambiguity*, New York: Citadel Press.

Beauvoir, Simone de ([1949] 1997), *The Second Sex*, trans. H. M. Parsley, London: Vintage.

Becker, Gail and Robert D. Nachtigall (1992), 'Eager for Medicalisation: The Social Production of Infertility as a Disease', *Sociology of Health and Illness*, 14: 456–71.

Bellhouse, Clare, Meredith J. Temple-Smith and Jade E. Bilardi (2018), '"It's just one of those things people don't seem to talk about …" Women's Experiences of Social Support Following Miscarriage: A Qualitative Study', *BMC Women's Health*, 18 (1): 76.

Bennett, Jane (2010), *Vibrant Matter: A Political Ecology of Things*, Durham, NC: Duke University Press.

Berend, Zsusza (2012), 'Surrogate Losses: Failed Conception and Pregnancy Loss among American Surrogate Mothers', in Sarah Earle, Carol Komaromy and Linda Layne (eds), *Understanding Reproductive Loss: Perspectives on Life, Death, and Fertility*, Farnham: Ashgate, 79–91.

Berlant, Lauren (1994), 'America, "Fat", the Fetus', *boundary 2*, 21 (3): 145–95.

Berlant, Lauren (2011), *Cruel Optimism*, Durham, NC: Duke University Press.

Berlant, Lauren (2016), 'The Commons: Infrastructures for Troubling Times', *Environment and Planning D: Society and Space*, 34 (3): 393–419.

Beynon-Jones, Sian (2016), 'Gestating Times: Women's Accounts of the Temporalities of Pregnancies That End in Abortion in England', *Sociology of Health & Illness*, 39 (6): 832–46.

Bhabha, Homi (1994), *The Location of Culture*, London: Routledge.

Bhattacharya, Tithi (ed) (2017), *Social Reproduction Theory: Remapping Class, Re-Centering Oppression*, London: Pluto.

Bianchi, Emmanuela (2014), *The Feminine Symptom: Aleatory Matter in the Aristotelian Cosmos*, New York: Fordham University Press.

Bigwood, Carol (1991), 'Renaturalizing the Body (With the Help of Merleau-Ponty)', *Hypatia*, 6 (3): 54–73.

Blewitt, Emily (2017), 'An (Un)familiar Story: Exploring Ultrasound Poems by Contemporary British Women Writers', in Gill Rye, Victoria Browne, Adalgisa Giorgio, Emily Jeremiah, Abigail Lee Six (eds), *Motherhood in Literature and Culture: Interdisciplinary Perspectives from Europe*, London and New York: Routledge.

Blows, Emma, Lydia Bird, Jane Seymour and Karen Cox (2012), 'Liminality as a Framework for Understanding the Experience of Cancer Survivorship: A Literature Review', *Leading Global Nursing Research*, 68 (10): 2155–64.

Bommaraju, Aalap, Megan L. Kavanaugh, Melody Y. Hou. and Danielle Bessett (2016), 'Situating Stigma in Stratified Reproduction: Abortion Stigma and Miscarriage Stigma as Barriers to Reproductive Healthcare', *Sexual & Reproductive Healthcare*, 10: 62–9.

Bond Stockton, Kathryn (2009), *The Queer Child, or Growing Sideways in the Twentieth Century*, Durham, NC: Duke University Press.

Boorse, Christopher (1977), 'Health as a Theoretical Concept', *Philosophy of Science*, 44: 542–73.

Bordo, Susan (1993), *Unbearable Weight: Feminism, Western Culture and the Body*, Berkeley, CA: University of California Press.

Borg, Susan and Judith N. Lasker (1982), *When Pregnancy Fails: Coping with Miscarriage, Stillbirth and Infant Death*, London: Routledge & Kegan Paul.

Bornemark, Jonna and Nicholas Smith (eds) (2016), *Phenomenology of Pregnancy*, Huddinge: Södertörn University Press.

Borok, Michelle (2019), 'April Is the Cruelest Month', in Shannon Gibney and Kao Kalia Yang (eds), *What God Is Honored Here? Writings on Miscarriage and Infant Loss by and for Native Women and Women of Color*, Minneapolis: University of Minnesota Press, 23–37.

Boster, Dea H. (2015), *African American Slavery and Disability: Bodies, Property, and Power in the Antebellum South, 1800–1860*, New York: Routledge.

Bourne, Stanford (1968), 'The Psychological Effects of Stillbirths on Women and Their Doctors', *Journal of the Royal College of General Practitioners*, 16 (2): 103–12.

Breslow, Jacob (2021), *Ambivalent Childhoods: Speculative Futures and the Psychic Life of the Child*, Minneapolis: University of Minnesota Press.

Bridges, Khiara (2011), *Reproducing Race: An Ethnography of Pregnancy as a Site of Racialization*, Oakland, CA: University of California Press.

Briggs, Laura (2017), *How All Politics Became Reproductive Politics: From Welfare Reform to Foreclosure to Trump*, Oakland, CA: University of California Press.

British Medical Association (2016), 'A Guide to Effective Communication: Inclusive Language in the Workplace'. Available at: https://www.

northstaffslmc.co.uk/website/LMC001/files/BMA-guide-to-effective-communication-2016.pdf (accessed 23 January 2022).

Brooks-Gardner (2003), 'Pregnant Women as a Social Problem', in Donileen R. Loseke and Joel Best (eds), *Social Problems: Constructionist Readings*, New York: Routledge.

Brown, Jenna (2019), *Queer + Pregnant: A Pregnancy Journal*, Independently Published.

Brown, Jessica Autumn and Myra Marx Ferree (2005), 'Close Your Eyes and Think of England: Pronatalism in the British Print Media', *Gender and Society*, 19 (1): 5–24.

Brown, Wendy (2015), *Undoing the Demos: Neoliberalism's Stealth Revolution*, Cambridge, MA: MIT Press.

Browne, Victoria (2014), *Feminism, Time and Nonlinear History*, New York: Palgrave.

Browne, Victoria (2016a), 'Scholarly Time and Feminist Time: Gillian Howie on Education and Intellectual Inheritance', in Victoria Browne and Daniel Whistler (eds), *On the Feminist Philosophy of Gillian Howie: Materialism and Mortality*, London: Bloomsbury, 81–103.

Browne, Victoria (2016b), '"The Money Follows the Mum": Maternal Power as Consumer Power', *Radical Philosophy* 199: 2–7.

Browne, Victoria (2017), 'The Temporalities of Pregnancy: On Contingency, Loss and Waiting', in Gill Rye, Victoria Browne, Adalgisa Giorgio, Emily Jeremiah and Abigail Lee Six (eds), *Motherhood in Literature and Culture: Interdisciplinary Perspectives from Europe*, London and New York: Routledge, 33–46.

Browne, Victoria (2018), 'The Politics of Miscarriage', *Radical Philosophy* 203: 61–72.

Browne, Victoria (2022), 'A Pregnant Pause: Pregnancy, Miscarriage and Suspended Time', *Hypatia*, 37 (2): 447–468.

Brubaker, Sarah Jane and Christie Wright (2006), 'Identity Transformation and Family Caregiving: Narratives of African American Teen Mothers', *Journal of Marriage and Family* 68 (5): 1214–28.

Bruce, Sylvia J. (1962), 'Reactions of Nurses and Mothers to Stillbirths', *Nursing Outlook*, 10 (2): 88–91.

Buchan, Lizzy (2018), 'Abortion Debate: MPs Say "We Are Not Criminals" as They Share Stories about Their Terminations', *Independent*, 5 June. Available at: https://www.independent.co.uk/news/uk/politics/nothern-ireland-abortion-irish-referendum-rules-pro-choice-life-pregnancy-mps-a8384976.html (accessed 23 January 2022).

Bueno, Julia (2019), *The Brink of Being: Talking about Miscarriage*, London: Virago.

Burke, Megan (2019), *When Time Warps: The Lived Experience of Gender, Race, and Sexual Violence*, Minneapolis: University of Minnesota Press.

Butler, Judith (1993), *Bodies That Matter: On the Discursive Limits of 'Sex'*, London: Routledge.

Cahill, Ann (2015), 'Miscarriage and Intercorporeality', *Journal of Social Philosophy*, 46 (1): 44–58.

Cahill, Ann J., Kathryn J. Norlock and Byron J. Stoyles (eds) (2015a), 'Miscarriage, Reproductive Loss, and Fetal Death', Special issue, *The Journal of Social Philosophy*, 46 (1).

Cahill, Ann J., Kathryn J. Norlock and Byron J. Stoyles (2015b), 'The Philosophical Treatments of Miscarriage and Pregnancy Loss', *The Philosopher's Eye*, 24 March. Available at: https://philosophycompass.wordpress.com/2015/03/24/the-philosophical-treatments-of-miscarriage-and-pregnancy-loss/ (accessed 23 January 2022).

Callahan, Joan C. and James W. Knight (1993), 'On Treating Prenatal Harm as Child Abuse', in Diana Tietjens Meyers, Kenneth Kipnis and Cornelius F. Murphy Jr. (eds), *Kindred Matters: Rethinking the Philosophy of the Family*, Ithaca, NY: Cornell University Press, 143–70.

Cancellero Cecilia A. (2001), *Pregnancy Stories: Real Women Share the Joys, Fears, Thrills and Anxieties of Pregnancy from Conception to Birth*, Oakland, CA: New Harbinger Publications.

Carmon, Irin (2021), 'The End of the Viability Line', *The Intelligencer – New York Magazine*, 23 November. Available at: https://nymag.com/intelligencer/2021/11/abortion-fetal-viability-line.html (accessed 23 January 2022).

Carson, Ronald (2002), 'The Hyphenated Space: Liminality in the Doctor-Patient Relationship', in R. Charon and M. Montello (eds), *Stories Matter: The Role of Narrative in Medical Ethics*, New York: Routledge, 171–82.

Carty-Williams, Candice (2019), *Queenie*, London: Trapeze.

Catapang Podosky, Paul-Mikhail (2021), 'Gaslighting, First and Second Order', *Hypatia*, 36 (1): 207–27.

Cavarero, Adriana (1995), *In Spite of Plato: A Feminist Rewriting of Ancient Philosophy*, trans. Serena Anderlini d'Onofrio and Aine O'Healy, Cambridge: Polity.

Ceballo, Rosario (1999), 'The Only Black Woman Walking the Face of the Earth Who Cannot Have a Baby:' Two Women's Stories', in M. Romero and A. J. Stewart (eds), *Women's Untold Stories: Breaking Silence, Talking Back, Voicing Complexity*, New York: Routledge, 3–19.

Ceballo, Rosario, Erin T. Graham and Jamie Hart (2015), 'Silent and Infertile: An Intersectional Analysis of the Experiences of Socioeconomically Diverse African American Women with Infertility', *Psychology of Women Quarterly*, 39 (4): 497–511.

Chakrabarty, Dipesh (2000), *Provincializing Europe: Postcolonial Thought and Historical Difference*, Princeton, NJ: Princeton University Press.

Chamberlain, Gethin and Valerie Elliott (2013), '11 Hours Labour and All Natural! How Serene Kate Sailed through a Textbook Delivery as She Goes through the Perfect Birth She Was Hoping For', *Daily Mail Online*, 28 July. Available at: https://www.dailymail.co.uk/news/article-2380237/11-hours-labour-

natural-How-serene-Kate-sailed-textbook-delivery-goes-perfect-birth-
hoping-for.html (accessed 23 January 2022).

Chatterjee, Rhitu and Rebecca Davis (2017), 'How Racism May Cause Black
Mothers to Suffer the Death of Their Infants', December 20. Available
at: https://www.npr.org/sections/health-shots/2017/12/20/570777510/
how-racism-may-cause-black-mothers-to-suffer-the-death-of-their-infants
(accessed 23 January 2022).

Chatzadakis, Andreas, Jamie Hakim, Jo Littler, Catherine Rottenberg and
Lynne Segal (2020), *The Care Manifesto: The Politics of Interdependence*,
London: Verso.

Chinyere Oparah, Julia and Linda Jones, Dantia Hudson, Talita Oseguera and
Helen Arega (2018), *Battling over Birth: Black Women and the Maternal
Healthcare Crisis*, Amarillo, TX: Praeclarus Press.

Cicerchia, Lillian (2019), 'What Medicare for All Means for Abortion Rights',
Jacobin, 18 January. Available at: https://jacobinmag.com/2019/01/
medicare-for-all-abortion-hyde-trap-laws-reproductive-justice (accessed
23 January 2022).

Clack, Beverley (2020), *How to Be a Failure and Still Live Well: A Philosophy*,
London and New York: Bloomsbury.

Clark Miller, Sarah (2015), 'The Moral Meanings of Miscarriage', *Journal of
Social Philosophy*, 46 (1): 141–57.

Colen, Shellee (1986), '"With Respect and Feelings": Voices of West Indian Child
Care Workers in New York City', in Johnnetta B. Cole (ed), *All American
Women: Lines That Divide, Ties That Bind*, New York: Free Press, 46–70.

Collins, Patricia Hill (2005), 'Black Women and Motherhood' in Sarah Hardy,
Caroline Wiedmer (eds), *Motherhood and Space*, New York: Palgrave
Macmillan, 149–59.

Connolly, William E. (2011), *A World of Becoming*, Durham, NC: Duke
University Press.

Cooper, Harriet (2020), *Critical Disability Studies and the Disabled Child:
Unsettling Distinctions*, London and New York: Routledge.

Cooper, Melinda (2017), *Family Values: Between Neoliberalism and the New
Social Conservatism*, Cambridge, MA: Zone Books.

Cornell, Drucilla (2002), 'Wandering Wombs and Dismembered Selves', in
Janet Halley and Wendy Brown (eds), *Left Legalism/Left Critique*, Durham,
NC: Duke University Press, 337–73.

Cosgrove, Lisa (2004), 'The Aftermath of Pregnancy Loss: A Feminist Critique
of the Literature and Implications for Treatment', *Women and Therapy*, 27
(3–4): 107–22.

Cosslett, Tess (1994), *Women Writing Childbirth: Modern Discourses of
Motherhood*, Manchester: Manchester University Press.

Côté-Arsenault, Denise, Davya Brody and Mary-Therese Dombeck (2009),
'Pregnancy as a Rite of Passage: Liminality, Rituals & Communitas', *Journal
of Prenatal & Perinatal Psychology & Health*, 24 (2): 69–87.

Craig, Claudia (2018), 'It's Perfectly Safe – So Why Can't Women Take Abortion Pills at Home?', *Guardian*, 1 August. Available at: https://www.theguardian.com/commentisfree/2018/aug/01/abortion-pill-law-scotland-women-english (accessed 23 January 2022).

Craven, Christa and Elizabeth Peel (2014), 'Stories of Grief and Hope: Queer Experiences of Reproductive Loss', in Margaret Gibson (ed), *Queering Motherhood: Narrative and Theoretical Perspectives*, Bradford, ON: Demeter Press, 97–113.

Crawford, Sara, Ruben A. Smith, Sachiko A. Kuwabara and Violanda Grigorescu (2017), 'Risk Factors and Treatment Use Related to Infertility and Impaired Fecundity among Reproductive-Aged Women', *Journal of Women's Health*, 26 (5): 500–10.

Crosby, Cristina (2016), *A Body Undone: Living on after Great Pain*, New York: New York University Press.

Currah, Paisley (2008), 'Expecting Bodies: The Pregnant Man and Transgender Exclusion from the Employment Non-Discrimination Act', *Women's Studies Quarterly*, 36 (3): 330–6.

Curtis, Sally C., Joyce C. Abma and Kathryn Kost (2010), '2010 Pregnancy Rates among U. S. Women', *National Centre for Health Statistics*. Available at: https://www.cdc.gov/nchs/data/hestat/pregnancy/2010_pregnancy_rates.htm (accessed 23 January 2022).

Davis, Angela ([1981] 1999), *Women, Race and Class*, London: Penguin Modern Classics.

Davis, Dána-Ain Davis (2019), 'Obstetric Racism: The Racial Politics of Pregnancy, Labor, and Birthing', *Medical Anthropology*, 38 (7): 560–73.

Davis, Lennard J. (1995), *Enforcing Normalcy: Disability, Deafness, and the Body*, London: Verso.

Davis-Floyd, Robbie E. (1992), *Birth as an American Rite of Passage*, Berkeley, LA and Oxford: University of California Press.

Denbow, Jennifer (2016), 'Abortion as Genocide: Race, Agency, and Nation in Prenatal Nondiscrimination Bans', *Signs*, 41 (3): 603–26.

Department of Health and Social Care (2012), 'The Health and Social Care Act 2012', 30 April. Available at: https://assets.publishing.service.gov.uk/government/uploads/system/uploads/attachment_data/file/138257/A1.-Factsheet-Overview-240412.pdf (accessed 23 January 2022).

Deutscher, Penelope (2016), *Foucault's Futures: A Critique of Reproductive Reason*, New York: Columbia University Press.

Deveau, Angie and Emily Lind (eds) (2017), *Interrogating Pregnancy Loss: Feminist Writings on Abortion, Miscarriage and Stillbirth*, Bradford, ON: Demeter Press.

Dey, Claudia (2018), 'Mothers as Makers of Death', *The Paris Review*, 14 August. Available at: https://www.theparisreview.org/blog/2018/08/14/mothers-as-makers-of-death/ (accessed 23 January 2022).

Dingli, Sophie and Thomas N. Cooke (2019), *Political Silence: Meanings, Functions and Ambiguity*, London and New York: Routledge.

Dinshaw, Carolyn (2015), 'Response Time: Linear, Nonlinear, Queer', *Studies in Gender and Sexuality*, 16 (1): 40–3.

Diprose, Rosalyn (2002), *Corporeal Generosity: On Giving with Nietzsche, Merleau-Ponty, and Levinas*, Albany, NY: State University of New York Press.

Dissanayake, Mekhala V., Blair G. Darney, Aaron B. Caughey and Willi Horner-Johnson (2020), 'Miscarriage Occurrence and Prevention Efforts by Disability Status and Type in the United States', *Journal of Women's Health*, 29 (3): 345–52.

Doka, Kenneth J. (ed) (2002), *Disenfranchised Grief: Recognizing Hidden Sorrow*, Lexington, MA: Lexington Books.

Dolezal, Luna (2015), 'The Phenomenology of Self-Presentation: Describing the Structures of Intercorporeality with Erving Goffman', *Phenomenology and the Cognitive Sciences*, 16 (2): 237–54.

Dotson, Kristie (2011), 'Tracking Epistemic Violence, Tracking Practices of Silencing', *Hypatia*, 26 (2): 236–57.

Dowling, Emma (2021), *The Care Crisis: What Caused It and How Can We End It?*, London: Verso.

Doyle, Jennifer (2009), 'Blind Spots and Failed Performance: Abortion, Feminism, and Queer Theory', *Qui Parle* 18 (1): 25–52.

Dubow, Sarah (2011), *Ourselves Unborn: A History of the Fetus in Modern America*, Oxford: Oxford University Press.

Duden, Barbara (1993), *Disembodying Women: Perspectives on Pregnancy and the Unborn*, trans. Lee Hoinaki, Cambridge, MA: Harvard University Press.

Earle, Sarah, Carol Komaromy and Linda Layne (2012), 'An Introduction to Understanding Reproductive Loss', in Sarah Earle, Carol Komaromy and Linda Layne (eds), *Understanding Reproductive Loss: Perspectives of Life, Death and Fertility*, Farnham: Ashgate, 1–7.

Edelman, Lee (2004), *No Future: Queer Theory and the Death Drive*, Durham, NC: Duke University Press.

Eichenbaum, Efrat (2012), 'African American Women's Experiences of Pregnancy Loss: Examining Coping', PhD Thesis, Drexel University. Available at: https://idea.library.drexel.edu/islandora/object/idea%3A4114 (accessed 23 January 2022).

El-Gingihy, Youssef (2015), *How to Dismantle the NHS in Ten Easy Steps*, Winchester, UK and Washington, DC: Zero Books.

Epstein-Gilboa, Keren (2017), 'Reframing the Devastation and Exclusion Associated with Pregnancy Loss: A Normal and Growth-Enhancing Component of the Physiological Female Continuum', in Angie Deveau and Emily Lind (eds), *Interrogating Pregnancy Loss: Feminist Writings on Abortion, Miscarriage and Stillbirth*, Bradford, ON: Demeter Press, 109–32.

Ergas, Yasmine (2017), 'Pregnant Bodies and the Subjects of Rights: The Surrogacy–Abortion Nexus', in Yasmine Ergas, Jane Jenson and Sonya

Michel (eds), *Reassembling Motherhood: Procreation and Care in a Globalized World*, New York: Columbia University Press, 99–125.

Farquharson, Roy G. (ed) (2002), *Miscarriage*, Abingdon: Quay.

Faulkner, Sandra L. (2012), 'That Baby Will Cost You: An Intended Ambivalent Pregnancy', *Qualitative Inquiry*, 18 (4): 333–40.

Fausto-Sterling, Ann (1993), 'The Five Sexes: Why Male and Female Are Not Enough', *The Sciences*, March/April: 20–24.

Federici, Silvia (2004), *Caliban and the Witch: Women, the Body and Primitive Accumulation*, New York: Autonomedia.

Fine, Michelle and Adrienne Asch (1988), 'Shared Dreams: A Left Perspective on Disability Rights and Reproductive Rights', in Michelle Fine and Adrienne Asch (eds), *Women with Disabilities: Essays in Psychology, Culture, and Politics*, Philadelphia, PA: Temple University Press, 233–41.

Firestone, Shulamith ([1970] 1999), *The Dialectic of Sex: The Case for Feminist Revolution*, London: Verso.

Franklin, Sarah (1991), 'Fetal Fascinations: New Dimensions to the Medical-Scientific Construction of Fetal Personhood', in Sarah Franklin, Celia Lury and Jackie Stacey (eds), *Off-Centre: Feminism and Cultural Studies*, London: HarperCollins Academic, 190–205.

Franklin, Sarah (1995), 'Postmodern Procreation: A Cultural Account of Assisted Reproduction', in Faye D. Ginsburg and Rayna Rapp (eds), *Conceiving the New World Order: The Global Politics of Reproduction*, Berkeley, CA: University of California Press, 323–45.

Fraser, Nancy (2009), 'Feminism, Capitalism and the Cunning of History', *New Left Review* (56), 97–117.

Frederick, Angela (2017), 'Risky Mothers and the Normalcy Project: Women with Disabilities Negotiate Scientific Motherhood', *Gender & Society*, 31 (1): 74–95.

Freidenfelds, Lara (2020), *The Myth of the Perfect Pregnancy: A History of Miscarriage in America*, Oxford: Oxford University Press.

Frost, Julia, Harriet Bradley, Ruth Levitas, Lindsay Smith and Jo Garcia (2007), 'The Loss of Possibility: The Scientisation of Death and the Special Case of Early Miscarriage', *Sociology of Health and Illness*, 29 (7): 1003–22.

Funk, Nanette (2013), 'Contra Fraser on Feminism and Neoliberalism', *Hypatia*, 28 (1): 179–96.

Gago, Veronica (2020), *Feminist International: How to Change Everything*, London: Verso.

Garbes, Angela (2016), 'What I Gained from Having a Miscarriage: When It Comes to Pregnancy Loss, There's so Much We Don't Talk about or Understand', *The Stranger*, 27 April. Available at: https://www.thestranger.com/features/2016/04/27/24011632/what-i-gained-from-having-a-miscarriage/ (accessed 23 January 2022).

Garbes, Angela (2018), *Like a Mother: A Feminist Journey through the Science and Culture of Pregnancy*, New York: HarperCollins.

Garland-Thomson, Rosemarie (1997), *Extraordinary Bodies: Figuring Physical Disability in American Culture and Literature*, New York: Columbia University Press.

Garland-Thomson, Rosemarie (2012), 'The Case for Conserving Disability', *Journal of Bioethical Inquiry*, 9 (3): 339–55.

Gatens, Moira (1996), *Imaginary Bodies: Ethics, Power and Corporeality*, London: Routledge.

Guardian (2021), 'Tackling Inequalities Often Not a Main Priority in Healthcare, says CQC', 22 October. Available at: https://www.theguardian.com/society/2021/oct/22/tackling-inequalities-often-not-a-main-priority-in-healthcare-says-cqc (accessed 23 January 2022).

Gentile, Katie (2014), 'Exploring the Troubling Temporalities Produced by Fetal Personhood', *Psychoanalysis, Culture & Society*, 19 (3): 279–96.

Gerber, Nancy (2017) 'Grief, Shame, and Miscarriage', in Angie Deveau and Emily Lind (eds), *Interrogating Pregnancy Loss: Feminist Writings on Abortion, Miscarriage and Stillbirth*, Bradford, ON: Demeter Press, 47–61.

Gerber-Epstein, Paula, Ronit D. Leichtentritt and Yael Benyamini (2009), 'The Experience of Miscarriage in First Pregnancy: The Women's Voices', *Death Studies*, 33 (1): 1–29.

Geronimus, Arline T. (1992), 'The Weathering Hypothesis and the Health of African-American Women and Infants: Evidence and Speculations', *Ethnicity & Disease*, 2 (3): 207–21.

Gibney, Shannon (2019), 'Sianneh: The Trip Was Good', in Shannon Gibney and Kao Kalia Yang (eds), *What God Is Honored Here? Writings on Miscarriage and Infant Loss by and for Native Women and Women of Color*, Minneapolis: University of Minnesota Press, 99–107.

Gibney, Shannon and Kao Kalia Yang (2019), 'Introduction: Reclaiming Life', in Shannon Gibney and Kao Kalia Yang (eds), *What God Is Honored Here? Writings on Miscarriage and Infant Loss by and for Native Women and Women of Color*, Minneapolis: University of Minnesota Press, 1–7.

Gibson, Margaret (2014), *Queering Motherhood: Narrative and Theoretical Perspectives*, Bradford, ON: Demeter Press.

Gilson, Erinn (2021), 'The Problems and Potentials of Vulnerability', in Victoria Browne, Jason Danely and Doerthe Rosenow (eds), *Vulnerability and the Politics of Care: Transdisciplinary Dialogues*, Oxford: Oxford University Press, 85–108.

Ginsburg, Faye D. and Rayna Rapp (ed) (1995), *Conceiving the New World Order*, Oakland, CA: University of California Press.

Greengrass, Jessie (2018), *Sight: A Novel*, London: John Murray.

Gregory, Andrew (2021), 'Thousands of Adverse Birth Outcomes in England Down to "Alarming" Inequality', *Guardian*, 1 November. Available at: https://www.theguardian.com/lifeandstyle/2021/nov/01/thousands-of-adverse-birth-outcomes-in-england-down-to-alarming-inequality (accessed 23 January 2022).

Greil, Arthur L., J. McQuillan and K. Slauson-Blevins (2011), 'The Social Construction of Infertility', *Philosophy Compass*, 5: 736–46.

Grigorovich, Alisa (2014), '"Pregnant with Meaning": An Analysis of Online Media Response to Thomas Beatie and His Pregnancy', in Margaret Gibson (ed). *Queering Motherhood: Narrative and Theoretical Perspectives*, Bradford, ON: Demeter Press, 81–97.

Grose, Jessica (2015), 'The Cost of a Miscarriage', *The Slate*, 26 March. Available at: http://www.slate.com/articles/double_x/doublex/2015/03/the_cost_of_a_miscarriage_we_talk_about_the_emotional_pain_but_not_the_financial.html (accessed 23 January 2022).

Grosz, Elizabeth (1990), *Jacques Lacan: A Feminist Introduction*, London and New York: Routledge.

Grosz, Elizabeth (1994), *Volatile Bodies: Toward a Corporeal Feminism*, Sydney: Allen and Unwin.

Guenther, Lisa (2006), *The Gift of the Other: Levinas and the Politics of Reproduction*, Albany, NY: State University of New York Press.

Guenther, Lisa (2008), 'Being from Others: Reading Heidegger after Cavarero', *Hypatia*, 23 (1): 99–118.

Guenther, Lisa (2013a), *Solitary Confinement: Social Death and Its Afterlives*, Minneapolis: University of Minnesota Press.

Guenther, Lisa (2013b), 'The Most Dangerous Place: Pro-Life Politics and the Rhetoric of Slavery,' *Postmodern Culture*, 22 (2).

Guenther, Lisa (2016), 'Life behind Bars: The Eugenic Structure of Mass Incarceration,' in Hasana Sharp and Chloe Taylor (eds), *Feminist Philosophies of Life*. Kingston, ON: McGill-Queen's University Press, 217–39.

Guenther, Lisa (2019), 'Critical Phenomenology', in Gail Weiss, Ann V. Murphy and Gayle Salamon (eds), *50 Concepts for a Critical Phenomenology*, Evanston, IL: Northwestern University Press.

Gumbs, Alexis Pauline (2016), 'M/other Ourselves: A Black Queer Feminist Genealogy for Radical Mothering', in China Materns, Alexis Pauline Gumbs and Mai'a Williams (eds), *Revolutionary Mothering: Love on the Front Lines*, Toronto: PM Press, 19–32.

Guttmacher Institute (2021), '26 States Are Certain or Likely to Ban Abortion without Roe: Here's Which Ones and Why', 28 October. Available at: https://www.guttmacher.org/article/2021/10/26-states-are-certain-or-likely-ban-abortion-without-roe-heres-which-ones-and-why (accessed 23 January 2022).

Guttmacher Institute (2022a), 'State Facts about Abortion: Mississippi', January. Available at: https://www.guttmacher.org/fact-sheet/state-facts-about-abortion-mississippi (accessed 23 January 2022).

Guttmacher Institute (2022b), 'Substance Use during Pregnancy', 1 January. Available at: https://www.guttmacher.org/state-policy/explore/substance-use-during-pregnancy (accessed 23 January 2022).

Hacking, Ian (1990), *The Taming of Chance*, Cambridge: Cambridge University Press.

Halberstam, Jack (2010), 'The Pregnant Man', *The Velvet Light Trap*, 65: 77–8.

Halberstam, Jack (2011), *The Queer Art of Failure*, Durham, NC: Duke University Press.

Halberstam, Judith (2005), *In a Queer Time and Place: Transgender Bodies, Subcultural Lives*, New York: New York University Press.

Hall, Gary (2022), 'Defund Culture', *Radical Philosophy*, 2.12.

Hamilton, Brady E., Joyce A. Martin and Michelle J.K. Osterman (2021), 'Births: Provisional Data for 2020', *National Centre for Health Statistics*, May. Available at: https://www.cdc.gov/nchs/data/vsrr/vsrr012-508.pdf (accessed 23 January 2022).

Hamilton, Chloe (2013), 'Forced C-Section Was "the Stuff of Nightmares": Social Services Condemned for Forcibly Removing Unborn Child from Woman', *Independent*, 1 December. Available at: https://www.independent.co.uk/news/uk/home-news/social-services-forcibly-remove-unborn-child-from-woman-by-caesarean-after-she-suffered-mental-health-breakdown-8975808.html (accessed 23 January 2022).

Han, Sally (2018), 'Pregnant with Ideas: Concepts of the Foetus in Twenty-First Century United States', in Sally Han, Tracy K. Betsinger and Amy B. Scott (eds), *The Anthropology of the Fetus: Biology, Culture, and Society*, Oxford: Bergahn Books.

Hardy, Sarah and Rebecca Kukla (2015), 'Making Sense of Miscarriage Online', *Journal of Social Philosophy*, 46 (1): 106–25.

Harraway, Donna J. (1997), *Modest_Witness@Second_Millennium. FemaleMan_Meets_OncoMouse: Feminism and Technoscience*, New York and London: Routledge.

Hartouni, Valerie (1992), 'Fetal Exposures: Abortion Politics and the Optics of Allusion', *Camera Obscura*, 29: 131–51.

Harvey, David (2005), *A Brief History of Neoliberalism*, Oxford: Oxford University Press.

Heidegger, Martin ([1927] 2009), *Being and Time*, trans. John Macquarrie and Edward Robinson, Oxford: Blackwell.

Heinämaa, Sara (2003), *Toward a Phenomenology of Sexual Difference: Husserl, Merleau-Ponty, Beauvoir*, Lanham, Boulder, New York and Oxford: Rowman & Littlefield.

Hemmings, Clare (2011), *Why Stories Matter*, Durham, NC: Duke University Press.

Hensley, Erica and Nick Judin (2021), 'Disrupted Care: Mississippi Legislature Kills Postpartum Medicaid Extension, Affecting 25,000 Mothers Yearly', *Mississippi Free Press*, 2 April. Available at: https://www.mississippifreepress.org/10868/disrupted-care/ (accessed 23 January 2022).

Herald Scotland (2021), 'Covid Scotland: Pregnant "People" Vaccine Tweet Sparks Row over Inclusiveness', 29 July. Available at: https://www.heraldscotland.com/politics/19476587.covid-scotland-pregnant-people-vaccine-tweet-sparks-row-inclusiveness/ (accessed 23 January 2022).

Herman, Katya (2020), 'The Things You Only Know If You Had a Miscarriage during Lockdown', *Vogue*, 31 May. Available at: https://www.vogue.co.uk/arts-and-lifestyle/article/miscarriage-lockdown (accessed 23 January 2022).

Hester, Helen (2018), *Xenofeminism*, Cambridge: Polity.

Hey, Catherine Itzin, Lesley Saunders and Mary Anne Speakman (eds) (1989), *Hidden Loss: Miscarriage and Ectopic Pregnancies*, London: Women's Press.

Hines, Sally, Ruth Pearce, Carla A. Pfeffer, Damien W. Riggs and Francis Ray White (2021), 'Trans Pregnancy: Fertility, Reproduction and Body Autonomy', *International Journal of Transgender Health*, 22 (1–2): 1–5.

Hintz-Zimbrano, Katie (2015), 'Miscarriage Stories: 10 Women Share Their Loss', *Mother*, 31 August. Available at: http://www.mothermag.com/miscarriage-stories/ (accessed 23 January 2022).

Hird, Myra (2007), 'The Corporeal Generosity of Maternity', *Body & Society*, 13 (1): 1–20.

Hodge, Joanna (1994), 'Irigaray Reading Heidegger', in Carolyn Burke, Naomi Schor and Margaret Whitford (eds), *Engaging with Irigaray*, New York: Columbia University Press, 191–209.

Hoffe, Otfried (2003), *Aristotle*, trans. Christine Salazar, Albany, NY: SUNY Press.

Hoffkling, Alexis, et al. (2017), 'From Erasure to Opportunity: A Qualitative Study of the Experiences of Transgender Men around Pregnancy and Recommendations for Providers', *BMC Pregnancy and Childbirth*, 17 (332): 7–20.

Howes, Sarah Agaton (2019), 'Lessons from Dying', in Shannon Gibney and Kao Kalia Yang (eds), *What God Is Honoured Here? Writings on Miscarriage and Infant Loss by and for Native Women and Women of Color*, Minneapolis: University of Minnesota Press, 19–23.

Htut Maung, Hane (2018), 'Is Infertility a Disease and Does It Matter?' *Bioethics*, 33 (1): 43–53.

Husserl, Edmund ([1928] 1964), *The Phenomenology of Internal Time-Consciousness*, ed. Martin Heidegger, trans. James S. Churchill, Indiana: Indiana University Press.

Irigaray, Luce (1985a), *Speculum of the Other Woman*, trans. Gillian C. Gill, Ithaca, NY: Cornell University Press.

Irigaray, Luce (1985b), *This Sex Which Is Not One*, trans. Catherine Porter with Carolyn Burke, Ithaca, NY: Cornell University Press.

Irigaray, Luce (1993), *je, tu, nous: Toward a Culture of Difference*, trans. Alison Martin, New York: Routledge.

Jacobson, Heather (2016), *Labor of Love: Gestational Surrogacy and the Work of Making Babies*, New Brunswick, NJ: Rutgers University Press.

Jansen, Julia and Maren Wehrle (2018), 'The Normal Body: Female Bodies in Changing Contexts of Normalization and Optimization', in Clara Fischer and Luna Dolezal (eds), *New Feminist Perspectives on Embodiment*, London and New York: Palgrave Macmillan, 37–55.

Jarman, Michelle (2015), 'Relations of Abortion: Crip Approaches to Reproductive Justice', *Feminist Formations*, 27 (1): 46–66.

Jensen, Tracy and Imogen Tyler (2015), '"Benefits Broods": The Cultural and Political Crafting of Anti-welfare Commonsense', *Critical Social Policy*, 35 (4): 470–91.

Jones, Sophie, Harriet Cooper and Fran Bigman (2014), 'Non-Reproduction: A Conversation', *Studies in the Maternal*, 6 (1).

Kafer, Alison (2013), *Feminist Queer Crip*, Bloomington: Indiana University Press.

Kamal, Soniah (2019), 'The Face of Miscarriage', in Shannon Gibney and Kao Kalia Yang (eds), *What God Is Honoured Here? Writings on Miscarriage and Infant Loss by and for Native Women and Women of Color*, Minneapolis: University of Minnesota Press, 177–87.

Kaplan, Laura (2019), *The Story of Jane: The Legendary Underground Feminist Abortion Service*, Chicago: Chicago University Press.

Katz Rothman, Barbara (1986), *The Tentative Pregnancy: How Amniocentesis Changes the Experience of Motherhood*, New York: W. W. Norton & Company.

Kilshaw, Susie (2017a), 'Birds, Meat, and Babies: The Multiple Realities of Fetuses in Qatar', *Anthropology & Medicine*, 24 (2): 189–204.

Kilshaw, Susie (2017b), 'How Culture Shapes Perceptions of Miscarriage', *Sapiens*, https://www.sapiens.org/biology/miscarriage-united-kingdom-qatar/.

Kilshaw, Susie (2020), *Pregnancy and Miscarriage in Qatar: Women, Reproduction and the State*, London: Bloomsbury.

Kilshaw, Susie and Katie Borg (2020), *Navigating Miscarriage: Social, Medical and Conceptual Perspectives*, New York and Oxford: Berghann Books.

Kilshaw, Susie, Nadia Omar, Stella Major, Mona Mohsen, Faten El Taher, Halima Al Tamimi, Kristina Sole and Daniel Miller (2017), 'Causal Explanations of Miscarriage amongst Qataris', *BMC Pregnancy and Childbirth*, 17 (250): 1–12.

Kimball, Alexandra (2015), 'Unpregnant: The Silent, Secret Grief of Miscarriage', *The Globe and Mail*, 3 December. Available at: https://www.theglobeandmail.com/life/parenting/unpregnant-the-silent-secret-grief-of-miscarriage/article27576775/ (accessed 23 January 2022).

Knight, Kelly Ray (2015), *addicted.pregnant.poor*, Durham, NC: Duke University Press.

Knowles, Charlotte (2019), 'Beauvoir on Women's Complicity in Their Own Unfreedom', *Hypatia*, 34 (2): 242–65.

Komaromy, Carol (2012), 'Managing Emotions at the Time of Stillbirth and Neonatal Death', in Sarah Earle, Carol Komaromy and Linda Layne (eds), *Understanding Reproductive Loss: Perspectives on Life, Death and Fertility*, Aldershot: Ashgate, 193–205.

Kortsmit, Katherine, Michele G. Mandel, Jennifer A. Reeves, H. Elizabeth Clark, Pamela Pagano, Antoinette Nguyen, Emily E. Petersen and Maura

K. Whiteman (2021), 'Centre for Disease Control and Prevention: Abortion Surveillance – United States, 2019', *Surveillance Summaries*, 70 (9): 1–29, 26 November. Available at: https://www.cdc.gov/mmwr/volumes/70/ss/ss7009a1.htm (accessed 23 January 2022).

Kowal, Emma (2009), 'Waiting for the Baby', in Ghassan Hage (ed), *Waiting*, Melbourne: Melbourne University Press, 210–18.

Kristeva, Julia (1986), *The Kristeva Reader*, ed. Toril Moi, Oxford: Blackwell.

Kukla, Rebecca (2005), *Mass Hysteria: Medicine, Culture, and Mothers' Bodies:* Lanham, MD: Rowman & Littlefield.

Kukla, Rebecca (2009), 'Introduction: Maternal Bodies', *Hypatia*, 21 (1): vii–ix.

Kukla, Rebecca (2014), 'Medicalization, "Normal Function", and the Definition of Health', in John D. Arras, Elizabeth Fenton and Rebecca Kukla (eds), *The Routledge Companion to Bioethics*, London and New York: Routledge, 515–31.

LaChance Adams, Sarah and Caroline Lundquist (eds) (2013), *Coming to Life: Philosophies of Pregnancy, Childbirth, and Mothering*, New York: Fordham University Press.

Lahad, Kinneret (2017), *A Table for One: A Critical Reading of Singlehood, Gender and Time*, Manchester: Manchester University Press.

The Lancet (2021), 'Miscarriage: Worldwide Reform of Care Is Needed', *Editorial*, 26 April. Available at: https://www.thelancet.com/journals/lancet/article/PIIS0140-6736(21)00954-5/fulltext (accessed 23 January 2022).

Landsman, Gail (1998), 'Reconstructing Motherhood in the Age of "Perfect" Babies: Mothers of Infants and Toddlers with Disabilities', *Signs*, 24 (1): 69–99.

Layne, Linda (1997), 'Breaking the Silence: An Agenda for a Feminist Discourse of Pregnancy Loss', *Feminist Studies*, 23 (2): 289–315.

Layne, Linda (2003), *Motherhood Lost: A Feminist Account of Pregnancy Loss in America*, New York: Routledge.

Layne, Linda (2012), '"Troubling the Normal": "Angel Babies" and the Canny/Uncanny Nexus', in Sarah Earle, Carol Komaromy and Linda Layne (eds), *Understanding Reproductive Loss: Perspectives on Life, Death and Fertility*, Aldershot: Ashgate, 129–41.

Leach, Brittany (2020), 'Abjection and Mourning in the Struggle over Fetal Remains', *Contemporary Political Theory*, 20 (1): 141–64.

Lee-Ortiz, Janet (2019), 'Kamali's Stillbirth', in Shannon Gibney and Kao Kalia Yang (eds), *What God Is Honoured Here? Writings on Miscarriage and Infant Loss by and for Native Women and Women of Color*, Minneapolis: University of Minnesota Press, 149–71.

Leroy, Margaret (1988), *Miscarriage*, London: MacDonald Optima.

Letherby, Gayle (1993), 'The Meanings of Miscarriage', *Women's Studies International Forum*, 16 (2): 165–80.

Letherby, Gayle (2009), 'Experiences of Miscarriage', in Sarah Earle, Caroline Bartholomew and Carol Komaronomy (eds), *Making Sense of Death and Dying and Bereavement*, London: Sage, 140–2.

Lewis, Emanuel (1976), 'The Management of Stillbirth: Coping with an Unreality', *Lancet* 308 (7986): 619–20.

Lewis, Sophie (2017), 'Gestational Labors: Care Politics and Surrogates' Struggle', in Susanne Hofmann and Adi Moreno (eds), *Intimate Economies: Bodies, Emotions, and Sexualities on the Global Market*, New York: Palgrave Macmillan, 187–213.

Lewis, Sophie (2018), 'Cyborg Uterine Geography: Complicating "Care" and Social Reproduction', *Dialogues in Human Geography*, 8 (3): 300–16.

Lewis, Sophie (2019), *Full Surrogacy Now: Feminism against the Family*, London: Verso.

Lind, Emily (2017), 'Fatphobia, Pregnancy Loss, and My Hegemonic Imagination: A Story of Two Abortions', in Angie Deveau and Emily Lind (eds), *Interrogating Pregnancy Loss: Feminist Writings on Abortion, Miscarriage and Stillbirth*, Bradford, ON: Demeter Press, 139–50.

Lindemann, Hilde (2015), 'Miscarriage and the Stories We Live by', *Journal of Social Philosophy*, 46 (1): 80–90.

Little, Margaret Olivia (1999), 'Abortion, Intimacy, and the Duty to Gestate', *Ethical Theory and Moral Practice*, 2 (3): 295–312.

Littlewood, Jenny (1999), 'From the Invisibility of Miscarriage to an Attribution of Life', *Anthropology and Medicine*, 6 (2): 217–30.

Long, Robyn (2018), 'Sexual Subjectivities within Neoliberalism: Can Queer and Crip Engagements Offer an Alternative Praxis?' *Journal of International Women's Studies*, 19 (1): 78–93.

Longhurst, Robyn (1999), 'Pregnant Bodies, Public Scrutiny: Giving "Advice" to Pregnancy Women', in Elizabeth Kenworthy Teather (ed), *Embodied Geographies: Spaces, Bodies and Rites of Passage*, London and New York: Routledge, 77–90.

Longhurst, Robyn (2001), *Bodies: Exploring Fluid Boundaries*, London and New York: Routledge.

Lovell, Alice (1983), 'Some Questions of Identity: Late Miscarriage, Stillbirth and Perinatal Loss', *Social Science and Medicine*, 17 (11): 755–61.

Lowe, Pam (2016), *Reproductive Health and Maternal Sacrifice: Women, Choice and Responsibility*, London and New York: Palgrave Macmillan.

Luce, Jacquelyne (2010), *Beyond Expectation: Lesbian/Bi/Queer Women and Assisted Conception*, Toronto: University of Toronto Press.

Lundquist, Caroline (2008), 'Being Torn: Toward a Phenomenology of Unwanted Pregnancy', *Hypatia*, 23 (3): 136–55.

Lymer, Jane (2016), *The Phenomenology of Gravidity: Reframing Pregnancy and the Maternal through Merleau-Ponty, Levinas and Derrida*, London: Rowman & Littlefield.

Mackenzie, Catriona (1992), 'Abortion and Embodiment', *Australasian Journal of Philosophy*, 70 (2): 136–55.

Mahmood, Saba (2005), *Politics of Piety: The Islamic Revival and the Feminist Subject*, Princeton: Princeton University Press.

Mahoney, Mary and Lauren Mitchell (2016), *The Doulas: Radical Care for Pregnant People*, New York: Feminist Press.

Malhotra, Sheena and Aimee Carrillo Rowe (2013), 'Still the Silence: Feminist Reflections at the Edge of Sound,' in Malhotra Sheena and Aimee Carrillo Rowe (eds), *Silence, Feminism, Power: Reflections at the Edges of Sound*, New York: Palgrave Macmillan, 1–16.

Mamo, Laura (2007), *Queering Reproduction: Achieving Pregnancy in the Age of Technoscience*, Durham, NC: Duke University Press.

Mann, Bonnie (2018), 'The Difference of Feminist Phenomenology: The Case of Shame', *Puncta: A Journal of Critical Phenomenology*, 1 (1): 41–73.

Manninen, Bertha Alvarez (2010), 'Pro-Choice Philosopher Has Baby: Reflections on Fetal Life', in Sheila Lintott (ed), *Motherhood – Philosophy for Everyone: The Birth of Wisdom*, Chichester: Wiley-Blackwell, 41–51.

Mansfield, Becky (2008), 'The Social Nature of Natural Childbirth', *Social Science & Medicine*, 66 (5): 1084–94.

Martin, Emily (2001), *The Woman in the Body: A Cultural Analysis of Reproduction*, Boston, MA: Beacon Press.

Maternity Action (2018), 'What Price Safe Motherhood? Charging for NHS Maternity Care in England and Its Impact on Migrant Women', 1 October. Available at: https://www.maternityaction.org.uk/wp-content/uploads/WhatPriceSafeMotherhoodFINAL.October.pdf (accessed 23 January 2022).

Matthews, Susan (2021), 'While Hearing the Case That Could Overturn Roe, Amy Coney Barrett Suggests Adoption Could Obviate the Need for Abortion Anyway', *The Slate*, 1 December. Available at: https://slate.com/news-and-politics/2021/12/amy-coney-barrett-abortion-adoption-comments.html (accessed 23 January 2022).

Matthiesen, Sara (2021), *Reproduction Reconceived: Family Making and the Limits of Choice After Roe v. Wade*, Oakland, CA: University of California Press.

MBRRACE-UK (Mothers and Babies: Reducing Risk though Audits and Confidential Enquiries across the UK), (2020), *Saving Lives, Improving Mothers' Care: Lessons Learned to Inform Maternity Care from the UK and Ireland Confidential Enquiries into Maternal Deaths and Morbidity 2016–18*. Available at: https://www.npeu.ox.ac.uk/assets/downloads/mbrrace-uk/reports/maternal-report-2020/MBRRACE-UK_Maternal_Report_Dec_2020_v10.pdf (accessed 23 January 2022).

McLenahan, Irene G. (1962), 'Helping the Mother Who Has No Baby to Take Home', *American Journal of Nursing*, 62 (4): 70–1.

McLeod, Carolyn (2002), *Self-Trust and Reproductive Autonomy*, Cambridge, MA: MIT Press.

McMahon, M. (1995), *Engendering Motherhood: Identity and Self-transformation in Women's Lives*. New York: The Guilford Press.

McNay, Lois (2000), *Gender and Agency, Reconfiguring the Subject in Feminist and Social Theory*, Cambridge: Polity.

McRobbie, Angela (2013), 'Feminism, the Family and the New "Mediated" Maternalism', *New Formations*, 80 (1): 119–37.

McRuer, Robert (2006), *Crip Theory: Cultural Signs of Queerness and Disability*, New York: New York University Press.

McWhorter, Ladelle (2005), 'Foreword', in Shelley Tremain (ed), *Foucault and the Government of Disability*, Ann Arbor: University of Michigan Press.

Merck, Mandy and Stella Sandford (eds) (2010), *Further Adventures of the Dialectic of Sex: Critical Essays on Shulamith Firestone*, London and New York: Palgrave Macmillan.

Merleau-Ponty, Maurice (1964), 'The Child's Relations with Others', in James M. Edie (ed), *The Primacy of Perception*, trans. William Cobb, Evanston: Northwestern University Press, 96–159.

Merleau-Ponty, Maurice (1968), *The Visible and the Invisible*, trans. Alphonso Lingis, Evanston: Northwestern University Press.

Mezzadri, Alessandra (2019), 'On the Value of Social Reproduction: Informal Labour, the Majority World and the Need for Inclusive Theories and Politics', *Radical Philosophy*, 2.04: 33–41.

Middlemiss, Aimee (2021), 'Pregnancy Remains, Infant Remains, or the Corpse of a Child? The Incoherent Governance of the Dead Foetal Body in England', *Mortality*, 26 (3): 299–315.

Midwives Alliance of North America (2015), 'Position Statement on Gender Inclusive Language', 9 September. Available at: https://mana.org/healthcare-policy/position-statement-on-gender-inclusive-language (accessed 23 January 2022).

Millar, Erica (2016), 'Mourned Choices and Grievable Lives: The Anti-Abortion Movement's Influence in Defining the Abortion Experience in Australia since the 1960s', *Gender & History*, 28 (2): 501–19.

Millar, Erica (2018), *Happy Abortions: Our Bodies in the Era of Choice*, London: Zed Books.

Mills, Catherine (2014), 'Making Fetal Persons: Fetal Homicide, Ultrasound, and the Normative Significance of Birth', *PhiloSophia: A Journal of Continental Feminism*, 1: 88–107.

Miscarriage Association (2014), 'Waiting', Available at: http://www.miscarriageassociation.org.uk/wp-content/uploads/2017/01/Waiting.pdf (accessed 23 January 2022).

Miscarriage Association (2016), 'Néna's Story', Available at: https://www.miscarriageassociation.org.uk/story/nenas-story/ (accessed 23 January 2022).

Miscarriage Association (2021), 'Slowly Losing My Baby', Available at: https://www.miscarriageassociation.org.uk/story/slowly-losing-my-baby/ (accessed 23 January 2022).

Mitchell, M. (2004), *Righteous Propagation: African Americans and the Politics of Racial Destiny after Reconstruction*, Chapel Hill: University of North Carolina Press.

Moi, Toril (1999), *What Is a Woman? And Other Essays*, Oxford: Oxford University Press.

Mol, Annemarie (2003), *The Body Multiple: Ontology in Medical Practice*, Durham, NC: Duke University Press.

Mol, Annemarie (2014), 'A Reader's Guide to the Ontological Turn, Part 4', *Somatosphere*, 19 March. Available at: http://somatosphere.net/2014/a-readers-guide-to-the-ontological-turn-part-4.html/ (accessed 23 January 2022).

More, Sam Dylan (1998), 'The Pregnant Man – An Oxymoron', *Journal of Gender Studies* 7 (3): 319–28.

Morgan, Lynn M. (1999), 'Materializing the Fetal Body, or, What Are Those Corpses Doing in Biology's Basement?', in Morgan, Lynn M. and Meredith Wilson Michaels (eds), *Fetal Subjects, Feminist Positions*, Philadelphia: University of Pennsylvania Press, 43–61.

Morgan, Lynn M. and Meredith Wilson Michaels (eds) (1999), *Fetal Subjects, Feminist Positions*, Philadelphia: University of Pennsylvania Press.

Moscucci, O. (2003), 'Holistic Obstetrics: The Origins of "Natural Childbirth" in Britain', *Postgraduate Medical Journal*, 79: 168–73.

Moua, Chue, with Kao Kalia Yang (2019), 'Either Side', in Shannon Gibney and Kao Kalia Yang (eds), *What God Is Honoured Here? Writings on Miscarriage and Infant Loss by and for Native Women and Women of Color*, Minneapolis: University of Minnesota Press, 247–59.

Mukherjee, Sudeshna, Digna R. Velez Edwards, Donna D. Baird, David A. Savitz and Katherine E. Hartmann (2013), 'Risk of Miscarriage among Black Women and White Women in a US Prospective Cohort Study', *American Journal of Epidemiology*, 177 (11): 1271–8.

Mullin, Amy (2005), *Reconceiving Pregnancy and Childcare: Ethics, Experience and Reproductive Labor*, Cambridge: Cambridge University Press.

Muñoz, Jose Esteban (2009), *Cruising Utopia: The Then and There or Queer Futurity*, New York: New York University Press.

Murkhoff, Heidi (2017), *What to Expect When You're Expecting*, 5th edn, New York: Workman Publishing.

Murphy, Fiona and Susan Philpin (2010), 'Early Miscarriage as "Matter Out of Place": An Ethnographic Study of Nursing Practice in a Hospital Gynaecological Unit', *International Journal of Nursing Studies*, 47 (5): 534–41.

Murphy, Samantha L. (2010), *Lost Futures: Stillbirth and the Social Construction of Grief*, Saarbrücken, Germany: Lambert Academic Press.

Murray, Nic and Hannah Summers (2021), 'Jailed Women in UK Five Times More Likely to Suffer Stillbirths, Data Shows', *The Guardian*, 5 December. Available at: https://www.theguardian.com/society/2021/dec/05/jailed-women-in-uk-five-times-more-likely-to-suffer-stillbirths-data-shows (accessed 23 January 2022).

Nakamura Lin, Jami (2019), 'The Night Parade', in Shannon Gibney and Kao Kalia Yang (eds), *What God Is Honoured Here? Writings on Miscarriage and Infant Loss by and for Native Women and Women of Color*, Minneapolis: University of Minnesota Press, 247–59.

Nash, Jennifer C. (2021a), 'Love Warriors: Women of Color Doulas in a Time of Crisis', *Literary Hub*, August 20. Available at: https://lithub.com/love-warriors-women-of-color-doulas-in-a-time-of-crisis/ (accessed 23 January 2022).

Nash, Jennifer C. (2021b), *Birthing Black Mothers*, Durham, NC: Duke University Press.

National Advocates for Pregnant Women (NAPW) (2007), 'Open Letter to the Oklahoma County District Attorney', 25 June. Available at: https://www.nationaladvocatesforpregnantwomen.org/open-letter-to-the-oklahoma-county-district-attorney/ (accessed 23 January 2022).

National Advocates for Pregnant Women (NAPW) (2018), 'Victory in Indiana', 29 November. Available at: https://www.nationaladvocatesforpregnantwomen.org/victory-in-indiana/ (accessed 23 January 2022).

National Advocates for Pregnant Women (NAPW) (2021a), 'NAPW Factsheet: Arrests and Other Deprivations of Liberty of Pregnant Women, 1973–2020', September. Available at: https://www.nationaladvocatesforpregnantwomen.org/wp-content/uploads/2021/09/Arrests-of-Pregnant-Women-1973-2020-Fact-Sheet.pdf (accessed 23 January 2022).

National Advocates for Pregnant Women (NAPW) (2021b), 'NAPW Factsheet: Pregnancy and Drug Use: The Facts', September. Available at: https://www.nationaladvocatesforpregnantwomen.org/wp-content/uploads/2021/09/FINAL_Pregnancy-and-Drug-Use-Factsheet.docx-1.pdf (accessed 23 January 2022).

National Advocates for Pregnant Women (NAPW) (2021c), 'National Advocates for Pregnant Women Files Brief on Behalf of 45 Organizations, Experts, and Advocates, Including Actor Amy Schumer, in Support of Arizona Mother Found to Have Committed Child Neglect for Legally Using Medical Marijuana to Treat Hyperemesis Gravidarum during Her Pregnancy', 6 July. Available at: https://www.nationaladvocatesforpregnantwomen.org/national-advocates-for-pregnant-women-files-brief-on-behalf-of-45-organizations-experts-and-advocates-including-actor-amy-schumer-in-support-of-arizona-mother-found-to-have-committed-child-neglect/ (accessed 23 January 2022).

National Advocates for Pregnant Women (NAPW) (2021d), 'National Advocates for Pregnant Women Files Brief with U.S. Supreme Court Focusing on the Impact of Mississippi's Abortion Ban on All Pregnant People, Not Only Those Seeking to End a Pregnancy', 20 September. Available at: https://www.nationaladvocatesforpregnantwomen.org/dobbs-brief-release-9-2021/ (accessed 23 January 2022).

National Advocates for Pregnant Women (NAPW) (2021e), 'Support Brittany Poolaw', 22 October. Available at: https://www.nationaladvocatesforpregnantwomen.org/support-brittney-poolaw/ (accessed 23 January 2022).

Neiterman, Elena (2012), 'Doing Pregnancy: Pregnant Embodiment as Performance', *Women's Studies International Forum* 35 (5): 372–83.

Neiterman, Elena and Bonnie Fox (2017), 'Controlling the Unruly Maternal Body: Losing and Gaining Control over the Body during Pregnancy and the Postpartum Period', *Social Science Medicine*, 174: 142–8.

Nelson, Elizabeth (2021), 'Abortion Was Legalised in Northern Ireland in 2019 – So Why Are We Still Waiting for It?', *Guardian*, 29 October. Available at: https://www.theguardian.com/commentisfree/2021/oct/29/abortion-legalised-2019-northern-ireland-human-rights (accessed 23 January 2022).

Nelson, Jennifer (2003), *Women of Color and the Reproductive Rights Movement*, New York: New York University Press.

Nelson, Maggie (2015), *The Argonauts*, Minneapolis: Graywolf Press.

O'Brien, Mary (1981), *The Politics of Reproduction*, New York: Routledge & Kegan Paul.

O'Donnell, Kelly Suzanne (2017), 'Reproducing Jane: Abortion Stories and Women's Political Histories', *Signs*, 43 (1): 77–96.

O'Donnell, Lucy (2019), *Sitting with Uncertainty*, Grundon Graphics.

O'Farrell, Maggie (2017), *I am, I am, I am: Seventeen Brushes with Death*, London: Tinder Press.

Oakley, Ann, Ann McPherson and Helen Roberts (1990), *Miscarriage*, London: Penguin.

Obama, Michelle (2018), *Becoming*, New York: Viking Press.

Office for National Statistics (2020), 'Births in England and Wales: 2019', 22 July. Available at: https://www.ons.gov.uk/peoplepopulationandcommunity/birthsdeathsandmarriages/livebirths/bulletins/birthsummarytablesenglandandwales/2019 (accessed 23 January 2022).

Office for National Statistics (2021), 'Conceptions in England and Wales: 2019', 5 August. Available at: https://www.ons.gov.uk/peoplepopulationandcommunity/birthsdeathsandmarriages/conceptionandfertilityrates/bulletins/conceptionstatistics/2019 (accessed 23 January 2022).

Oksala, Johanna (2014), 'In Defense of Experience', *Hypatia*, 29 (2): 388–403.

Oliver, Kelly (1998), *Subjectivity without Subjects: From Abject Fathers to Desiring Mothers*, Oxford: Rowman & Littlefield.

Oliver, Kelly (2010), 'Motherhood, Sexuality, and Pregnant Embodiment: Twenty-Five Years of Gestation', *Hypatia*, 25 (4): 760–77.

Oliver, Kelly (2012), *Knock Me Up, Knock Me Down: Images of Pregnancy in Hollywood Films*, New York: Columbia University Press.

Osborne, Peter (2015), 'Problematizing Disciplinarity, Transdisciplinary Problematics,' *Theory, Culture and Society*, 32 (5–6): 3–35.

Paltrow, Lynn M. (2005), 'Abortion Issue Divides, Distracts Us from Common Threats and Threads', *Perspectives* 13 (3). Available at: https://www.

americanbar.org/content/dam/aba/publishing/perspectives_magazine/
women_perspectives_voicesabortion.pdf (accessed 23 January 2022).

Paltrow, Lynn M. (2021), 'Why I Refuse to Feel Hopeless about the Texas
Abortion Case', *Ms Magazine*, 8 September. Available at: https://
msmagazine.com/2021/09/08/texas-abortion-rights-ban-feminists-roe-v-
wade-pregnancy/ (accessed 23 January 2022).

Paltrow, Lynn M. and Jeanne Flavin (2013), 'Arrests of and Forced
Interventions on Pregnant Women in the United States, 1973–2005:
Implications for Women's Legal Status and Public Health', *Journal of Health
Politics, Policy and Law*, 38 (2): 299–343.

Paltrow, Lynn M. and Lisa K. Sangoi (2016), 'The Dangerous State Laws That
Are Punishing Pregnant People: In the Past 10 Years, Arrests and Forced
Interventions of Pregnant Women Have Skyrocketed', *ThinkProgress*,
28 September. Available at: https://archive.thinkprogress.org/
criminalization-pregnancy-us-43e4741bb514/ (accessed 23 January 2022).

Pande, Amrita (2014), *Wombs in Labor: Transnational Commercial Surrogacy
in India*, New York: Columbia University Press.

Park, Shelley M. (2013), *Mothering Queerly, Queering Motherhood: Resisting
Monomaternalism in Adoptive, Lesbian, Blended, and Polygamous
Families*, Albany, NY: State University of New York Press.

Parker, George and Cat Pausé (2018), '"I'm Just a Woman Having a Baby":
Negotiating and Resisting the Problematization of Pregnancy Fatness',
Frontiers in Sociology, 3 (5).

Parker, Rozsika (1995), *Torn in Two: The Experience of Maternal Ambivalence*,
London: Virago.

Parker, Willie (2016), "Afterword" to Mary Mahoney and Lauren Mitchell, *The
Doulas: Radical Care for Pregnant People*, New York: The Feminist Press,
282–4.

Parsons, Kate (2010), 'Feminist Reflections on Miscarriage, in Light of Abortion',
International Journal of Feminist Approaches to Bioethics, 3 (1): 1–22.

Pauly Morgan, Kathryn (1989), 'Of Woman Born? How Old Fashioned! New
Reproductive Technologies and Women's Oppression', in Christine Overall
(ed) *The Future of Human Reproduction*, Toronto: The Women's Press.

Peel, Elizabeth and Ruth Cain (2012), '"Silent" Miscarriage and Deafening
Heteronormativity: A British Experiential and Critical Feminist Account',
in Sarah Earle, Carol Komaromy and Linda Layne (eds), *Understanding
Reproductive Loss: Perspectives on Life, Death and Fertility*, Aldershot:
Ashgate, 79–92.

Petchesky, Rosalind (1980), 'Reproductive Freedom: Beyond "A Woman's
Right to Choose"', *Signs*, 5 (4): 661–85.

Petchesky, Rosalind Pollack (1987), 'Fetal Images: The Power of Visual Culture
in the Politics of Reproduction', *Feminist Studies*, 12 (2): 263–92.

Phillips, Jess (2018), 'I Had an Abortion and I Will Keep Fighting for This Right
for All', *Guardian*, 27 May. Available at: https://www.theguardian.com/

commentisfree/2018/may/27/jess-phillips-i-had-an-abortion-and-will-fight-for-rights-for-everyone (accessed 23 January 2022).

Phipps, Alison (2014), *The Politics of the Body*, Cambridge: Polity.

Picard, Caroline (2021), 'What to Eat for Lunch during Pregnancy', *What to Expect*, 31 March. Available at: https://www.whattoexpect.com/pregnancy/pregnancy-health/lunch-during-pregnancy/ (accessed 23 January 2022).

Pidd, Helen (2021), 'Three Miscarriage Rule before Receiving Help Is Unacceptable, Says MP', *Guardian*, 16 June. Available at: https://www.theguardian.com/society/2021/jun/16/three-miscarriage-rule-before-receiving-help-is-unacceptable-says-mp (accessed 23 January 2022).

Poovey, Mary (1995), *Making a Social Body: British Cultural Formation, 1830–1864*, Chicago: University of Chicago Press.

Prager, Sarah (2020), 'Pregnancy Loss Is Lonely – Especially for Transgender People', *Healthline*, 9 December. Available at: https://www.healthline.com/health/pregnancy/transgender-pregnancy-loss (accessed 23 January 2022).

Presser, Lizzie (2018), 'Inside the Secret Network Providing Home Abortions across the US', *Guardian*, 27 August. Available at: https://www.theguardian.com/world/2018/aug/27/inside-the-secret-network-providing-home-abortions-across-the-us (accessed 23 January 2022).

Price, Janet and Margrit Shildrick (1999), *Feminist Theory and the Body: A Reader*, London and New York: Routledge.

Public Health England (2014), 'Public Health England Marketing Strategy, 2014–2107', July. Available at: https://assets.publishing.service.gov.uk/government/uploads/system/uploads/attachment_data/file/326548/PHE_StrategyDoc_2014_10.pdf (accessed 23 January 2022).

Pugliese, Alice (2016) 'Phenomenology of Drives: Between Biological and Personal Life', in Jonna Bornemark and Nicholas Smith (eds), *Phenomenology of Pregnancy*, Huddinge: Södertörn University, 71–91.

Puig de la Bellacasa, Maria (2017), *Matters of Care: Speculative Ethics in More than Human Worlds*, Minneapolis: University of Minnesota Press.

Rajendra, Dania (2019), 'Binding Signs', in Shannon Gibney and Kao Kalia Yang (eds), *What God Is Honoured Here? Writings on Miscarriage and Infant Loss by and for Native Women and Women of Color*, Minneapolis: University of Minnesota Press, 107–15.

Raphael-Leff, Joan (2016), '"Two-in-one-body": Unconscious Representations and Ethical Dimensions of Inter-corporeality in Childbearing', in Jonna Bornemark and Nicholas Smith (eds), *Phenomenology of Pregnancy*, Huddinge: Södertörn University, 157–99.

Rapp, Rayna (1999), *Testing Women, Testing the Fetus: The Social Impact of Amniocentesis in America*, London and New York: Routledge.

Reagan, Leslie J. (2003), 'From Hazard to Blessing to Tragedy: Representations of Miscarriage in Twentieth-Century America', *Feminist Studies*, 29 (2): 356–78.

Reiheld, Alison (2015), '"The Event That Was Nothing": Miscarriage as a Liminal Event', *Journal of Social Philosophy*, 46 (1): 9–26.

Reynolds, Joel (2020), '"What If There's Something Wrong with Her?" – How Biomedical Technologies Contribute to Epistemic Injustice in Healthcare', *Southern Journal of Philosophy* 58 (1): 161–85.

Reza, Seema (2019), 'Pity', in Shannon Gibney and Kao Kalia Yang (eds), *What God Is Honoured Here? Writings on Miscarriage and Infant Loss by and for Native Women and Women of Color*, Minneapolis: University of Minnesota Press, 193–207.

Rice, Carla, Eliza Chandler, Jen Rinaldi, Nadine Changfoot, Kirsty Liddiard, Roxanne Mykitiuk and Ingrid Mündel (2017), 'Imagining Disability Futurities', *Hypatia*, 32 (2): 213–29.

Rich, Adrienne ([1976] 1992), *Of Woman Born: Motherhood as Experience and Institution*, London: Virago.

Riggs, Damien W. (2013), 'Transgender Men's Self-Representations of Bearing Children Post-Transition', in Fiona Joy Green and May Friedman (eds), *Chasing Rainbows: Exploring Gender Fluid Parenting Practices*, Bradford, ON: Demeter Press, 62–71.

Roberts, Dorothy E. (1997), *Killing the Black Body: Race, Reproduction, and the Meaning of Liberty*, New York: Pantheon.

Roberts, Dorothy E. (2018), 'The Ethics of Biosocial Science', *Faculty Scholarship at Penn Law*. Available at: https://scholarship.law.upenn.edu/faculty_scholarship/2505 (accessed 23 January 2022).

Robertson, Rachel (2015), 'Out of Time: Maternal Time and Disability', *Studies in the Maternal*, 7 (1): 1–13.

Rosenblum, Darren, Noa Ben-Asher, Mary A. Case, Elizabeth Emens, Berta E. Hernandez-Truyol, Vivian M. Gutierrez, Lisa C. Ikemoto, Angela Onwuachi-Willig, Jacob Willig-Onwuachi, Kimberly Mutcherson, Peter Siegelman and Beth Jones (2010), 'Pregnant Man?: A Conversation', *Yale Journal of Law& Feminism*, 22: 102. Available at: https://digitalcommons.law.yale.edu/yjlf/vol22/iss2/3 (accessed 23 January 2022).

Ross, Loretta J. (2008), 'Re-enslaving African American Women,' *On the Issues*, 24 November. Available at: https://www.ontheissuesmagazine.com/cafe2.php?id=22 (accessed 23 January 2022).

Ross, Loretta J. (2016), 'Thank God for the Doulas!' Foreword to Mary Mahoney·and Lauren Mitchell, *The Doulas: Radical Care for Pregnant People*, New York: The Feminist Press, ix–xvi.

Ross, Loretta J. (2017), 'Reproductive Justice as Intersectional Feminist Activism', *Souls* 19 (3): 286–314.

Ross, Loretta J. and Rickie Solinger (2017), *Reproductive Justice: An Introduction*, Oakland, CA: University of California Press.

Ross, Loretta J., Lynn Roberts, Erika Derkas, Whitney Peoples and Pamela Bridgewater Toure (eds) (2017), *Radical Reproductive Justice: Foundations, Theory, Practice, Critique*, New York: Feminist Press.

Royal College of Midwives (2019), 'The NHS Long Term Plan', 7 January. Available at: https://www.rcm.org.uk/media/2871/nhs-long-term-plan-jan-2019.pdf (accessed 23 January 2022).

Ruddick, Sue (2007), 'At the Horizons of the Subject: Neo-liberalism, Neo-conservatism and the Rights of the Child', *Gender, Place and Culture: A Journal of Feminist Geography*, 14 (5): 513–27.

Ruse, Michael (2002), 'Evolutionary Biology and Teleological Thinking', in Andre Ariew, Robert Cummins and Mark Perlman (eds), *Functions: New Essays in the Philosophy of Psychology and Biology*, Oxford: Oxford University Press, 33–63.

Russell, Neal James, Lisa Murphy, Laura Nellums, Jonathon Broad, Sarah Boutros, Nando Sigona and Delan Devakumar (2019), 'Charging Undocumented Migrant Children for NHS Healthcare: Implications for Child Health', *Archives of Disease in Childhood*, 104: 722–4.

Ryan-Flood, Róisín and Rosalind Gill (2010), 'Introduction', in Ryan-Flood and Gill (eds), *Secrecy and Silence in the Research Process: Feminist Reflections*, London and New York: Routledge, 1–13.

Sabin, Lamiat (2015), 'Mother-of-Six with Learning Difficulties Can Be Put through Forced Sterilisation, Rules Judge', *Independent*, 4 February. Available at: https://www.independent.co.uk/news/uk/home-news/mother-of-six-who-has-learning-difficulties-can-be-put-through-forced-sterilisation-rules-judge-10023496.html (accessed 23 January 2022).

Salamon, Gayle (2018), 'What's Critical about Critical Phenomenology?', *Puncta: Journal of Critical Phenomenology*, 1 (1): 8–17.

Salem, Sarah (2018), 'Race, Nation and Welfare: Eugenics and the Problem of the "Anti-Social" Citizen', *The Disorder of Things*, 29 June. Available at: https://thedisorderofthings.com/2018/06/29/race-nation-and-welfare-eugenics-and-the-problem-of-the-anti-social-citizen/ (accessed 23 January 2022).

Samuels, Ellen (2017), 'Six Ways of Looking at Crip Time', *Disability Studies Quarterly*, 37 (30). Available at: https://dsq-sds.org/article/view/5824 (accessed 23 January 2022).

Sandford, Stella (2008), '"All Human Beings Are Pregnant": The Bisexual Imaginary in Plato's Symposium', *Radical Philosophy*, 150: 24–35.

Sandford, Stella (2015), 'Contradiction of Terms: Feminist Theory, Philosophy and Transdisciplinarity', *Theory, Culture & Society*, 32 (5–6): 159–82.

Sandford, Stella (2016), 'Feminist Phenomenology, Pregnancy and Transcendental Subjectivity', in Jonna Bornemark and Nicholas Smith (eds), *Phenomenology of Pregnancy*, Huddinge: Södertörn University, 51–71.

Sartre, Jean-Paul [1943] 2003), *Being and Nothingness: An Essay on Phenomenological Ontology*, trans. Hazel E. Barnes, Abingdon: Routledge.

Scott, Joan W. (1991), 'The Evidence of Experience', *Critical Inquiry*, 17 (4): 773–97.

Scully, Jackie Leach (2021), 'The Politics of Care: From Biomedical Transformation to Narrative Vulnerability', in Victoria Browne, Jason

Danely and Doerthe Rosenow (eds), *Vulnerability and the Politics of Care: Transdisciplinary Dialogues*, Oxford: Oxford University Press, 151–68.

Scuro, Jennifer (2017), *The Pregnancy [does-not-equal] Childbearing Project: A Phenomenology of Miscarriage*, London: Rowman & Littlefield.

Scuro, Jennifer (2018), 'Thoughts on the Postpartum Situation', *Frontiers in Sociology*, 3 (13).

Scuro, Jennifer (2021), 'What You Do Hurts All of Us!" When Women Confront Women through Pro-life Rhetoric"', in Rachel Alpha Johnson Hurst (ed), *Representing Abortion*, New York: Routledge, 207–20.

Shemkus, Sarah (2014a), 'Losing the Baby: My Week of Gestational Limbo', *The Slate*, 24 January. Available at: https://slate.com/human-interest/2014/01/having-a-miscarriage-all-the-confusion-sadness-foolishness-relief-and-anticipation-of-losing-a-baby.html (accessed 23 January 2022).

Shemkus, Sarah and Michel Martin (2014b), 'The Truth about Miscarriage: Being in "Gestational Limbo"', *New York Public Radio*, 10 February. Available at: https://www.npr.org/2014/02/10/274687103/the-truth-about-miscarriage-being-in-gestational-limbo (accessed 23 January 2022).

Sherwin, Susan (1991), 'Abortion through a Feminist Ethics Lens', *Dialogue*, 30 (3): 327–42.

Shildrick, Margrit (1997), *Leaky Bodies and Boundaries: Feminism, Postmodernism and (Bio)ethics*, London: Routledge.

Shildrick, Margrit (2001), *Embodying the Monster. Encounters with the Vulnerable Self*, London: Sage.

Shilliam, Robbie (2018), *Race and the Undeserving Poor: From Abolition to Brexit*, Newcastle: Agenda Publishing.

Shilling, Chris (1993), *The Body and Social Theory*, London: Sage.

Silbergleid, Robin (2017), 'Missed Miscarriage', in Angie Deveau and Emily Lind (eds), *Interrogating Pregnancy Loss: Feminist Writings on Abortion, Miscarriage and Stillbirth*, Bradford, ON: Demeter Press, 150–7.

skelton, j. wallace (2017), 'Failing', in Angie Deveau and Emily Lind (eds), *Interrogating Pregnancy Loss: Feminist Writings on Abortion, Miscarriage and Stillbirth*, Bradford, ON: Demeter Press, 132–9.

Sky News (2019) 'Beyonce: Miscarriage and Child Birth Caused Star to "Search for Deeper Meaning"', 12 December. Available at: https://news.sky.com/story/beyonce-miscarriage-and-child-birth-caused-star-to-search-for-deeper-meaning-11882456 (accessed 23 January 2022).

Smalkoski, Kari (2019), 'Untranslation', in Shannon Gibney and Kao Kalia Yang (eds), *What God Is Honoured Here? Writings on Miscarriage and Infant Loss by and for Native Women and Women of Color*, Minneapolis: University of Minnesota Press, 87–93.

Smith, Andrea (2005), 'Beyond Pro-Choice versus Pro-Life: Women of Color and Reproductive Justice', *NWSA Journal*, 17 (1): 119–40.

Sofia, Zoe (1984) 'Exterminating Fetuses: Abortion, Disarmament, and the Sexo-Semiotics of Extraterrestrialism', *Diacritics*, 14 (2): 47–59.

Spillers, Hortense (1987), 'Mama's Baby, Papa's Maybe: An American Grammar Book', *Diacritics*, 17 (2): 64–81.

Spivak, Gayatri Chakravorty (1999), *A Critique of Postcolonial Reason: Toward a History of the Vanishing Present*, London and Cambridge, MA: Harvard University Press.

Squires, Catherine R. (2019), 'Calendar of the Unexpected?', in Shannon Gibney and Kao Kalia Yang (eds), *What God Is Honoured Here? Writings on Miscarriage and Infant Loss by and for Native Women and Women of Color*, Minneapolis: University of Minnesota Press, 207–25.

Srinivasan, Amia (2021), *The Right to Sex*, London and New York: Bloomsbury.

Stacey, Jackie (1997), *Teratologies: A Cultural Study of Cancer*, London and New York: Routledge.

Stanworth, Michelle (ed) (1987), *Reproductive Technologies: Gender, Motherhood and Medicine*, Cambridge: Polity.

Stein, Gary L. (2010), 'Ashley's Case: The Ethics of Arresting the Growth of Children with Serious Disability', *Journal of Social Work in Disability & Rehabilitation*, 9 (2–3): 99–109.

Stephenson, Niamh, Kim McLeod and Catherine Mills (2016), 'Ambiguous Encounters, Uncertain Foetuses: Women's Experiences of Obstetric Ultrasound', *Feminist Review*, 113 (1): 17–33.

Stern, Mark Joseph (2021), 'The Alternative to Overturning *Roe* That Terrifies Anti-Abortion Advocates', *The Slate*, 30 November. Available at: https://slate.com/news-and-politics/2021/11/dobbs-abortion-roe-casey-supreme-court.html (accessed 23 January 2022).

Stone, Alison (2007), *An Introduction to Feminist Philosophy*, Cambridge: Polity.

Stone, Alison (2010), 'Natality and Mortality: Rethinking Death with Cavarero', *Continental Philosophy Review*, 43 (3): 353–72.

Stone, Alison (2011), *Feminism, Psychoanalysis and Maternal Subjectivity*, London: Routledge.

Sufrin, Carolyn (2017), *Jailcare: Finding the Safety Net for Women behind Bars*, Oakland, CA: University of California Press.

Sukovic, Masha and Margie Serrato (2017), 'Communicating Miscarriage: Coping with Loss, Uncertainty and Self-Imposed Stigma', in Angie Deveau and Emily Lind (eds), *Interrogating Pregnancy Loss: Feminist Writings on Abortion, Miscarriage and Stillbirth*, Bradford, ON: Demeter Press, 21–40.

Summers, A. K. (2014), *Pregnant Butch: Nine Long Months Spent in Drag*, New York: Soft Skull Press.

Szkupinski-Quiroga, Seline (2002), *Disrupted Bodies: The Effect of Infertility on Racialized Identities*, Berkeley, CA: University of California Press.

Teman, Elly (2009), 'Embodying Surrogate Motherhood: Pregnancy as a Dyadic Body-project', *Body & Society*, 15 (3): 47–69.

Teman, Elly (2010), *Birthing a Mother: The Surrogate Body and the Pregnant Self*, Oakland, CA: University of California Press.

Thomson, Judith Jarvis (1971), 'A Defense of Abortion', *Philosophy and Public Affairs*, 1 (1): 47–66.

Throsby, Karen (2004), *When IVF Fails: Feminism, Infertility and the Negotiation of Normality*, New York: Palgrave Macmillan.

Tilley, Elizabeth, Jan Walmsley, Sarah Earle and Dorothy Atkinson (2012), '"The Silence Is Roaring": Sterilization, Reproductive Rights and Women with Intellectual Disabilities', *Disability & Society*, 27 (3): 413–26.

Tonkin, Lois (2012), 'Haunted by a Present Absence', *Studies in the Maternal*, 4 (1).

Toze, Michael (2018), 'The Risky Womb and the Unthinkability of the Pregnant Man: Addressing Trans Masculine Hysterectomy', *Feminism & Psychology*, 28 (2): 194–211.

Transport for London (2017), 'New Figures Show Huge Success of "Please Offer Me a Seat" Badge', 20 December. Available at: https://tfl.gov.uk/info-for/media/press-releases/2017/december/new-figures-show-huge-success-of-please-offer-me-a-seat-bad (accessed 23 January 2022).

Tremain, Shelley (2010), 'Stemming the Tide of Normalisation: An Expanded Feminist Analysis of the Ethics and Social impact of Embryonic Stem Cell Research', *Hypatia*, 25 (3): 577–609.

Turner, Victor (1964), 'Betwixt and between: The Liminal Period in *rites de passage*', *The Proceedings of the American Ethnological Society*, Symposium on New Approaches to the Study of Religion: 4–20.

Turner, Victor (1977), 'Variations on a Theme of Liminality', in Sally F. Moore and Barbara Myerhoff (eds), *Secular Ritual*, Assen/Amsterdam: Van Gorcum.

Tyler, Imogen (2000), 'Reframing Pregnant Embodiment', in Sara Ahmed, Jane Kilby, Celia Lury, Maureen McNeil and Beverley Skeggs (eds), *Transformations: Thinking through Feminism*, London and New York: Routledge, 288–301.

Tyler, Imogen (2008), 'Chav Mum, Chav Scum: Class Disgust in Contemporary Britain', *Feminist Media Studies*, 8 (2): 17–34.

Tyler, Imogen (2013), *Revolting Subjects: Social Abjection and Resistance in Neoliberal Britain*, London and New York: Zed Books.

Vácha, Jiri (1978), 'Biology and the Problem of Normality', *Scientia*, 113: 823–46.

Valmidiano, Elsa (2019), 'Blighted', in Shannon Gibney and Kao Kalia Yang (eds), *What God Is Honoured Here? Writings on Miscarriage and Infant Loss by and for Native Women and Women of Color*, Minneapolis: University of Minnesota Press, 225–37.

Van der Sijpt, Erica (2018), *Wasted Wombs. Navigating Reproductive Interruptions in Cameroon*, Nashville: Vanderbilt University Press.

Van Gennep, Arnold (1960), *The Rites of Passage*, trans. M.B. Vizedom and G.L. Caffee, Chicago: University of Chicago Press.

Van, Paulina (2001), 'Breaking the Silence of African American Women: Healing after Pregnancy Loss', *Health Care for Women International*, 22: 229–243.

Vergès, Françoise (2020), *The Wombs of Women: Race, Capital, Feminism*, trans. Kaiama L. Glover, Durham, NC: Duke University Press.

Villarmea, Stella (2020), 'Reasoning from the Uterus: Casanova, Women's Agency, and the Philosophy of Birth', *Hypatia*, 36 (1): 22–41.

Volscho, Thomas W. (2011), 'Racism and Disparities in Women's Use of the Depo-Provera Injection in the Contemporary USA', *Critical Sociology*, 37 (5): 673–88.

Vora, Kalindi (2015), *Life Support: Biocapital and the New History of Outsourced Labor*, Minnesota: University of Minnesota Press.

Wallace, J. (2010), 'The Manly Art of Pregnancy', in Kate Bornstein and S. Bear Bergman (eds), *Gender Outlaws: The Next Generation*, Seattle: Seal Press, 188–94.

Watkins, Elizabeth Siegel (2010), 'From Breakthrough to Bust: The Brief Life of Norplant, the Contraceptive Implant', *Journal of Women's History*, 22 (3): 88–111.

Watts, Jonathan (2015), 'El Salvador: Where Women Are Thrown into Jail for Losing a Baby', *Guardian*, 17 December. Available at: https://www.theguardian.com/global-development/2015/-dec/17/el-salvador-anti-abortion-law-premature-birth-miscarriage-attempted-murder(accessed 23 January 2022).

Weinbaum, Alyse Eve (2004), *Wayward Reproductions: Genealogies of Race and Nation in Transatlantic Modern Thought*, Durham, NC: Duke University Press.

Weintrobe, Sally (ed) (2012), *Engaging with Climate Change: Psychoanalytic and Interdisciplinary Perspectives*, London: Routledge.

Weiss, Gail (1998), *Body Images: Embodiment as Intercorporeality*, New York: Routledge.

Weiss, Gail (1999), *Perspectives on Embodiment: The Intersections of Nature and Culture*, New York: Routledge.

Wendell, Susan (1997), *The Rejected Body: Feminist Philosophical Reflections on Disability*, New York: Routledge.

Winnubst, Shannon (2006), *Queering Freedom*, Bloomington: Indiana University Press.

Wojnar, Danuta (2009), *The Experience of Lesbian Miscarriage: Phenomenological Inquiry*, Saarbrücken: Lambert.

Wolff, John R., Paul E. Neilson and Patricia Schiller (1970), 'The Emotional Reaction to a Stillbirth', *American Journal of Obstetrics and Gynecology*, 101 (1): 73–6.

Woliver, Laura (2008), *The Political Geographies of Pregnancy*, Urbana and Chicago: University of Illinois Press.

Wollstonecraft, Mary ([1792] 1993), *A Vindication of the Rights of Woman*, Oxford: Oxford University Press.

Wood, H and Beverly Skeggs (2020), 'Clap for Carers? From Care Gratitude to Care Justice', *European Journal of Cultural Studies*, 23 (4): 641–7.

World Health Organization (2020), 'Factsheet: Infertility', 14 September. Available at: https://www.who.int/news-room/fact-sheets/detail/infertility (accessed 23 January 2022).

Young, Iris Marion ([1984] 2005), 'Throwing Like a Girl: A Phenomenology of Feminine Body Comportment, Motility, and Spatiality', in *Throwing Like a Girl and Other Essays*, Chicago: University of Chicago Press, 27–46.

Young, Iris Marion ([1984] 2005), 'Pregnant Embodiment: Subjectivity and Alienation', in *Throwing Like a Girl and Other Essays*, Chicago: University of Chicago Press, 46–61.

Yuval-Davis, Nira (1997), *Gender and Nation*, London: Sage.

Zandy, Janet (2004), *Hands: Physical Labor, Class, and Cultural Work*, New Brunswick, NJ: Rutgers University Press.

Ziarek, Ewa Plonowska (1999), 'At the Limits of Discourse: Heterogeneity, Alterity and the Feminine', in Christina Hendricks and Kelly Oliver (eds), *Language and Liberation: Feminism, Philosophy and Language*, Albany, NY: SUNY Press, 323–46.

Ziarek, Ewa Plonowska (2010), '"Women on the Market": On Sex, Race, and Commodification', in Elena Tzelepis and Athena Athanasiou (eds), *Rewriting Difference: Luce Irigaray and 'The Greeks'*, Albany, NY: SUNY Press, 203–17.

Zucker, Jessica (2021), *I Had a Miscarriage: A Memoir, a Movement*, New York: Feminist Press.

Index